Roudinesco was
...acan's Ecole Freudienn...
...80. Her books include...
...conscient et ses ...
...e la psychanalyse...
...la psychanalyse en...
...has recently appea...
...n and Co. A Histo...
...1925–1985.

Théroigne de Méricourt

Théroigne de Méricourt

A Melancholic Woman during the French Revolution

ELISABETH ROUDINESCO

Translated by
Martin Thom

VERSO

London · New York

First published by Editions du Seuil 1989
This edition published by Verso 1991
© Editions du Seuil 1989
Translation © Martin Thom 1991
All rights reserved

Verso
UK: 6 Meard Street, London W1V 3HR
USA: 29 West 35th Street, New York, NY 10001–2291

Verso is the imprint of New Left Books

British Library Cataloguing in Publication Data

Roudinesco, Elisabeth
Théroigne de Méricourt : a melancholic woman during the
French Revolution.
1. France. Revolutionaries
I. Title
944.04092

ISBN 0–86091–324–4

US Library of Congress Cataloging-in-Publication Data

Roudinesco, Elisabeth, 1944–
[Théroigne de Méricourt, English]
Théroigne de Méricourt : a melancholic woman during the French
Revolution / Elisabeth Roudinesco; translated by Martin Thom.
p.   cm.
Translation of : Théroigne de Méricourt.
Includes bibliographical references (p.   ) and index.
ISBN 0–86091–324–4
1. Théroigne de Méricourt, 1762–1817. 2. France—Biography.
3. France—History—Revolution, 1789–1799—Women.
4. Revolutionaries—France—Biography.   5. Feminists—France—
Biography. 6. Mentally ill—France—Biography.   I. Title.
DC146.T36R6813   1991
944.04′2′092—dc20
[B]

Typeset in Bembo by Leaper & Gard Limited, Bristol
Printed in Great Britain by Biddles Ltd.

To my mother, Jenny Aubry
1903–1987

CONTENTS

ACKNOWLEDGEMENTS

I am particularly grateful to Élisabeth Badinter, who gave me access to her own documentation on the women of the Revolution, encouraged me to write this book and was kind enough to read it in manuscript.

My thanks also go to Professor Pierre Morel, who located a number of documents for me, and who helped me to look more closely at Théroigne's madness.

A further debt of gratitude is owed to Agnès Ploteny, who pursued various researches at my request in the Vienna State Archives, and who forwarded to me all the still unpublished documents having some bearing on Théroigne's life.

I would also like to thank Michel Guerin and Nicole Gergely at the Institut français in Vienna, for the valuable help they gave me; Michel Vovelle and Danielle Le Monnier, who gave me access to the library of the Institut d'histoire de la Révolution française; Philippe Raxhon, who drew my attention to a number of valuable documents written by Belgian historians; and Olivier Bétourné, who gave the manuscript a second reading.

Finally, I would like to thank the following people, each of whom assisted me in my research: François Dupuigrenet des Roussilles (Bibliothèque nationale); Nadine Simon (musée de l'Assistance publique); Veronique Leroux-Hugon (bibliothèque Charcot de la Salpêtrière); Florence Greffe (Archives des hôpitaux); Jacques Postel (bibliothèque de l'hôpital Saint-Anne); Michel Collée (Société internationale d'histoire de la psychiatrie et de la psychanalyse); Aglaia I. Hartig, Odile Rapp, Hélène Bétourné, Noël Mormont, René Moureau, Didier Cromphout, Diederik Bakhuys, Denis Roche, Claude Simion, Jean-Pierre Lefranc, Michèle

Acknowledgements

Montrelay, Élisabeth Biro, Sylvain Roumette, Jackie Pigeaud, Yvette Azoulay (musée de l'Homme).

Elisabeth Roudinesco

SOURCES OF ILLUSTRATIONS

Portrait by Selles: musée Carnavalet, Paris. Physionotrace portraits by Chrétien: Bibliothèque nationale and musée Carnavalet, Paris. Portrait attributed to Lagrenée: Charles Rocour collection, Liège. Anonymous portrait: Bibliothèque nationale, Paris. Portrait by Raffet: Bibliothèque nationale, Paris. Image from Épinal: Bibliothèque nationale, Paris. Boilly's *Triumph of Marat*, musée de Lille. Théroigne and Madame de Staël: Bibliothèque nationale, Paris. Handwritten confessions: Hof-u-Staats Archiv, Vienna. Busts of Théroigne: musée de l'Homme, Paris. Gabriel's portrait of Théroigne: musée Carnavalet. Sarah Bernhardt as Théroigne: Sirot-Angel collection.

If we are agreed that no portion of humanity should suffer . . . let us put inscriptions above the gates of our asylums which declare that they will soon disappear. For if, when the Revolution has ended, we still have some unfortunates among us, our revolutionary labours will have been in vain.

BARÈRE, 23 Messidor Year II

I

The Conquest of Liberty

August 1762 to December 1790

HUMILIATIONS

For some time the inhabitants of Brabant and Liège, in the Low Countries, had been aware of confused rumours from France. The Bastille, symbol of absolutism, had fallen. Peasants were burning châteaux, seizing property deeds and dividing up estates. The countryside was in the grip of a fear which spread hour by hour, from village to village. In Paris itself, the king had been awarded the title of 'restorer of the nation'. In the course of a single, already famous night, the nobility's privileges had been abolished. The old world seemed to have toppled over into the adventure of liberty.

Galvanized by the French example, the patriots of Brabant and Liège prepared to challenge the might of Austria. Joseph II, the Habsburg emperor and the brother of Marie-Antoinette, had changed the status of the provinces and granted reforms inspired by the spirit of the Enlightenment. The patriots, however, wished to follow the example of the Constituent Assembly in France and to replace Joseph's enlightened despotism with the principle of national sovereignty. Whereas the emperor claimed to establish the happiness of the people by means of changes from above, imposed by a foreign power, the patriots called for the independence of their country and for a government based on the general will.

In Brabant, the patriots, led by Jean-François Vonck, were in the minority. They therefore entered into alliance with the conservative Catholics, whose leader was Van der Noot. The latter enjoyed ancient privileges, and their nationalism and their rejection of enlightened despotism made them hostile to the *philosophe* emperor. The poor, uneducated peasantry, who were in the majority, supported the Catholics, whose fraternization with the patriots was to prove short-lived. The Catholics, preferring the restoration of the imperial cause to the triumph of new ideas, were prepared to let the Revolution perish.

In the pays Liégois, on the other hand, the patriots forged an alliance with the workers, the peasants and the manufacturing bourgeoisie. Since their hostility was aimed less at Austria than at the Ancien Régime, they began by attacking the vestiges of what seemed to them to be a wholly discredited despotism. Lawyers and members of the liberal bourgeoisie therefore made the slogans of the French Constituent Assembly their own, and fomented rebellion among the people.

On 18 August 1789, the streets of Liège were in a state of revolt. Cockades of red and yellow, the town's traditional colours, could be seen everywhere. Fabry and Bassenge, the leaders of the Revolution, were carried through the streets in triumph; the hero of the day, meanwhile, a valiant colonel by the name of Ransonnet-Bosfort, was the object of deep admiration, as he, like La Fayette, had played a part in the liberation of the American colonies. At dawn he had ordered that the gates of the citadel be opened, and the rebels had swarmed in. The town hall had been stormed by midday, and a new town council installed. A huge and motley crowd gathered there and marched on the château de Seraing, the residence of Hoensbroech the prince-bishop, a clumsy and brutal man. Hoensbroech was brought back to Liège and, cowed by the uproar, he tremulously ratified the election of the revolutionary magistrates. That same evening, by candlelight, the Ancien Régime was abolished.[1] However, less than two months later, it was restored – by Austrian troops. The 'two Revolutions', the Brabantine and the Liégois, had therefore failed, although for different reasons, and the people of the Low Countries would have to wait until 1830 for modern Belgium to be constituted. As Michelet noted: 'Having taken refuge in great numbers among us, the Liégois shone in our armies by their ardent courage, and they were no less distinguished in our clubs for their choleric eloquence. They were our brothers or our children.'[2]

On 18 August 1789, Anne-Josèphe Terwagne, a native of the Ardennes, was not yet called Théroigne de Méricourt. She was not present at the insurrection in Liège, and so she did not follow the people to the tyrant's palace or exhort the crowd to conquer liberty. She was not disguised in a riding-habit, nor did she straddle a cannon, wear a purple plume or brandish a sabre or pistol. On that particular day, Anne-Josèphe was travelling from Paris to Versailles, where she hoped to follow the debates at the National Assembly.

Since her return from Rome, on 11 May, she had wholly changed: the opening of the Estates-General had made a new woman of her. Before she had been gloomy, sick at heart and often ill; now she was in a receptive and triumphant frame of mind, drawn by rumours to a cause whose deeper reasons she wished to understand. Anne-Josèphe could have returned to Liège and supported her compatriots in their struggle, and once more seen the village of her childhood, but she preferred Paris, the radiant symbol of all her hopes. The Swiss banker Jean-Frédéric Perregaux, the future founder of the Banque de France and later to be a Count of the Empire, had taken a fancy to her. His entourage included both writers and artists. On his advice, Anne-Josèphe had sold her silver plate and pawned her jewels, so that she might be in a position to devote all her energies to the great cause of liberty. Fascinated by intellectual questions, and dazzled by the flamboyant representatives of the Constituent Assembly, she embarked upon a new life. She dreamed of happiness, wisdom and equality, and gradually she forgot her past existence, in which she had been a part of the demi-monde and a failed singer, in order to give herself unreservedly to the love of the Revolution. It was not hard for Anne-Josèphe to renounce the pleasures of the flesh, for she had never known them. In June, she moved into a town house in the rue des Vieux-Augustins,[3] and then sought out lodgings in Versailles, so that she might live nearer her beloved Assembly.

It was at the Palais-Royal, early in the summer of 1789, that she discovered the 'dawn of new times'. This famous garden was the school in which she first learned something of the Revolution and, although the instruction she gained there could not match what she was to receive a month later at the Assembly, she encountered a particular sensibility, an unthinking enthusiasm which took the place for her of family love. As she was to write in her *Confessions*:

> What most impressed me was the atmosphere of general benevolence; egoism seemed to have been banished, so that everyone spoke to each other, irrespective of distinctions [of rank]; during this moment of upheaval, the rich mixed with the poor and did not disdain to speak to them as equals; finally, everyone's countenance seemed to me to have altered; each person had developed his character and his natural faculties. I saw many who, though covered in rags, had a heroic air. Even the most insensitive could not fail to be moved by a spectacle of this nature, and I too was so stirred that I resolved to go to Versailles and witness the debates of the national assembly, not from the very beginning, as I later deeply regretted, but when the debate on the Declaration of the Rights of Man was beginning.[4]

The Palais-Royal was by no means so idyllic a place as the young woman from the Ardennes claimed. Prostitution was rife, and the duc d'Orléans, who owned the property, had attempted to pay off his debts by building shops, which were then leased out to shopkeepers. He had opened up a series of streets in the area, each of which bore the name of one of his sons (Chartres, Montpensier and Beaujolais). Ever since the Estates-General had first met, the cafés, theatres and gambling houses had become talking-shops, where rumours and opinions circulated freely. Comment was offered on the events of the day, which might range from revolutionary 'plots' to the shadowy plans of the court and the intrigues of 'the Austrian she-wolf'.

On Sunday 12 July, the Palais-Royal was in turmoil. The news had just broken that Necker, the liberal minister, had been dismissed by the king. The tribunes included the timid Camille Desmoulins, who began to harangue the crowd, exhorting it to take up arms against tyranny: 'Let us all don a green cockade, for green is the colour of hope.' He grabbed such a cockade and fixed it to his hat. The flames of revolution began to spread.[5]

As had been her practice every day since her arrival in Paris, Anne-Josèphe Terwagne was taking a walk that afternoon in the galleries of the garden. Yet, as chance would have it, she did not hear Camille Desmoulins's harangue. She was not at the Palais-Royal when the tribune was speaking, and it was only in the evening that, becoming conscious of a groundswell of unrest, she asked some soldiers she passed if they belonged to the Third Estate. They were too surprised to arrest her. On the following day, she learned of the existence and meaning of the green cockade, and immediately donned it. The next day, she heard of the fall of the Bastille. On 17 July, when the king went to the Hôtel de Ville to receive the tricolour cockade from the hands of Bailly, the new mayor, and from La Fayette, she was present, with the people. For the first time, she had assumed the dress which was to make her famous, and ultimately legendary: namely, a white riding-habit and a round hat. Still unknown to the crowd, she walked in front of the sovereign.

Anne-Josèphe Terwagne was born in the village of Marcourt on 13 August 1762 of a well-to-do family from the Ardennes peasantry. The surname was fairly common in the area, although known in a number of different variants, such as Terevaine, Terwaigne, Terwoine, Teroine and Terovène. *Terwagne* was the Walloon spelling, while *Théroigne* was the Frenchified form. On the eve of the Revolution, the young woman was known as Mlle

Théroigne, or Anne-Josèphe Théroigne, although she often assumed a number of other names. The appellation Théroigne de Méricourt — formed from a transposition of her surname and from a corruption of *Marcourt* — was an invention of the royalist press, and one which Anne-Josèphe never acknowledged.

Marcourt lies on the right bank of the river Ourthe, about one league from La Roche, and is dominated by a fortified castle perched upon a precipitous rock. The setting is a magnificent one, a landscape consisting of wooded hills, meadows and caves. Further to the south are the peat bogs and sands of the Ardennes, then, to the north-east, the undulating valleys of the Condroz and, finally, to the north-west, the country of La Herve, where geometrically shaped meadows have gradually replaced the former tillage. Less than a hundred kilometres away, one comes to Liège, a thriving region which was characterized by the wide range of activities which had arisen in the course of the sixteenth century, ranging from gunpowder and saltpetre manufacture to the cloth trade, and markets which thrived on a peasantry grown rich through its property.

Pierre Terwagne was born in 1731, the offspring of one of these families of peasant proprietors. His own family lived at Xhoris, in the county of Logne. Aged thirty, in the autumn of 1761, Pierre married Anne-Élisabeth Lahaye, a native of Marcourt. The couple lived in a 'mancion', a kind of house built of oak and covered in slates. Pierre's wife was not in her first youth, being only one year younger than her husband. In both her father's and her mother's line, she was descended from peasant proprietors. One branch of her family, the Campinado, lived in Germany and in Austria, while another resided in the province of Luxembourg.

When Anne-Josèphe was born, ten months after her parents' marriage, she was named after her mother, Anne, and her father's brother, Joseph Terwagne; the latter inspired the names of the two sons born subsequently, Pierre-Joseph Terwagne (on 25 December 1764) and Nicolas-Joseph Terwagne (on 28 September 1767).

Élisabeth Lahaye did not recover from her third pregnancy. At her death, her daughter, who was then five years old, was left on her own with her father and her two brothers, the elder of whom was just beginning to mumble a few words, while the younger was still in his cradle. From this time on, Anne-Josèphe's life was a chapter of misfortunes. She was taken in by an aunt, who lived in Liège, but was quickly dispatched to a convent, where she learned dress-making. Anne-Josèphe remained there until her first communion, but her aunt, now married with two children of her own, refused to pay her maintenance any longer. Hired as a maid by her aunt, ill-treated and perhaps beaten, Anne-Josèphe decided to return to Marcourt, where she hoped that her father might provide her with some of the affection she so sorely missed. Yet her father too had remarried; his second wife, Thérèse Ponsard, from the village of Erpigny, was in due course to have ten children by him.

Théroigne hoped that her troubles would now be at an end, and that her young stepmother would give her the love that her aunt had denied her, but these hopes were soon dashed. Her father's second wife displayed the utmost indifference to the child, tyrannizing over her and subjecting her to humiliations of every kind.

The years passed, and Pierre Terwagne's affairs took a turn for the worse. He lost law-suits, of the kind in which peasants are often involved, he mortgaged his land and sold his possessions. His family, which had once seemed privileged, was inexorably being ruined. Théroigne had no wish to share the same fate, and therefore decided that it was better to flee the moral wretchedness which surrounded her. At the age of thirteen, she took her young brothers with her. Pierre-Joseph then set out for Germany, and asked a relation in the Campinado family to give him shelter; Nicolas-Joseph stayed with his sister, who acted as a mother to him, and the two of them took refuge in Xhoris, with their paternal grandparents, also peasant proprietors. But the same melancholy tale unfolded once more, although this time it was the humiliations rather than the physical tasks which caused Anne-Josèphe the most suffering:

> I was forced to do work that was heavier than a child of my age could properly cope with, but it was not this that made me most unhappy, for I was far less prepared to tolerate the slights to which I was subjected; when I could bear them no more, I returned to my aunt's house in Liège, but I was still unhappier there, for she continued to treat me as she had done the first time.[6]

Tired of the injustices she had suffered, the young girl again tried to run away, but her aunt confiscated her clothes and her personal belongings. She then decided to set out for the Limbourg, where she found a job as a cowherd. After a year of the most terrible boredom, she found a post in Liège as a children's governess. Finally, at Anvers in 1778, she met Mme

Colbert, the only woman who was ever to show her any affection, and became her lady companion. This woman taught her to write, and then arranged for her to study music and singing, at first in order to accompany her daughter in duets and then with a view to encouraging her to pursue an artistic career. Théroigne played the pianoforte.

Mme Colbert, who was beautiful and attractive, was attached to the young peasant girl, who reminded her of her own lost youth. She gave Théroigne a taste for books and for culture, and took her with her on her travels. Théroigne believed that her existence had now come to have some meaning, for it was through this maternal figure that she acquired a passion for music. She dreamed of luxury, fame and a career as a singer. Her happiness lasted four full years, during which she left her adolescence behind and became a woman. Pretty, blue-eyed, with a fresh complexion and chestnut hair, Théroigne was small and her hands and feet were exceptionally delicate. Her features, though mobile, conveyed neither laughter nor tears.[7]

At the age of twenty, Théroigne made the acquaintance of an English infantry officer, who struck her as being both honest and sensitive. He turned out, however, to be a run-of-the-mill seducer. He declared himself 'captivated by her siren's voice' and dangled before her the fortune which he stood to inherit when he came of age. He courted her relentlessly and promised to marry her. Théroigne held out for a year, then abandoned herself to passion. The Englishman immediately forgot his promises and, once he had become rich, dragged his mistress to Paris in order that she might give herself up to debauch. Théroigne tried in vain to educate him, to 'reform' him, and to instil in him some morality. Her first love, the only one she was ever to know, seemed to be yet another betrayal. However, the officer proved to be generous, and gave her 200,000 livres, which she converted into stocks and jewels.

The young woman from the Ardennes then embarked upon a *déclassé* existence in Paris and in London, uneasily suspended between literary bohemianism, polite society and moral degradation. During one of her stays in France, Théroigne met Anne-Nicholas Doublet, Marquis de Persan, a masochistic old man, whose numerous liaisons had already all but ruined him. Yet he was *Maître de requêtes* at the Paris *parlement*, and still a rich man, with several châteaux to his name. Mad with desire and in the grip of a profound narcissism, he hid his true feelings from Théroigne, while lavishing presents upon her, which were dispatched as if from an unknown admirer. Théroigne believed that he was astute in financial matters, and therefore entrusted the management of her money affairs to him. But, just as she was getting ready to rejoin her lover in London, the Marquis declared his passion for her. He had presented himself as someone who would concern himself with her welfare, advise her and 'teach her French', whereas in reality his absurd jealousy led him to heap bitter reproaches upon her and to have her house watched.

Théroigne took care over her financial affairs, and therefore came to an agreement with the Marquis, the terms being that he would pay her a life annuity of 5,000 livres, payable every six months until her death, in exchange for a sum of 50,000 livres, which she entrusted to him. This contract therefore ensured Théroigne a considerable fortune, and gave her every appearance of being a kept woman. Yet she knew neither carnal passion nor genuine affection. Her lover was a rake; her protector a formidable businessman who relied upon his money to win him love and who would not be able to pay the annuity when Théroigne would be most in need of it. Wishing to have his way and to make her his official mistress, he offered her jewellery, silver plate, a coach and horses, and a fabulous diamond necklace as well. Théroigne remained unmoved. She reckoned that she 'owed' the Marquis nothing, since he gave such presents of his own accord, and since she had exchanged a quarter of her fortune for the 'Persian annuity'. The Marquis never tired of belabouring her, and of complaining of the expenses she caused him.

Théroigne thus spent her days in a very curious situation. The world saw her as a mysterious, proud and kept woman, but in private she led a sad existence. As Thomas d'Espinchal wrote:

> Those persons who went a great deal to plays and to public places, as I myself did, will recall that, a few years before, an unknown woman who went by the name of Mme Campinado used to make frequent appearances at the Opera and, more particularly, at the *Concert spirituel*. She used to sit on her own, covered in diamonds, in a large box; she had a coach and horses, and was a foreigner, with very much the air of being a kept woman, although she never let it be known who provided her with funds. This was the very same person who, since the Revolution, has reappeared under the name of Mlle Théroigne de Méricourt.[8]

It was not long before she fell in love with a famous tenor, Giacomo David, and made plans to follow him to Italy and to sing with him. But the affair came to nothing. Then misfortune struck again. Théroigne gave birth to a little girl, whom she named Françoise-Louise Septenville. Her English lover refused to acknowledge the child as his own. In spite of the care which Théroigne lavished on her daughter, the child died in 1788 from the after-effects of smallpox. She had by this time become embroiled with a castrato by the name of Ferdinand-Justin Tenducci. The Marquis, stricken with jealousy, complained unceasingly about his own situation, and a letter which he wrote to her at the time read as follows:

> Do you want to take your leave of me, and use your talents to win fame and fortune? You must be out of your mind. I felt that I was bringing you round to a more sensible attitude, and, after I had chatted with you for a while, you yourself had ended up by agreeing with me. You made me pay you a year's more annuity than I actually owed you, since you were provided with all that you required. Nevertheless, I did as you asked.... Since you wish to take your leave of me, I expect the blow to fall any day now, though I still doubt that you will strike it, for I confess to you that the very idea of you living off your talents and going on to the stage is at odds with the good opinion I have of you. I find this unworthy of you. I sacrificed everything two years ago in order to stop you embarking upon this foolish escapade with David. If you really are determined not to return to France, I ask you to sell your furniture to me rather than to someone else. You will find it waiting for you if ever you return.[9]

Before leaving for Italy with Tenducci, Théroigne paid a visit to her own village. In order not to seem a kept woman, she assumed the name of Spinster and affected to be the widow of an English colonel. Upon her arrival, she learned of the death of her father, which had taken place in 1786. Her stepmother was living in the direst poverty, and was barely able to bring up her ten children. Anne-Josèphe was touched by her plight and, setting aside the humiliation which she had suffered in the past, decided to take with her both her two full brothers and her half-brother, the eldest son from Pierre Terwagne's second marriage. She sent Pierre-Joseph to Perregaux, the banker, requesting him to use some money from her fortune to buy him a post as an inspector in a bank in Liège, and her younger brother, Nicolas-Joseph, was placed as an apprentice painter in Rome. Théroigne thus displayed great generosity towards the offspring of her family, who had proved unable to cope for themselves.

Tenducci, a singer in the Sistine chapel, was a cantankerous man, both brutal and repulsively ugly. Théroigne had encountered him in Paris at the *Concert spirituel*. He had a scandalous reputation, and his amorous adventures were both derisory and fantastical. His abduction of a rich heiress in England had very nearly cost him his neck but, since the young girl was returned still a virgin to her family, he had been released from prison. When he met Théroigne, his hope was that she would 'dote' upon him. But he was above all aware that he could easily extort from her a part of her annuities by promising to make her dreams come true. She therefore signed a contract with him, in which she appeared under three different names: 'Anna Gioseppa Le Compte, generally known by the name of Anna Gioseppa Campinado, formerly Gioseppa Théroigne Spinster.'[10] *Le Compte* was Tenducci's own invention, *Campinado* referred to Théroigne's mother's family. Nevertheless, in affecting to be the widow of an English colonel who had in fact not wished to marry her, the name which she had assumed was plainly a curious one.

The Italian journey proved a nightmare from the outset. No sooner had they arrived in Genoa, than Théroigne demanded that her contract be annulled. She claimed that she had never read it, and she took the castrato to court. She won the case, but the music master disappeared, cheating her both of the costs of the journey and of the money she had earned by her teaching.

Letters from two different doctors reveal that Théroigne had contracted a venereal disease some time previously. Although cured by means of mercury, she complained of various pains, of tiredness and of the digestive troubles which the treatment had occasioned. In January 1788, a doctor prescribed some pills and decoctions made of celery leaves, which had a diuretic effect. In May, a surgeon recommended mercury rubs all over her body, and maintained that the virus had invaded her bone marrow. Finally, he advised a course of treatment involving daily baths at home and a vegetarian diet. In March 1789, the first doctor took charge of her once more, and suggested that the quantities of food that she ate should be adjusted to fit her condition and her appetite, that she live an abstemious life in order not to tire her stomach and that she drink *tisanes* of chervil and celery. He emphasized that the pain she felt in her nose was due to a caries or to an ulceration, and that the swelling above her eye was an exostosis.[11]

Dealt a cruel blow by this 'shameful illness', Théroigne stayed for a year in Genoa, where she spent a few happy hours. She moved in the best society, spent some evenings at the house of the British consul and contemplated a return to London. However, she went to Rome and to Naples instead, in part for the pleasure of the journey and in part to see her favourite brother, Nicolas-Joseph, the apprentice painter. In order to cover her living expenses, she borrowed some money from the Marchese Giovanni-Luca Durazzo, a wealthy financier. In her letters to Perregaux, Théroigne praised the Marchese highly:

> I am most eager to serve as the means whereby you might enter into corre-spondence with so agreeable a gentleman, who has the most extensive business interests in Paris, especially as regards loans.... If I may be of any use to you in this respect, I am entirely at your service.[12]

In March 1789, shortly before her return to Paris, Théroigne, with the support of Perregaux, proved herself to be a ruthless creditor towards the Marquis de Persan. In a letter to the former, she wrote as follows:

> Sir, I am most grateful to you for the trouble you have taken to rid me of the Marquis de Persan. I enclose my *certificat de vie*, which is completely up to date, in order to prevent him from stalling any longer, and so that you may forthwith pay me the six months due and those which will become due next April, and so that you will be entitled, as I hereby affirm, to act with all the rigour of the law in order to force him to settle with me immediately.[13]

The Marquis tried to pretend that Théroigne was dead, in order to renege upon his agreement. He was not to know how right he was, for she was in fact soon to 'disappear', and to put an end herself to her former existence as a member of the demi-monde and as a failed singer. From May 1789, the peasant woman from Marcourt gradually became a *Femme de la Révolution*.

CONCEPTIONS OF FEMININITY
UNDER THE ANCIEN RÉGIME

If we are to understand Théroigne's trajectory during the Revolution, we need to examine the history of the feminine condition on the eve of this great event.

There had been two different schools of thought in the Enlightenment as regards the nature of women. The first, which stemmed from the earlier theory of temperaments, posited a separate and invariable feminine nature. The chief reference-points here were the writings of Jean-Jacques Rousseau — *La Nouvelle Héloïse* and the fifth part of *Émile* in particular. Rousseau had reversed the Christian perspective, and had maintained that woman was the human archetype, but that, having lost the state of nature, she had become a worldly, factitious and artificial being. In order to regenerate herself, she would therefore have to learn to live in a way that was consonant with her real origin. Regeneration would be accompanied by a return to a language that had existed before words and before thought; one which was capable of expressing conjugal and maternal love. This language was related to a physiological essence of femininity; the implication being that woman was a sensitive, instinctive and corporeal being, whose faculties were weak, and who was particularly ill-adapted to logic and to reason. Her nature committed her to activities serving to complement man, who embodied the powers of the intellect.

This thesis was advanced, to great acclaim, in a book entitled *Système physique et moral de la femme*, which was written by a doctor, Pierre Roussel, and published in 1775.[14] The author popularized Rousseauist perspectives, which were likewise propounded in the article in the *Encyclopédie* on

'Woman'. Being uterine in temperament, woman was defined by her softness and her dampness. She was subject to specific sicknesses, such as vapor-
ous conditions, and was always quasi-childlike. The texture of her organs
was characterized by a congenital weakness. Her bones were smaller and
more brittle than those of men, and her thoracic cage was narrower. Her
spongy tissues might readily become inflamed, her muscles were frail and
her skin was delicate. A woman's hips had to be balanced for her to find her
centre of gravity, which made her progress when walking a little unsteady
and prevented her from running fast. These facts proved that her destiny lay
in giving birth, in nursing and in protecting. If a woman were ever to display
any excesses in the sexual domain, she would become lubricious, as
Messalina or Cleopatra had been. Moreover, the colder a woman remained,
the more effectively she would retain the sperm and the better, therefore,
she could conceive. If her whole destiny lay in procreation, old age would
clearly cause her to lose her essential nature. Sexual desire in an old woman
was therefore always something to be condemned. Indeed, it aroused disgust
and indignation. However, since the menopause turned her in some respects
into a man, an elderly woman earned a degree of freedom, which thereby
allowed her to live for herself. Now that her life was no longer lived wholly
in the service of the species, she became more responsible than a young wife,
who was subject to the authority of her husband. This accounts in part for
the idea, current during the Revolution, that widows and spinsters of a
certain age ought to be granted rights of which other women were deprived.

This thesis, which lent credence to a hypothetical, and in fact completely
imaginary, 'feminine nature', was sustained by the self-evident anatomical
and physiological difference between the sexes. But it led to a conception of
femininity based upon little more than the nature of a woman's organs.
Given this perspective, the difference between the sexes served to justify a
cultural and moral inequality. Indeed, if woman was by nature a weaker and
more sensitive being than man, one would have to forbid her access to
reason and intelligence, which were in essence masculine, in order to keep
her in her natural state. For any acquisition on her part of a 'culture' would
make her manly, artificial and unsuited to procreation.

The sole current within Enlightenment philosophy to challenge this
naturalistic discourse had arisen out of positions articulated a century before
by Poullain de la Barre[15] and theorized by Antoine Caritat, the Marquis de
Condorcet, the only philosopher actually to participate in the Revolution.[16]

Condorcet denied that the admission of a difference between the sexes entitled one to assert the so-called 'natural' primacy of a hypothetical feminine essence, whose destiny consisted solely of procreation. By the same token, he rejected the inegalitarian conclusion that had been drawn: namely, that woman was forbidden all access to reason. Rather than dispute the question of 'natural femininity', Condorcet's thinking about the feminine condition was based upon the category of natural right, which subjected all individuals to the same laws. Just as women were an integral part of humanity in general, so were they, like men, beings endowed with reason. They were thus entitled to obtain identical rights to those enjoyed by their male companions, namely, civil rights and political rights. Condorcet therefore preferred the rule of a right which made all equal before the law, irrespective of their racial, physical or natural differences, to that of a nature capable of justifying an equality or inequality of a physiological kind. Consequently, if women often seemed inferior to men, it was for historical reasons: society subjected women to the authority of their husbands, denied them civil rights and deprived them of education.[17]

A century after Poullain de la Barre, who was the first thinker to apply the method of Cartesian doubt to the inegalitarian prejudice, Condorcet would therefore seem to have been the first philosopher to consider the feminine condition in terms of a radical rupture between a necessarily egalitarian juridical order and a differentiated anatomical order. Historians therefore acknowledge him to have been in this respect the precursor of feminism, inasmuch as this movement, which emerged in the course of the Revolution through the clubs and the legions of amazons, would be concerned throughout the nineteenth century with a fierce struggle for the conquest of political rights.

During the period in which Enlightenment representations of femininity were forged, women themselves were wholly deprived of civil and political rights. Their dependence upon father, spouse or extended family was absolute. As Jean-Paul Bertaud has observed:

> A woman's private possessions, her dowry, constituted an inalienable inheritance, and she was not entitled to dispose of them. She was also forbidden to enter into any financial dealings without her husband's consent. She was not deemed fully capable of owning and running on her own behalf a property. Even her will was valid only if her spouse accepted it. If she were widowed, a woman could remarry only if certain conditions were met, and

her family always had the right to scrutinize her conduct. It was the husband, and the husband alone, who decided upon the marriage and education of his children. A widow who paid taxes was subject to *corvées*, and she had to pay both royal and seigneurial tolls. She was, however, debarred from all public office. Every judicial post was, for example, closed to her, and she had no right to plead in court.[18]

But, as an indirect result of this regime of enslavement, a woman might sometimes have rights which would subsequently, through the abolition of privileges, be lost. For example, women who were fiefholders were entitled to play a role in the electoral system of the provincial and municipal assemblies. When the Estates-General were convoked, some women were therefore involved in the election of representatives.[19]

In spite of all the deprivations which they suffered, the situation of women was not the exact opposite of that of men, for the feudal system worked in such a way that they enjoyed a situation of inferiority similar to that of other groups comprising both sexes — namely, serfs, actors, Protestants, Jews and Blacks.[20] The inegalitarian prejudice in terms of gender seemed therefore to be inscribed twice, at every rung of the law: it first affected the feminine part of the human species, and then, in addition, it struck those women who belonged to groups which had no rights.

The situation was not quite as simple as this, however. Social inequality so prevailed over sexual inequality that it tended to mask it; rather than accentuating the specific injustice which women suffered, it served to reinforce a sense of class division. Women also identified themselves with the political ideals of the groups to which they belonged, before recognizing themselves in a formation in which their own particular identity might be enshrined. It was not until the abolition of privileges, the Declaration of Rights of Man and the Citizen, the fall of the monarchy and the founding of the republic that they would arrive at a historical awareness of their identity. The Revolution therefore represented the symbolic birth certificate of French feminism, although it gave women merely a civil semi-equality and no political equality at all. When the revolutionary process began, only a handful of women, either of high rank or conversely *déclassé*, marginal or 'foreign', actually laid claim to a genuine egalitarianism. Condorcet, moreover, was the only person to advocate a programme of this kind.

The Revolution resulted, however, in the large-scale involvement of women in political action. They participated either en masse, during the popular insurrections and festivals, or in groups, in one of the many fraternal societies, or else as individuals, depending upon their particular personalities, their political situation or their origin. The Revolution made 'heroes' of men who otherwise would very probably have remained unknown. A similar transfiguration occurred in the case of the few great heroines of the revolutionary period.

Four famous women dominated the Revolution, and seem to incarnate, at each of its stages, the ideals of the various factions. Marie-Antoinette is the quintessence of the nobility's conception of femininity, sometimes vested in all of its caste privileges and sometimes stripped of every mark of its former glory. Subsequently, Madame Roland expressed the faltering sensibility of the Girondin party, and combined the Rousseauist figure of the maternal companion with the still aristocratic one of the directress of one's conscience. Then there was Charlotte Corday, the criminal virgin of the young Republic, who was seen by the moderates as a female Brutus, by the *Amis du roi* as a new Joan of Arc, and by the supporters of Marat as a bloodstained monster. Finally, with the advent of the Directory, the beautiful face of Madame Tallien can be discerned, a courtesan of the Thermidor period who served as a symbol both of the defeat of the Terror and of the recovery of pleasure.

However, between the crowds of anonymous women who invaded the *faubourgs* and the individual acts of the heroines of the Revolution, another form of political involvement emerged after the night of 4 August. The abolition of privileges had rendered the former status of women null and void, and there was consequently a need to define their whole situation afresh. It was at this moment, therefore, that the stage was set for a struggle for the recognition of women's civil and political rights. It was through the action of the clubs and the fraternal societies that this was advanced. This fight was, tragically enough, that of a tiny minority; it was repudiated by society as a whole, and suppressed before it had any chance of flourishing. The women who were its leaders had nothing in common either with the great feminine figures of the Revolution or with the crowds of poor women begging for bread. Either unmarried, kept women, unhappily married or charlatans, their names were Etta Palm d'Aelders, Olympe de Gouges, Théroigne de Méricourt and Claire Lacombe. Each was marginal, and yet very different from the other, for one was a false baroness from the Low Countries, the second a prolific yet untalented writer, the third a Luxembourgian peasant and the fourth a failed actress. Far more than the other women, these figures embody an egalitarianism which was to take a century and a half to prevail in France. When we read their speeches, study their personalities or observe their destinies, we feel them to have been as misunderstood in their own time as they are close to us in the present. For they were struggling for a recognition which is now so much part of our everyday existence that it is hard for us to imagine that it is not in fact self-evident. It was very probably because of this seeming kinship that these women have become an object of study for us, and it is likewise because of this former incomprehension that they were execrated during their own lifetimes and then belittled by posterity. They were heaped with ridicule for having defended what seemed then to be a preposterous notion, and dragged through the mud for their supposed fanaticism. A sentence from Madame Roland sums up fairly accurately the opinion, shared by both sexes at the time, that it was impossible for women to obtain political rights, and, by the same token, shows that only marginal figures could possibly have laid claim to such rights:

> I do not believe that our morality yet allows women to show themselves in public. They should serve as the inspiration for good and foster it, fan all such sentiments as are useful to the fatherland, but not involve themselves in political work as such.... They will be able to act openly only when the French have all deserved the name of free men. Until that time, our frivolity and our dubious morality would render ridiculous whatever was ventured upon by women, and would thereby destroy whatever might otherwise be achieved.[21]

Under the Ancien Régime, women's status was defined first and foremost in genealogical terms, rather than through any reference to nature. Beggars, procuresses, prostitutes, working women and poor peasants were at the very bottom of the scale, and, as their lives drew to a close, they were always haunted by the spectre of the Hôpital général, the famous site of the Great Confinement and the ultimate destination of the wayward. A momentary lapse in morals, an amorous adventure, after the manner of Manon Lescaut, or even a mere trifle might land these women of the people in La Salpêtrière, or earn them a place on the prisoners' convoy to the islands.

At the other end of the scale, the aristocratic woman enjoyed a comfortable degree of freedom. She was not yet the 'servant-and-mother' which bourgeois mores desired, and she neither brought up her own children nor lived as an uneducated spouse confined to the hearth. She dictated the ruling ideas of the day, defined the fashions, steered public opinion or practised the art of libertinage. Such women were educated in luxurious convents, so that, under cover of a marriage of convention, they might choose their own lovers, exercise their wits, advise princes and dabble in philosophy. However, deprived of all rights, they had no direct access either to the running of society or to the government of the kingdom. Thus, in spite of their privileges, which seemed to guarantee that La Salpêtrière would always be kept at arm's length, they were nevertheless threatened by an awesome condition, namely, ennui, which was the first sign of the onset of melancholia.[22]

During the last two decades prior to the Revolution, society seemed to be in the grip of a general melancholia. Various names were given to this condition, and various origins were ascribed to it. Sometimes it was seen as 'climatic' in nature, and was thought to have come from England, the heartland of spleen and fogs; sometimes it was attributed to the spleen itself, the source of black bile. Diderot reckoned that it was the product of fanaticism and, being religious in nature, that it presupposed death-dealing gloominesses which destroyed its victim. If, however, this same force were rid of its dogmatic form, it would become creative and beneficent.

Ever since Homer had described the inexplicable sadness of Bellerophon, a hero pursued by the hatred of the gods, and ever since Aristotle had theorized the 'melancholic temperament',[23] the condition had been thought to involve a virtually unchanging set of symptoms — dark moods, a sense of a bottomless abyss, the loss of all desire and of the faculty of speech, an almost irresistible attraction towards suicide, ruins or nostalgia. However, each period constructed its own representations of melancholia in order to inscribe in it the stigmata of its own particular history. Just as, in the aftermath of the 'traumatic shock' of the Commune, hysteria — a condition theorized by Charcot — was to become the chief illness of the closing years of the century, so too did melancholia seem, on the eve of the Revolution, to be the main symptom of the ennui produced by the poisonous atmosphere of the old society. Contemporaries believed that melancholia could as readily strike young bourgeois women deprived of the privileges of birth as *déclassé* persons who had lost their reference-points within the social fabric. But the condition also wreaked havoc among unemployed aristocrats, since the prejudice of derogation denied them the right to make their own fortunes. Where women were concerned, melancholia was often linked to the famous illness of the vapours, which was sometimes blamed upon the spleen, sometimes upon the uterus, the imaginary locus of sexuality.

Given this perspective, the melancholia of the latter half of the eighteenth century was associated with a condition which was feminine in nature, even though it might affect the two sexes indiscriminately. Whether it were an ennui arising out of happiness, or vice versa, or else a feeling of mockery or an aspiration towards a happiness which might release one from ennui, this condition seemed to mirror the general breakdown of a whole society. As Madame du Deffand wrote:

> All the universal histories and all the research into [natural] causes bores me;
> I have exhausted all the novels, stories and plays; there remain only letters,
> biographies and memoirs written by those who make their own history,
> which amuse me and awaken my curiosity a little. Ethics and metaphysics
> cause me a deadly boredom. What can I say? I have simply lived too much.[24]

It is not hard to understand how, in these circumstances, the ideas of the Austrian doctor Franz Anton Mesmer should have enjoyed such a triumphant success in Paris, in the years between 1778 and 1784. In order to recover psychic evil from its supposedly divine causes and thus reclaim it from the practice of exorcists and sorcerers, Mesmer used the mistaken theory of animal magnetism, which presupposed the existence of a 'universal fluid' exerting its 'influence' upon beings and plunging them into a state of mutual dependence. Mesmer argued that the act of magnetizing consisted of passing 'prophylactic fluids' between the doctor and the sick person. But it also served to activate the far more social notion of a human 'harmony'. One can readily discern how Mesmerism could have accompanied the revolutionary idea of a possible 'fraternity of peoples' and at the same time fuelled the mystical delirium of obscurantist sects.

The famous psychic condition attacked by Mesmer was not defined by any clinical criteria, since it was not until the invention by Philippe Pinel of modern alienism, in the wake of the Revolution, that a genuine classification of mental illnesses was established. But it was not until the advent of Charcot and the Freudian discovery that the historians of psychoanalysis were able to recognize Mesmer as the founder of the first dynamic psychiatry, for he was in fact the first person to 'dynamize' neurotic symptoms without at the same time making any reference to demonic possession. We are in a position today to understand, through Freud, how

Mesmer effected the transference without managing either to classify it or to theorize its sexual characteristics. He ascribed an unidentified relation of transference to 'magnetism'.

Mesmer would therefore seem to have been a precursor of psycho-analysis, at least as far as the cure of hysterical symptoms is concerned. However, we have no proof that the sick women upon whom he lavished his care, both in Vienna and in Paris, were in fact hysterics, since only the theory of hysteria derived from Charcot enables us retroactively to define them as such. This is further brought into question by the fact that no nineteenth-century alienist ever took Mesmer's experiments into account when defining hysteria. On the contrary, they all condemned them, starting with Pinel, who rejected magnetism in the name of the Enlightenment and reason.

Everything leads one to believe that Mesmer's patients, and especially the aristocrats of the court who thronged around the tub, suffered from a 'sick-ness of ennui' rather than a specifically hysterical condition, in which black bile, vapours, a uterine substratum and a scientific fascination were all inextricably intertwined. Consequently, if Mesmerism enjoyed such spec-tacular success on the eve of the Revolution, both as a means of fabricating symptoms and as a social theory, it was perhaps because it provoked a kind of convulsion within a society which saw itself as existing under the sign of a melancholic exaltation.[25]

The question of natural rights, in the form it assumed in Condorcet's writings, was concerned neither with defining a 'feminine nature' nor with 'magnetizing' relations between beings, but rather with identifying the place of women in society. We may learn something of this philosopher's position on the eve of the Revolution by studying two texts, published in 1787 and 1788 respectively: *Lettres d'un bourgeois de New Haven sur l'inutilité de partager les pouvoirs législatifs entre plusieurs corps* and *Essai sur la constitution et les fonctions des assemblées provinciales.*[26] In the latter, Condorcet outlined his plan for social and political reform, one of his demands being that women should take part in the election of representatives, because they were beings endowed with reason, who should therefore enjoy the same natural right as other human beings:

> Women would thereby not be deprived of civil rights, a privation which is contrary to justice, although justified by an almost universal practice. The

reasons advanced to justify refusing women access to public office, which are indeed only too easily refuted, can be motivated only by the wish to strip them of a right whose exercise would be so simple, and which men hold, not by virtue of their sex, but in their quality as reasonable and sensitive beings, which they have in common with women.[27]

At the same time, the attitude of the women of the Third Estate towards their own condition found expression in the *Cahiers de doléances des femmes*. In a petition sent to the king on 1 January 1789, the women laid claim neither to political equality nor to the right to send deputies to the Estates-General. On the other hand, they were adamant about three points in particular. They stressed the need for free education, which would demonstrate that they were not intellectually inferior. They asked that the trades of dress-making, embroidery and millinery be granted special privileges, and that men be debarred from them. Finally, they called for prostitutes to be condemned, and to be regarded as the dregs of humanity:

We would wish this class of woman to wear a distinctive emblem. Since nowadays they even go so far as to ape the modesty of our garb, and since they mingle with us, wearing any and every kind of dress, we often find ourselves being confused with them; some men have been mistaken and their error has caused us to blush. We ask that these women be obliged always to wear this emblem, under pain of being forced to work in the public workshops for the benefit of the poor (for we know that work is the heaviest penalty that one can inflict upon them). ... However, it strikes us that the rule of fashion would thereby be obliterated, and one would run the risk of seeing far too many women wearing the same stripe.[28]

Almost all the petitions of the *Cahiers de doléances* for 1789 express a similar hatred for prostitutes, a similar lack of concern for the notion of political equality and a similar emphasis upon corporate self-interest. If one excepts the concern for education, which was claimed as a right by the majority of women of the Third Estate, they thus seemed to have virtually the same opinions as the men regarding their own condition. However, Madame B.B., a woman from the Pays de Caux, evidently from a wealthy milieu, expressed a different point of view. Although she did not lay claim to equal rights in any real sense of the term, she emphasized the need for education and she did not vent her spleen upon prostitutes. She called for the abolition of male primogeniture, for the admission of female representatives to the Estates-General and for an emancipation of women equivalent to that planned for the Blacks. But, as far as punishment was concerned, Madame B.B. remained a moderate. She was in favour of the death penalty and of corporal punishment, and she advocated stigmatization through the branding of a letter on the cheek for bankrupts and for criminals who had not been punished by death.[29]

As the revolutionary process drew women ever closer to the political process, their claims became correspondingly more precise and coherent, indeed egalitarian. Thus, it was not until 1790 that a position was crystallized, although admittedly still a minority one, which aimed at a complete transformation in the civil, juridical and political situation of women. Two names were of particular importance in that year, namely, Etta Palm and Condorcet.

LOVE OF THE REVOLUTION

Shortly after the insurrection in Liège, which unfolded at a great distance from her, Théroigne became 'infatuated' with the Revolution. As she traversed this wholly unprecedented event, she gradually emerged from her ennui and began to build a new identity for herself. She forgot her past humiliations, although without therefore laying claim to any kind of political equality. She did not relish the company of women, she dreaded seducers and preferred abstract speeches to mellifluous oratory. Théroigne therefore disliked Mirabeau. As Michelet observed:

> She had had love affairs in the past, but from now on, she was to have but one love, the love of the Revolution, and it cost her her life.... There were to be no more lovers; she had declared that she wished for no one else but the great metaphysician, the sworn enemy of women, the abstract and cold abbé Sieyès.[30]

It is not difficult to see why Théroigne should have admired the abbé Sieyès. At first sight he would seem to be her complete antithesis. He was a fierce, sarcastic man, liable to unleash both withering irony and calculated coldness. His disdainful nature seemed to be at the furthest possible remove from her exalted state, and yet his abstract tendencies were matched by her more cerebral qualities. She may have reminded him of his own path in life, of the humiliations which he had suffered in childhood, of the sordid aspect of his financial affairs, of his dreams of social advancement, of recognition or even of fame. The sacrifices which his career had cost him had quite worn him out. Although he had not the slightest trace of a vocation, Sieyès had trained as a priest, and in the course of his religious education he had suffered an inhuman regime. When his involvement in the Revolution began, he was forty years old, and behind him there stretched a life characterized by disappointments, a contained rage and a sense of resignation. How could Théroigne have failed to respond to this man, who had declared that the Third Estate was nothing, ought to be everything and ought to claim for itself the right to become something? The peasant woman from Marcourt — who was nothing, ought to be everything and dreamed of becoming something — was its personification.[31]

In order not to miss any sessions at the Assembly, Théroigne moved to Versailles, in the rue de Noailles, where she rented lodgings from a widow. From now on, she dressed in a riding-habit, with the aim of looking like a man, thereby avoiding the kinds of humiliation she felt at being a woman.

The first time she sat in gallery number 6, she saw the deputies debating the Declaration of Rights of Man and the Citizen. Then she listened to the Bishop of Clerment demanding that the constitution remain tied to religion. She heard Mirabeau invoking the spirit of tolerance, and Rabaut Saint-Etienne calling for liberty for the Jews, 'these peoples who have always been outlaws, wanderers and vagabonds on the face of the earth, these peoples who have been condemned to humiliation'.[32] On 26 August, Théroigne was present at the reading of the Declaration of Rights:

> The Assembly seemed to me to be a beautiful and imposing spectacle, whose majesty impressed me deeply; I experienced some uplifting sentiments and my soul took wing. At first I did not understand much of all the debates that took place, but imperceptibly I found a way in, and finally I came to know the cause of the people and that of the privileged; my patriotism then increased in proportion as I was persuaded that justice and right were on the side of the people.[33]

Towards the end of August, Théroigne made the acquaintance of the abbé Sieyès's brother and of Jérôme Pétion. Upon several occasions, she entertained the two men at her own lodgings.

Michelet observed that 'what is most instinctive and inspired in the people is the women', and, in his view, the October uprisings marked the entrance of this 'instinct' upon the revolutionary stage. The crowd became a woman and the Revolution became feminized. The women set out on 5 October from the faubourg Saint-Antoine and from the quarter of Les Halles to assemble before the Hôtel de Ville and demand bread. Then, led by

Stanislas Maillard, who sported the title of 'captain of the Bastille volunteers', they continued onwards to Versailles in order to capture 'the baker, the baker's wife and the little baker's boy'. The march was sparked off by one incident in particular. A few days before, the officers of the royal bodyguard had staged a banquet at the castle for the Flanders regiment. A little the worse for drink, the merrymakers had trampled underfoot the tricolour cockade and had flaunted the black one instead, in honour of the queen. But unrest smouldered once the patriots sought to free the king from the influence of the court. At dawn, on 6 October, the palace was invaded, and the crowd climbed to the antechamber of Marie-Antoinette's apartments. After several hours of negotiations, the king agreed to return to Paris. In the evening, escorted by La Fayette and the crowd of women, he reached the Tuileries. 'Men had captured the Bastille', wrote Michelet, 'but it was women who captured the king.'[34]

During these two uprisings, Théroigne de Méricourt was not at the head of the women of the people. She did not march with the crowd, and she did not follow the convoy of those who returned to Paris. In short, she had no part in this episode of Year I of liberty, in which women had played so momentous a role. On 5 October, in the evening, she stayed at the Assembly with the deputies. Then, escorted by Pétion, she reached the corner of the rue de Noailles. From this vantage-point, she was able to watch the Flanders regiment, the royal bodyguard, the cannons, the women and the people march past. As she left, she happened upon three wretches, who were all but starving and she ran to find a loaf of bread so that she might share this meagre fare with them.

At dawn the following day, the Assembly opened its doors to a virtually empty chamber. Théroigne, who was invariably punctual, took her seat. She was present at the session during which it was decided to send a delegation to the king. On 19 October, when the Assembly followed the monarch to Paris, Théroigne herself followed the Assembly. She rented rooms at the Hôtel de Grenoble, which was at 20 rue du Bouloi,[35] and once again, every morning, she went to the Manège to attend the proceedings. Her patriotism, her blameless conduct and her amorous loyalty to the national cause had earned her the respect of numerous deputies. By the end of the autumn, everyone knew her as 'la belle Liégoise'.

Her hotel had become a salon, where one might dine after the Assembly had stopped work for the day. Publicists used to meet up there to chat with the most distinguished representatives. As the *deux amis de la liberté* recorded:

I have seen a number of wise men, who are widely respected, becoming amorously disposed towards this little person, although she rejected their advances with a Spartan pride, which they much laughed at subsequently, when they learned that this exceedingly scrupulous beauty was simply a kept woman.... The most innocent jests cause her to blush; the slightest provocation irritates her and yet she never spends her time in the company of anyone else but men.[36]

Théroigne therefore led a life which was austere, and full of intellectual novelties. She spent her time with Sieyès, Pétion, Brissot, Camille Desmoulins and Barnave, but her suppers were also attended by some of the more colourful characters in Parisian life, such as Anacharsis Cloots, an enigmatic Flemish baron, highly cosmopolitan in culture; Antoine Gorsas, the 'boss' of the *Courrier de Versailles à Paris*, famous for his article on the bodyguards' banquet; the poet Marie-Joseph Chénier, the elder brother of André Chénier, and a hothead and tireless talker.

The former singer's destiny was to change still further when she encountered Gilbert Romme, a mathematician, future member of the Convention and future Montagnard, who was to become to her a friend, a father and the director of her conscience:

I proposed to those who came most frequently to the gallery of the Feuillants, and whom I knew the best, to form a society; Monsieur Rome [*sic*] and Monsieur Maret and one other, whose name I cannot now recall, were in favour of my plan and agreed to come to my house to consider it in more detail; in the company of three or four others, whom I did not know at all, we drew up a plan for a society, which you should have found in my papers.... I proposed the motion in the gallery of the Feuillants that it was fitting that the people should give the best patriots of the national assembly civic crowns or cockades; my motion was carried and Monsieur Rome [*sic*], together with the other patriots, drafted an address, which the people signed; he gave seven cockades to the seven members of the constitution committee. Everybody was keen to meet this small expenditure, but I myself, through an excess of zeal, did not wish it, and I bore the cockades to the house of the abbé Sieyès, thinking him to be the most worthy of recognition and public esteem, and the abbé Sieyès came himself to my house to thank me.[37]

No sooner was Théroigne publicly known, than she became the butt of the royalist press. She was accused of every infamy, treated as if she were a whore, and her name was linked with any number of different imaginary lovers. Just when her life of liberty was beginning to blossom, she witnessed the formation of the phantastical legend which was to transform her personality, in the eyes of posterity, into its very antithesis. Théroigne was thus represented as a sensual, libertine amazon, bloodthirsty and murderous and with a taste for the low life.

Labels such as counter-revolutionary, aristocrat, royalist, *monarchiste* and *monarchien*, although they referred to publicists of various different hues, could all be subsumed within the larger category of those who defined themselves as *Amis du roi* — sometimes nicknamed 'white Jacobins'. Of all these adversaries, those who inflicted the most savage treatment upon Théroigne were known as the Apostles. For, since the October Days, they had felt a blind hatred for the people, and for the crowd of women who had dared to shake the pedestal of the monarchy. These men met at 'evangelical banquets', and published a newspaper, *Les Actes des Apôtres*, which appeared every two days in Paris. They specialized in humorous denunciations of the patriots' 'plots', and embraced the dogma of monarchy at a time when it seemed most threatened. These men were, however, mostly commoners by origin. The theoretician of the group, Antoine Rivarol, was the son of an innkeeper from Le Gard, who claimed to be descended from an illustrious Piedmontese family. He had known Voltaire, Buffon and Diderot, and had delivered an encomium upon the French language, which had earned him some fame. Rivarol was flanked by Champcenetz, a former lieutenant in the French guards, who gave the impression of being his sidekick. He was to die, in a mood of defiant cheerfulness, upon the scaffold. Rivarol said of him: 'I coin the epigrams and Champcenetz does the fighting.'[38] Jean-Gabriel Peltier, the founder of their newspaper and the man responsible for its title, was a Breton, educated by the Oratorians and nicknamed by his friends 'the troubadour from Nantes'. He had supported the Revolution initially, but turned his coat after the October Days in order to 'denounce the bloodbath which threatens France'.[39] He harried mercilessly both Philippe d'Orléans, the chief organizer, as far as he was concerned, of the women's march, and Mirabeau, his bête noire. Finally, the great orator's brother also embraced the cause of the Apostles. This man — a debauched alcoholic, the buffoon of the group, and a musketeer of bloated appearance — went by the name of Mirabeau the Barrel.

The Apostles also numbered in their ranks François Suleau, alias 'le chevalier de la difficulté,[40] a former Hussar who had become a lawyer under the Ancien Régime, had been a childhood friend of Camille Desmoulins, and had studied at the Lycée Louis-le-Grand. He had sat on the same benches as Robespierre, and had been taught by the same teacher, the abbé Royou (who subsequently founded a royalist newspaper also). Although courageous and a fine swordsman, his head was empty of everything save the din caused by his own passions. After some hesitation, he aligned himself with the counter-revolutionaries, and turned out to be a brilliant pamphleteer. 'In the midst of the most grievous dangers', Jean-Paul Bertaud observed, 'he is able, like Peltier, to laugh and to win his audience round.'[41]

On 10 November 1789, the Apostles opened fire upon Théroigne. Champcenetz, the author of the first diatribe, wrote as follows:

> Chance has led me to make the acquaintance of Mlle Théroigne de Méricourt. The charms of her person, the grace of her wit and, doubtless above all else, her ardent love of liberty, have drawn me towards this adorable woman. One could call her the muse of democracy, or else think of her as Venus giving lessons in public right. Her company is itself a *lycée*; her principles are those of the Porch. She would adopt those of the Arcades, if the need arose. She numbers among her pupils the abbé Sieyès, Pétion de Villeneuve, Barnave, the fortunate Populus, with whom, alas, she is soon to crown her inexhaustible love with a marriage which will prove to be the great misfortune of my life. The most loudly applauded, most elegant and most civic speeches delivered before the Assembly have either been composed or inspired by her. The Hôtel de Grenoble, in the rue de Bouloy [*sic*], where she resides, has become the focus for the regeneration of France.[42]

So it was that for the very first time Anne-Josèphe Théroigne was called *Théroigne de Méricourt*. This name stuck, thus serving to consolidate a mistaken identity with noble airs. *Théroigne de Méricourt* was to trip as readily off the tongue as did such names as *Olympe de Gouges* or *Brissot de Warville*. As for 'Méricourt', which replaced 'Marcourt', it seems to refer us today to a very Parisian topography, namely, La Folie-Méricourt. There is, however, no connection between this famous street and the celebrated madwoman of La Salpêtrière and heroine of the Revolution.

A little later, the Apostles celebrated the life and loves of the woman from the Ardennes in a stage play, written in the style of Corneille and entitled *Théroigne et Populus ou le triomphe de la démocratie*. Populus was in fact a real person, the representative for Bourg-en-Bresse at the Assembly, whose name and somewhat gauche appearance made him the model of an ordinary Frenchman. By linking Théroigne's name to that of this man, the people as a whole was represented as being her lover, and the implication was that she was the patriots' 'whore'.[43]

The Apostles were not content simply to recount Théroigne's imaginary orgies with the people, for they also fabricated the legend of which she was to be the victim for a whole century. An engraving represented her as the conductor of an orchestra, wearing a costume identical to the one she was supposed to have worn at Versailles 'when, at the head of the army of the nation, she bested a brigade of bodyguards. Her scarlet riding-habit and her black plume served as a rallying-point. She was ever to be found where the unrest was greatest.'[44]

Having turned Théroigne into a female war chief, the Apostles dubbed her 'Madelon-Dulcinea-Friquet-Terouenne' — the point of the joke was to compare her to the divorced wife of Cromwell, and to bestow upon her as lover a mournful Don Quixote by the name of the Marquis de Saint-Huruge, whom they had used as their whipping boy. Born in 1750, this ex-officer was a part of the folklore of the Revolution. Cheated by his wife, who was a commoner, he had spent some time in prison before emigrating to England. When he returned to France, his heart was consumed with hatred for the Ancien Régime. He never stirred from the Palais-Royal, and his bellowing voice could invariably be heard above the clamour of the crowd. Self-styled 'Generalissimo of the patriots', he vented his hatred upon his 'persecutors', the aristocrats. By ascribing a lover of this sort upon Théroigne, the Apostles were effectively reducing the young woman's patriotic ideals to the status of casual love affairs, and pouring scorn upon the values which had enabled her to escape from her former predicament.

The more celebrated the civic deeds of the woman from the Ardennes made her, the more the Apostles heaped insults upon her and ascribed to her every sort of base action. They were not alone in this respect, for the first issue of another royalist rag, *La Chronique du Manège*, featured a particularly mean-spirited article, which recounted the story of 'The confinement of Mlle Théroigne de Méricourt':

> This nymph is a trollop, and obsessed by men; indeed, every representative may fairly claim to be the father of her child. In spite of being in an advanced state of pregnancy, she came that day, as usual, to her tribune in the National Assembly. Robespierre had just proposed a motion, which he had defended

with the most marvellous display of eloquence. Théroigne's admiration for the orator was such that she soon went into convulsions, which opened the path into the world of the 'National embryo'. The infant made a few wails and rolled past the president on the table of the National Assembly. It thereupon fell fast asleep, in the midst of Sieyès's files. The tiny body was subjected to the most minute scrutiny. A few drops of blood reminded one of Barnave, but it was observed that one leg was shorter than the other. This creature must plainly have come from the Bishop of Autun's factory. However, when this miraculous embryo began to babble, a chorus of voices cried out: 'that is the Count Mirabeau's'.[45]

A *Précis historique sur la vie de Théroigne de Méricourt*, which was published in 1790, provides us with a résumé of all the positions adopted by the counter-revolutionary press towards one who seemed to be the symbol of a liberated feminine condition. It was as if her prudery, her physical rejection of femininity, her cerebral attitudes and the mystery surrounding her past caused her to suffer many more attacks than did the other women who were the targets for gossip. In other words, the greater the misperception of her real life, the more her person became the key element in a formidable phantasmic construction.

In royalist parlance, the word 'Revolution' was associated with 'debauch', and the term 'Liberty' with 'libertinage'. The Rights of Man were likewise likened to the rights of the sexes to do as they wished. As a consequence, every 'free' man was a man who enjoyed the favours of women, and every 'free' woman a woman who enjoyed the favours of men. The men of the Constituent Assembly were therefore compared to fornicators, and the women who supported them were seen as courtesans. In this respect, the real sexual life of the deputies was less important than were the phantasies that were grafted on to their persons. The *Amis du roi* did not treat the libertine Mirabeau as more debauched than the chaste Robespierre.

In the *Précis historique*, which was a historical account of Théroigne's life, she was called 'Suzette-Madeleine-Agnès', and her mother was described as an infamous bawd who had succeeded in inculcating in her daughter, from the age of ten, an unbridled taste for the 'rights of man'. When she was twelve years old, Agnès became the mistress of a German baron whose perverse leanings she was able to assuage. But, finding him 'bizarre', she deceived him with his man-servant. To learn more of liberty, she bribed a large number of citizens, then led into debauch an English scholar in order to convince him to incite his country against tyranny. Having failed in this endeavour, she disembarked at Calais, became swept up in the course of the Revolution and led the crowd to Versailles.

As the imaginary figure of a debauched Théroigne was being consolidated, Anne-Josèphe was in fact living some moments of great exaltation. In mid-January 1790, she and Gilbert Romme founded the *Société des amis de la loi*. As the *deux amis de la liberté* recorded:

> Théroigne was pretty, while Romme was a kind of Quaker affecting the most austere modesty, with a face liable to strike fear into one's heart. He was an obscure metaphysician, a political alchemist whose bizarre disquisitions were quite impossible to follow. It was the funniest thing to hear little Théroigne striving to elaborate still further upon the mystic pronouncements of her master and, with countenances so different from each other, to see them laughing over their bold flights and their discoveries.[46]

In actual fact, many of their character traits complemented each other. Thus, while Théroigne was in search of a paternal authority, and an educator who was not a seducer, Gilbert Romme had the soul of a pedagogue. He must also have had only too much insight into the aspirations and obsessions of the young woman, for, on the eve of the Revolution, he was affected by the sickness of ennui. In April 1789, he wrote: 'My melancholy is an incurable illness', and he went on to say: 'My sombre melancholy is growing daily more intense.' Unlike Théroigne, he was aware of his condition, and was capable of self-analysis. He was initially carried along by events, then, having committed himself wholeheartedly to the cause of the Revolution, he remained loyal to the last, surrendering himself to death when the time came.[47]

Gilbert Romme was born at Riom in 1750. His father, who was an attorney without private means in the seneschalsy of Auvergne, died when he was still a child. Raised by his mother, an honourable woman whose piety was Jansenist in flavour, Gilbert studied at an Oratorian college. At Paris, where he had intended to become a doctor, he was initiated into the new ideas but did not immediately take up the struggle against the Ancien Régime. He was particularly fascinated by Rousseau, and wished to put into practice the educational methods outlined in *Émile*. His vocation as a pedagogue was confirmed in 1779, when Count Stroganov, the illustrious and extremely wealthy heir of the conquerors of Siberia, entrusted him with the education of his son, Pavel Alexandrovitch, who was nine years old. Romme then spent five years in Russia, mixing with the best St Petersburg society. He was presented to Catherine II and allowed himself to be convinced that her plans for reform were in good faith. He crossed the continent from one side to the other, visited Siberia, the Crimea and the coasts of the Arctic, and grew increasingly fond of his pupil. When he returned to the West, in 1786, he took him to Switzerland, and showed him something of France. Around January 1789, they were both resident in Paris. Although Romme was not strongly disposed to political action, he took an interest in the convocation of the Estates-General. He dreamed of a king who 'would be the father of the nation, the protector of the laws and the rewarder of services'.[48] He soon sided with the Third Estate. By July, he was in favour of insurrection and, after the night of 4 August, he agreed with the abolition of privileges.

Like Théroigne, Romme was therefore 'woken' by the Revolution, which was to give his life a new meaning. Although he was a follower of Rousseau, he refused to reduce women to the role of wives and mothers, and shared Condorcet's views on civil rights. He would later advocate the granting of civil and political equality to women.

In order to introduce Pavel Stroganov to the new ideas, Romme took him to the public galleries of the Assembly. The young man lost no time in taking out a subscription to the *Club des amis de la constitution*, the future Jacobin Club, where he used the pseudonym of Pavel Otcher, so that the nobility of St Petersburg might not discover that he had become 'the first Russian Jacobin in history'. But Catherine the Great's spies soon learned of the young man's activities, and she ordered his return to Russia, for she feared that Jacobinism might infect her own subjects. Meanwhile, Pavel played an active part in the meetings of the *Société des amis de la loi*, which had been Théroigne's brainchild. As Romme wrote:

> The project which I am outlining here was the outcome of several conver-
> sations, in the course of which Mlle Théroigne had argued that there was a
> pressing need at this time for a society whose purpose would be to establish
> the degree and means of influence of each member of the National
> Assembly.[49]

The label 'friends' derived from philanthropic traditions, and from eighteenth-century masonic lodges, but with the advent of the Revolution it acquired a new meaning, and served to designate the equality of citizens as against the hierarchical relations of the Ancien Régime. After 1791, there was a proliferation of 'popular' and 'fraternal' societies, which differed in turn from the societies of friends.

The initiative for the society was developed in the public gallery of the Feuillants.[50] From January, 1790 Romme assumed the role of representative of the public (that is, the people), which was then in attendance for the very first time at the proceedings of a modern assembly. His abstract vision of reality and his belief in the virtues of pedagogy led him to wish to transfer this form of representation outside the Assembly, and to conceive of an association which would serve as an extension of it. At this early date, the future Jacobin Club did not yet have the range of influence that it would have subsequently, and Romme, mindful of his native town, hoped that this new society could be used to support patriotic initiatives emanating from the provinces. The plan involved the establishment of six different committees, namely, a *Comité d'annotation*, designed to provide a record of the Assembly's sessions; a *Comité de bibliographie*, responsible for reading publications; a *Comité de rapport*, for taking note of whatever rumours were circulating in town; a *Comité de censure*, for the sorting of newspapers and documents; a *Comité des travaux*, which was concerned with the society itself; and, finally, a *Comité de redaction*, which was to be responsible for publishing a weekly account of the proceedings of all the other committees.[51]

The original kernel of this group consisted of Gilbert Romme, Pavel Stroganov, Théroigne de Méricourt and Bernard Maret, the future Duke of Bassano. New members soon joined, among them François Beaulieu, a historian and journalist who would later side with the Counter-Revolution; Chapsal, a lawyer; Mejan du Luc, Maret's collaborator on a paper entitled *Le Bulletin*, which would subsequently be amalgamated with *Le Moniteur*; Coquéan, an architect; Navier de Dijon, a patriot; Tailland, Romme's nephew; and, finally, ten or so persons whose identities are not known. During its brief existence, the society never managed to assemble more than around twenty members. Moderates were in the majority, and only three persons subsequently became genuine revolutionaries, namely, Gilbert Romme, Théroigne de Méricourt and Augustin Bosc d'Antic, the future Girondin and close friend of Madame Roland, who, after the death of the latter, would be the tutor of her daughter.

Bosc d'Antic, a man of a peaceable disposition and an expert in botany, launched himself into the whirlwind of the Revolution by accepting the

Platonic friendship of the beautiful Manon Roland, who would write him peremptory letters urging him to commit himself to a struggle that allowed of no mercy. On the eve of the October Days, when at the Constituent Assembly, his heart was won by a charming 'stranger'. Madame Roland wrote and reproached him for his fickleness:

> I do not know if you have fallen in love, but I know full well that, in the circumstances in which we find ourselves, an honest man may follow the torch of love only by having first lit it at the sacred fire of the fatherland. Your encounter was evidently of sufficient interest to merit a mention; I would be grateful if you would take me into your confidence; I would find it hard to forgive you if you kept me in the dark as to the name of so estimable a creature.[52]

Once Bosc had joined the *Société des amis de la loi*, he enlightened his beloved Manon, who was still intent upon discovering the famous stranger's name. 'Allow me to share', she wrote, 'in what you are seeing and thinking. You have not said another word about the Stranger, and your extreme discretion leads me to suppose that something of importance is afoot.'[53] Bosc knew now that the 'stranger' was called Théroigne de Méricourt, and he had very probably made his feelings for her known. The young woman, however, was interested only in the Revolution, and she was never to be Bosc's mistress. Furthermore, Madame Roland was never to meet the heroine of this story.

The first meetings of the society were held in the rue du Bouloi. Théroigne, who was the only woman in the group, acted as archivist. On 13 January, Romme was elected president. A few days later, it was deemed necessary to find another site for the society, because of the public reading rooms. Steps were taken to secure a suitable building in the Petits-Augustins, but a clause debarred women from having access to the convent, on pain of violating the rules of the order. At the beginning of February, the society decided to move its headquarters to Romme's apartment, which was more spacious than that of Théroigne.

By informing the people of the proceedings of the Assembly, the *Amis de la loi* sought to inculcate in it a loftier sense of its own rights and to enlighten it as to the benefits which the Revolution might bring it. But for a programme of this kind, virtuous men would have been mobilized. A vigorous process of selection would then be needed, for only persons known for their patriotic zeal, their enlightenment and their morality would have the right to join the society.[54] The latter's debates concerned three crucial moments in the Constituent Assembly's agenda, namely, the law of the silver mark, the question of the Jews and the freedom of the press.

Between 1789 and 1792, the electoral laws specified three degrees of citizens entitled to vote. The loftiest category consisted of those citizens who were eligible for the Constituent Assembly. Next came those citizens eligible for office in the departments and, finally, there were the 'active citizens', who had the right to vote for candidates and electors at municipal level, who in turn used their votes to elect either administrators at district and department level, or representatives at the Assembly. However, in order to be an active citizen, one had to be male, over twenty-five years old and resident in the electoral district for a year or more; bankrupts were debarred, and one had to pay taxes equivalent to three days' wages of an unskilled worker. In order to be eligible for the offices of administrator, at either commune, district or department level, one had to pay taxes equivalent to ten days of labourer's wages. Finally, in order to be elected a deputy, one had to pay taxes equivalent to, or higher than, a silver mark, that is to say, fifty-one days' wages.[55]

This system, which was gradually revised and amended, denied political rights to so-called *passive* citizens, including women, simply because they were women, and the poor, because they did not pay any direct taxes. In 1789, the Assembly's refusal to accept the principle of universal suffrage had therefore served to perpetuate a political inequality as regards both gender and class.

On 29 October 1789, the vote for the law of the silver mark occasioned some lively polemics. Condorcet and Robespierre were resolutely opposed to it. The former rejected the notion of introducing a hierarchy among active citizens in terms of money, while the latter contested the actual principle of a censitary regime.[56]

At their session of 27 January 1790, the *Amis de la loi* took note of Robespierre's declaration and expressed the wish that 'the National Assembly might finally find some means of abrogating the unjust law of the silver mark, or of rendering it inoperative through the administering of the powerful counterbalances to it'.[57]

The society's second debate concerned the Jewish question. At the end of December 1789, the Constituent Assembly had broached the problem of rights of citizenship for the Jews, it being necessary to decide whether non-

Catholics were admissible to public office. Clermont-Tonnerre, Robespierre, Custine and Adrien Duport spoke in defence of the Jews, while the abbé Maury, La Fare, Bishop of Nancy, and Reubell, the representative for Alsace, expressed open hostility. Robespierre then delivered a wholly admirable speech:

> How could one urge against the Jews the persecutions which they have suffered at the hands of different peoples? Indeed, these are national crimes, which we must expiate, by returning to them the imprescriptible rights of man, of which no human power may deprive them. We should bear in mind that it can never be politic, no matter what anyone may say, to condemn to humiliation and oppression a multitude of men who live in our midst.[58]

At their session of 29 January, the *Amis de la loi* condemned all forms of Judaeophobia:

> The decree on the Jews has reminded us that M. Reubell's opinion is exaggerated and contrary to all principles. Some members have tried to exonerate N. Reubell, observing that this opinion was motivated 1) by direct acquaintance of harm caused by the Jews to his constituents in Alsace; 2) by this representative's need, for the salvation of Alsace, to keep his constituents' confidence. The decree on the Jews then occasioned a fierce struggle between Patriotism and Aristocracy, with Rage on one side and Reason on the other. M. Romme was requested by the assembly to commit to the minutes that part of his report which depicted this struggle, which had proved so demeaning for the enemies of the Revolution.[59]

It was the debate on the freedom of the press which was to prove the most contentious, leading to conflicts within the *Société des amis de la loi*. On 20 January 1790, Sieyès proposed, in the name of the Constitution Committee, a bill designed 'to suppress those crimes which may be committed through use of printing'.[60] The *Amis de la loi* took this occasion to defend the principle of an unrestricted freedom, and to recall the risks involved in the censorship of written works:

> Think of all the excellent works which have been burned upon this specious excuse. As examples one could cite Rousseau, Voltaire, the abbé Raynal, Molière and La Fontaine. Think of all the magistrates, particularly if they

were priests, who would use this excuse to bring back the times of barbarism, and consequently, those of despotism and servitude.[61]

On 23 January, Théroigne received a letter from Joseph Chalier, a former conqueror of the Bastille, who had just arrived at Lyons with a view to propagating the ideas of the Revolution, and who proposed that she should become an honorary member of the Patriotic Society of Lyons. He wrote:

> Heaven alone knows how aristocratic this town is. But you may depend upon my resoluteness, my constancy and my unsullied devotion to the good of the Revolution, which makes us all brothers — and men. So, my dear sister, stay in Paris, for your presence there is of the utmost importance.

Around the same time, she received a note from Marat, who regretted that an indisposition prevented him from discussing in her club 'a sublime project' designed to guarantee 'the triumph of liberty'. Finally, in the public gallery of the Assembly, she earned the admiration of a member of the Jacobin Club, who asked to join the *Société des amis de la loi*: 'You will perhaps think it rash of me to behave so freely towards a person whose acquaintance I have not had the honour to make.'[62]

Through such exchanges, Théroigne became involved in a struggle which directly concerned her situation as a woman. Although she was neither a genuine militant as regards political rights, such as Olympe de Gouges or Etta Palm, nor the idol of a party, as Madame Roland was, she was nevertheless acquiring the sense that she was a free woman. When, therefore, at the session of 31 January, one of the members of the society commented upon the question of the state of nature by asserting that 'the rights of a man over his wife and, likewise, those of a father over his children are those of a protector over his protégés', Théroigne bridled, and stated her intention of drafting a report in defence of her own point of view. The offer was accepted, but Théroigne was the sole person to protest upon that particular occasion. Even Gilbert Romme, although he was well-versed in a wholly different conception of women's place in the polity, chose to keep his silence. Théroigne never wrote the report.[63]

However, she jotted down in a commonplace book a number of aphorisms upon 'the liberty of women, who have the same natural rights as men, so that, as a consequence, it is supremely unjust that we have not the same rights in society'.[64]

Towards the end of January, the society was confronted with a number of different problems. Various conflicts broke out between the moderates and the revolutionaries, and members began consequently to drift away. The club wielded no real influence. Its mode of operation had proved to be too elitist and too bureaucratic, at a time when action was based upon movement and upon daily volte-faces. Moreover, the rise of the *Club des amis de la constitution* had been accompanied by that of many similar ventures. Convinced that his society was about to disintegrate, Gilbert Romme made his way to the convent on the rue Saint-Honoré, where he hoped to win a degree of political recognition. At the end of March, the *Amis de la loi* broke up. For Théroigne, this was yet another setback.

Even if she was becoming increasingly aware of her isolation, as a woman, in the Revolution, she preferred to remain loyal to her ideal, although it brought her no rights, rather than renege upon the commitment which had turned her into a fighter for liberty. As she wrote:

> In all that I did then, I had no other aim in view but the love of glory, yet even this was adroitly managed. For it tended to work to the advantage of men, but I had neither sufficient talent nor sufficient experience, and besides I was a woman; this was the greatest of all shortcomings in the eyes of the other sex.[65]

As advocates of a Rousseauist vision of feminine nature, the patriots were able to appreciate women's actions in defence of liberty, but were neither prepared to admit them into their ranks on an equal footing, nor to grant them even the most restricted political rights. Théroigne was therefore thoroughly marginalized. She could bear, if she had to, the lies and calumnies of the royalist press, of counter-revolutionaries and of 'traitors' to the nation. But how could she ever come to accept this other, more covert form of rejection, which she suffered at the hands of her friends, the patriots?

On 4 February 1790, she was present at the solemn session at which the deputies swore the civic oath in the presence of the king. Ten days later, when the Assembly made its way to Notre Dame to celebrate a *Te Deum*, she was recognized by several men, who invited her to join their ranks. But she was soon forced to leave the procession:

> I walked a whole street alongside them; there were many who exclaimed:

Aha! a woman representative, now there's a curious sight! A few aristocratic priests, catching sight of me, cried out. Finally, I withdrew, in spite of the fact that there were many others who were marching, as I was, in the procession, and were not representatives either; but they were men, and it seems that what those aristocrats who had cried out upon seeing me had found so curious, was the notion that a woman would wish to do the same thing.[66]

Towards the end of the same month, sensing that the *Société des amis de la loi* was in a state of decline, Théroigne sought to gain admission to the Cordeliers Club, and thus obtain a consultative vote in the Assembly. She delivered a rousing speech before the members of the club, which was later described in dramatic terms by Camille Desmoulins:

It was the famous Théroigne who came to ask for the right to speak and to propose a motion. Only one person voted in favour of admitting her to the bar. Upon catching sight of her, an honourable member cried out in enthusiastic tones: 'It is the Queen of Sheba come to see the Solomon of the districts.'

In a formidable patriotic diatribe, Théroigne then proposed that a temple to the nation be built upon the site of the ruined Bastille. Camille Desmoulins reproduced what were reputedly Théroigne's own words:

Why are we tarrying, O illustrious Cordeliers, you who hearken unto me, paragons of the districts, republican patriots, Romans? ... Cut down the cedars of Lebanon, the pines of Mount Ida.... Prove that you are indeed Solomon, and that it was you who were meant by destiny to build the temple ...[67]

No sooner had Théroigne stopped speaking, than tumultuous applause broke out. Danton, Fabre d'Eglantine and Desmoulins set up a commission to look into the proposal. Of course, the idea never became a real architectural project. As for the *belle Ardennaise*, she was refused even the consultative vote for which she had asked. Upon the advice of its president, the Assembly merely gave her a vote of thanks. It but remained for Desmoulins to give a highly witty account of the whole episode:

[The president has concluded] that a canon of the Council of Mâcon having formally recognized that women have a soul and reason, just as men do, one could not prohibit them from making as good a use of it as the previous speaker; that Mlle Théroigne and those of her sex will always be at liberty to propose whatever they believe to be advantageous to the fatherland, but as regards the question of state, as to whether Mlle Théroigne should be admitted to the district with a consultative vote only, the assembly is not competent to take sides on this question, and this is not the place to settle it.[68]

Théroigne's courage was such that, in spite of this rebuff, she was still undaunted. Taking advantage of the fame she had won at the Cordeliers, she tried to rally the patriots and to found a new society, to be known as the *Club des droits de l'homme*. This society would preach fraternity, morality, justice, and virtue, and defend the oppressed by making their rights known to them. This ambitious programme was also doomed to fail. Théroigne knew no success either in persuading or in rallying. In addition, she was close to bankruptcy. She had pawned virtually her entire fortune and she was still supporting her brother Pierre-Joseph, who made no attempt to earn his own living and took every opportunity to profit from her generosity.

The royalist press seized upon the incident at the Cordeliers also, and heaped sarcasms upon Théroigne. A pamphlet written by an aristocrat and dedicated to the Assembly appeared in June. It contained the following poisonous piece:

> Théroigne, a second-rate courtesan, residing in furnished accommodation, living with Populus, Mirabeau and all the cads who care to present themselves, purse in hand. This heroine of the boudoir is causing something of a stir in her district. Finding the lodgings of the king somewhat too comfortable, and those of the Assembly quite the reverse, as if Cartouche* and his gang had been as well placed, Mlle Théroigne, through her truly masculine courage, her patriotism, her fiery eloquence has caused her audience to forget her sex, and would indeed perhaps forget it herself, were it not for the august functions which remind her of it daily, and which lovers of experimental physics do not allow her to dispense with.[69]

So numerous were such calumnies that, as far as public opinion was concerned, they lent credence to the notion that Théroigne was present at

---

*Louis-Dominique Cartouche Bourguignon, known as Cartouche (1693–1721), was a famous criminal and the leader of a band of robbers. [Trans.]

the October Days. Persuaded by rumours and by the perusal of rags, several 'eye-witnesses' believed that they had seen the famous riding-habit at the head or in the midst of the women's march. However, since 11 December, a trial had been in session at the Châtelet, whose express purpose was to round up and punish any rioters who had, in October, assailed the royal couple, and the queen in particular. Of the four hundred persons who were questioned, five claimed to have recognized Théroigne de Méricourt at the demonstration. Some stated that she was dressed in a black riding-habit, others reckoned that she had been dressed in red. Sometimes she was in the thick of the crowd, at other times she gambolled in front of the railings of the Orangerie.[70] In August 1790, when the inquiry ended, there was therefore the risk that a warrant would be issued for her arrest. Since Théroigne had not the slightest wish to go to prison for a crime which she had not committed, and since she was not prepared to humour the aristocrats and attempt to win round a court that was royalist in its sympathies, she decided to return to her own country:

> I left the French Revolution without too much regret, for every day I had suffered some degree of harassment in the public galleries of the National Assembly; there were invariably some aristocrats who, being offended by my zeal and my frankness, would heap sarcasms upon me; sometimes I was taunted, sometimes traps were laid for me; every day brought further annoyances, while the patriots, instead of encouraging me and treating me justly, ridiculed me. This is the plain and simple truth. I was therefore, so to speak, disgusted.[71]

This, then, was the predicament of Théroigne de Méricourt during the summer of 1790. To the insults from the royalist press and the ridicule of the patriots was added the graver threat of imprisonment. It is no wonder that Théroigne was disgusted by the Revolution.

ORIGINAL FEMINISM

We have so far considered two different perspectives on the participation of women in the Revolution, one of which was collective, the other individual.

On the one hand, women were heavily involved, alongside the men, in the attempt to create a system which would dispense with the inequalities of the Ancien Régime. In this type of action, the women were not fighting for their own objectives. The inferiority of their own condition seemed to them to be a secondary problem, either because they had no clear awareness of the specificity of that condition, or because the solution seemed to them to be dependent upon that which the Revolution brought to the general problem of inequality and of liberty.

On the other hand, there was a growing awareness on the part of an elite, composed of a handful of women, of philosophers and of politicians, of the specific forms of feminine inequality, and this served to justify a struggle for equal rights. This struggle was heightened during the early stages of the Revolution, since it had led to the fall of the Ancien Régime and to a plan for the general recasting of society.

I shall employ the terms *original feminism* or *early feminism* to describe this practice, which linked a struggle for equal rights for both sexes with a revolutionary project for the general transformation of society. Original feminism, which began with the French Revolution, was present as it unfolded, but was not connected with the collective involvement of women in the great demonstrations, itself something of a minority position, and one which was rejected by the majority of *patriotic* factions. On the political plane, the Girondins were less opposed to it than were the Montagnards. It nevertheless survived in one variant or another up until the ban on women's organizations in the autumn of 1793.

One can distinguish three separate phases in the development of original feminism. Up until January 1792, it was a *theoretical feminism*, which gave rise to a legalistic fight for civil and political rights. Those engaged in this struggle employed parliamentary eloquence, pamphleteering and the rhetoric of the clubs, and their demeanour tended to be elegant and elitist. The second phase of this movement began at the time of the debate over the war, which led to the fall of the monarchy. This was a *warrior feminism*, which advocated the levying of legions of amazons against the external enemy. This struggle saw orators going into the streets and rattling sabres, and it marked Théroigne's most intense involvement, alongside the Girondins, in the movement. Finally, after 10 August 1792, the history of original feminism entered its third phase, with the appearance on the stage of Claire Lacombe and of the *Club des citoyennes républicaines révolutionnaires*. This phase was a prolongation of the second, but it also led to a mobilization of women *sans-culottes*, who called for the arming of the women against the enemy within.

Original feminism should be distinguished from *radical feminism*, which was elaborated after the Revolution, in part through the invention of the phrase itself by Charles Fourier in 1837. According to Louis Devance, radical feminism may be defined as 'action having as its chief or even its sole aim the abolition of male supremacy and the liberation of women'.[72] In reality, this was conceived in terms of a struggle between the sexes, and made no allowances for the principle of a revolution, or even for egalitarian claims in general, as a precondition. Radical feminism might therefore readily lend itself to conservative ideals and culminate in a sexism which was itself inegalitarian. Even though this form of feminism was, historically speaking, a continuation of original feminism, it never appeared as such during the Revolution.

Théroigne de Méricourt was not actively involved in theorizing original feminism, and yet, even if she had not reflected deeply upon it, her growing awareness of her position as a woman, and her demands for liberty in the context of the egalitarian project of the Revolution, made her the spontaneous embodiment of it.

While the early stages of the revolutionary process were characterized by a high level of collective involvement on the part of women, it was during the second half of 1790 that original feminism took shape. Thus, in July, debate began in the Assembly on the question of women's civil rights. Upon this occasion, Condorcet gave a speech at the circus of the Palais-Royal, under the aegis of the *Cercle social*, a society founded by abbé Fauchet. This speech was a masterpiece, and may be considered the manifesto of early French feminism.

Condorcet's starting-point was the idea that the Declaration of Rights had been flouted, since half of the human species had been tacitly deprived of the right to play a part in the making of the laws:

> Since women have the very same qualities [as men], they must necessarily enjoy equal rights. Either no individual of the human species has genuine rights, or else all have the same rights; and he who votes against the rights of another, whatever that person's religion, colour or sex may be, has by the same token forsworn his own.

Condorcet went on to reject the idea that the physical constitution of women would be an obstacle to the equality of the sexes:

> Why should creatures subject to pregnancies and to passing indispositions not be able to exercise their rights, when no one has ever contemplated depriving people who have an attack of gout every winter, or who readily catch a cold?

He further emphasized that women were endowed with reason, but that, since unjust laws had meant that they had not had the same interests, their reason was determined by principles other than those which had moulded that of men: 'It is as reasonable for a woman to be preoccupied with the grace of her appearance as it was for Demosthenes to concern himself with his voice and his gestures.' Finally, he called upon people to cease ridiculing or making jokes about the struggle for equality between the sexes.[73]

This manifesto prompted numerous debates in the clubs and the salons. On 30 December 1790, a foreign woman, who presented herself as a Dutch baroness, delivered a great speech at the *Cercle social* on the injustice of the laws with regard to women. Etta Palm d'Aelders, who was blessed with good humour and a stout figure, was not afraid to admit that she was alone in the world and that she had been sacrificed, from childhood, to a powerful family. She was forty-seven years old, and her enemies were soon to denounce her as a spy in the hire of the Prussian court. Yet Etta Palm was responsible for founding the very first women's club of the Revolution. She declared:

Let us henceforth be your comrades rather than your slaves.... Gentlemen, women are your superiors in imagination, refinement of feeling, resignation in adversity, resolution when grief lays them low, patience in suffering and, finally, in generosity of soul and patriotic zeal.[74]

Alongside the debates held at the *Cercle social*, the first mixed club, known as the *Société fraternelle des amis de la Constitution*, saw the light of day in autumn 1790. Its founder, Claude Dansard, was a sympathetic boarding-house proprietor, who brought together each evening, in one of the rooms of the Jacobin Club, a number of artisans and merchants, together with their wives and children. He interpreted the Assembly's decrees by candlelight. When they had run out of candles, they clubbed together to buy a new one, and their discussions continued deep into the night. Madame Louise Robert-Kéralio, Madame Roland and Théroigne de Méricourt were among its participants.[75]

II
Exile and
Return

JANUARY 1791 TO AUGUST 1792

THE IDENTIFICATION OF A
MELANCHOLIC WOMAN

As Théroigne de Méricourt was returning to her native country, the Emperor Leopold II, who had succeeded his brother Joseph, was preparing to assume the imperial crown. He was an adroit tactician and a coldly calculating person, and the twenty-five years during which he had ruled the Grand-Duchy of Tuscany had given him a profound knowledge of political questions. Like his brother, he believed fervently in enlightened despotism, and he was convinced that pragmatism was superior to fine ideas. No sooner had he been crowned emperor than he issued a manifesto outlining a series of compromises aimed at checking the impetus of the revolution in the Low Countries while at the same time consolidating those liberal reforms which had already been put into effect. In July 1790, the emperor's authority was re-established in Belgium,[1] but Leopold declined to extend his sovereign rights there. With the support of Prussia, he nevertheless persevered with the policies that his predecessor had favoured. In place of liberty, the patriots were granted reforms and an amnesty. In this respect, the Josephine experiment had managed, in stark contrast to the French monarchy, to build a system of modern justice in which the search for truth and the respect for individual rights took precedence over arbitrary whim and intolerance. In 1787, a Penal Code, which had already been published during Maria Theresa's reign, was redrafted in a more liberal form, with the death penalty being abolished save in the case of court-martials. Patriots therefore benefited from these reforms.

Far removed from the turmoil of Paris, Théroigne was staying at Marcourt, where she spent a few truly happy hours. She revisited the house in which she had passed her childhood, spent a number of evenings with the villagers, taught the peasants patriotic songs and played tag in the meadows with the playmates of her youth. Gradually she was able to forget all the failures, bitterness and raillery to which she had been subjected, and to recover her belief in the revolutionary ideal. She fought with the village miller when he took too much flour from the peasants, and she quarrelled with the priest over the tithe. But she also sent him stockings and skirts for the poor, although she was careful to give him no money lest he refuse gifts deemed to be contrary to the Catholic faith. Being now short of funds, and concerned still to provide for her brothers, Théroigne pawned her diamond necklace. She made her way to Liège, and put up at the inn of the White Cross, in the hamlet of La Boverie. Soon patriots began to pay her visits, which she welcomed. She recovered her sense of revolutionary exaltation, and even dreamed of founding a revolutionary journal. As she still feared the law-suits directed against her, she asked Perregaux to send her the proceedings of the Châtelet, and was outraged to discover that she was mentioned by name, and that witnesses believed that they had sighted her, dressed in a riding-habit, on 5 October.

One day, her uncle and her paternal cousins invited her to the village fair at Xhoris. She stayed with them and felt so much at her ease that she decided to buy a plot of land there, and devote herself to a rural existence. A short way off, in the château de Fanson, there lived the Baron de Sélys, who was the podestà of the principality of Stavelot and the constable for the county of Logne. The baron was a conservative, a staunch defender of the Ancien Régime, who corresponded regularly with the aristocrats of the French court. He was also acquainted with Count Maillebois, a general and a counter-revolutionary agent responsible for the area between Liège and Koblenz. Sélys had known Théroigne since she had been a child, had watched her grow up and knew something of her career since. Eager to be of service to the royalist cause, he made Théroigne welcome. In this way he was able both to shine in provincial society by receiving a Parisian celebrity in his house and also aid his royalist friends by spying on the young woman. After each encounter, Sélys informed Count Maillebois of Théroigne's activities.[2] This was the origin of the rumour, rife in milieux frequented by the émigrés, that the little amazon had been sent by the Jacobins, armed with a huge fortune and aided and abetted by the patriots of Liège, to overthrow the Austrian monarchy. It was, in short, a classic conspiracy theory.

Théroigne was unaware of the old baron's machinations, and befriended his wife, who was the same age as her and much taken with liberal ideas. Théroigne's own favourite authors by this time were Seneca, Plato, Mably and Condillac. Whenever she happened upon passages which were to her liking, she would copy them into notebooks or on to sheets of writing paper. She also jotted down reflections of her own, and she took these notes wherever she went.[3]

Towards the end of December, the Austrian army advanced towards Liège. Fearing the looting and the patriot hunt that would inevitably follow, Théroigne preferred to return to La Boverie, although she had not finished paying for her plot of land. On 12 January 1791, the imperial troops entered the area. The patriots emigrated to France, taking the remnants of their army with them, and were to return to their own country only after the victories of Valmy and Jemappes. Marie-Christine de Saxe-Teschen, Leopold's sister and the wife of the governor who had been unseated by the Revolution, breathed a sigh of relief. She could now return from her enforced exile. Théroigne, however, was soon to face the emperor's judicial system.

Being informed of the presence in Liège of this celebrated woman, Count François-Claude de Mercy-Argenteau, the former Austrian ambassador to France, a confidant of Marie-Antoinette, and the guiding light behind the counter-revolutionary coalition, was convinced that Théroigne was a spy in the pay of the French government. Like many others, Mercy-Argenteau was certain that she had been involved in the October Days and that she had planned an attempt on the queen's life. This was reason enough, in his view, to seek to have her punished. On the prompting of those close to him, he planned to have her abducted and delivered into Austrian hands. Mercy-Argenteau immediately informed the old prince Anton von Kaunitz, the Imperial Chancellor, and asked him to pass the information on to his master, Leopold II. In a matter of weeks, Théroigne de Méricourt had thus become, in the minds of the émigrés, a political figure of the highest importance. Mercy-Argenteau sent a letter from Brussels to Baron Posch, the imperial president at Freibourg:

> I have recommended that she be taken in secret and conducted to Freibourg-en-Brisgau. I would therefore request of your Excellency that this lady be kept under extremely strict surveillance, until such time as His Majesty, our emperor, in consultation with the court of France, should have decided upon

her ultimate place of confinement. If, by some extraordinary mishap, the secret of such an imprisonment should come to the notice of the public, it is absolutely crucial that the actual identity of the person arrested should remain unknown. The documents which, in all probability, will be found when the planned arrest is carried out, are of the greatest importance to us. I therefore beg Your Excellency to be so kind as to seek out a person who is discreet, intelligent and to be trusted; this person's task will be to examine the papers in question and to put them into some sort of order. Those which are especially concerned with the court of France should be sent by special messenger to Monsieur Bastien, who is responsible for the handling of the whole affair.[4]

Being in the confidence of Mercy-Argenteau, Bastien had no difficulty in recruiting mercenaries competent to execute the plan effectively. There were many French officers of the old French army in the area between Worms and Koblenz at this time. Such men were both short of funds and tired of months of inactivity, and were therefore only too ready to embark upon an expedition which promised to release them from their boredom. Bastien was therefore quick to enrol three fortune-hunters, namely, the chevalier Maynard de La Valette, a former captain in the Armagnac regiment, Count Saint-Malon and Augustin-Lechoux, a former sergeant-major.

On 15 January 1791, in the middle of the night, the accomplices arrived in the hamlet of La Boverie on board a hired coach with drawn curtains. They entered the inn, seized Théroigne, who was asleep among her books, and forced her to get dressed, all the while seeking to convince her that they were ardent patriots, who had come to protect her from royalist attacks against her. Although mistrustful at first, Théroigne came to believe them and followed them without putting up any resistance.

In order to put themselves in the good graces of the Austrian authorities, the kidnappers decided to wring 'confessions' from the prisoner regarding her 'bloody involvement' in the Revolution. Assuming the pseudonym of Monsieur Legros, La Valette interrogated Théroigne and then drafted in his own hand some *Statements and Admissions*, which he attributed to her, and in which she was accused of a variety of differing crimes. La Valette later transmitted these confessions to Mercy-Argenteau, who passed them on to Count Metternich-Winneburg, the minister plenipotentiary of the emperor in the Low Countries. The latter immediately informed Prince Kaunitz.

Théroigne's fate had taken on every appearance of being an affair of state. Metternich wrote:

> While en route, Mlle Théroigne confessed to the French officers that, during the sinister night of 5 to 6 October, at Versailles, she had played a leading role. She has also acknowledged that, among her papers, she has a mass of documents and letters concerned with the French Revolution, with the uprising in the Netherlands and with the unrest in Liège and Stavelot. I have also learned that Mlle Théroigne has a great-uncle by the name of Campinado, who resides in Vienna. In addition to letters, she has on her person a sum of money, some letters of credit and some jewellery.[5]

La Valette had tried to rape Théroigne while their carriage was on the road to Freibourg, but she had resisted fiercely. Lechoux was present at the time, and although he did not approve of what he saw, he did not intervene either. After ten days of exhausting travelling, the three kidnappers delivered their prisoner into the hands of Baron Posch, who took her to be a dangerous criminal and threw her into a cell.

The secret of the abduction was so badly kept that the royalist press in Paris announced the event in the most triumphant of terms. For example, *Le Journal général* wrote as follows:

> The sweetheart of Populus, the confidante of Mirabeau, the famous Théroigne has been arrested near Luxembourg and taken to Vienna, in Austria. We have been assured that the Jacobin Club is going to threaten the emperor with an army of five hundred thousand national guards, if he refuses to hand over this heroine, because its chief members are anxious lest she betray their secrets.[6]

In a poem, the Apostles went still further; they explained that, although Théroigne had tried to seduce her kidnappers, they had resisted her charms. They went on to claim that she had been executed:

> And as we lightheartedly,
> Our ditties sing,
> Around the girl's neck,
> Is the executioner's string.
> Weep, then, unhappy Populus
> For your mistress is no more.[7]

A little later, a *Libertines' Catechism* was published, in which Théroigne was depicted as Lambertine, a procuress giving advice to streetwalkers:

> Théroigne in the district, as well as in the brothel
> has used her various talents to experiment
> with her tongue and her arse, which are so precious to France
> her name will live forever.[8]

In its issue for 10 April 1791, the *Moniteur*, although it hedged its bets, attempted to give an accurate account of the situation:

> There has been talk concerning a prisoner of state who has recently been taken to Vienna. The assumption is that this person came from the Low Countries or from Brussels. Rumour has it that this person is in fact a woman who was well-known in France during the Revolution. She answers to the name of Théroigne de Méricourt. Curious things are said of her. It is claimed, for example, that this young woman was implicated in the law-suit filed at the former Châtelet de Paris regarding the sinister *journées* of 5 and 6 October 1789 and that, having taken flight, the emperor had the right to seize her while in his domains, and that His Majesty has the right to try her in his own courts and even to condemn her to the extreme penalty. This outrageous claim is not even worth refuting. It would be preposterous for the emperor's subjects even to suspect His Majesty of being guilty of an assault combining indignity with barbarism.[9]

Théroigne was not transferred to Vienna, but to the fortress of Kufstein, in the Tyrol, where Kaunitz gave orders that she should be held in secret under the pseudonym of Madame de Théobald. This prison was a medieval castle with a drawbridge and thick stone towers built out of the rockface, ringed by deep moats and threatening ravines. There was no room left for hope in such a world, which seemed to be drawn directly from an English Gothic novel. However, in their counter-revolutionary fury, the organizers of the abduction would seem to have overlooked one crucial detail. Although Théroigne was indeed a patriot of the Revolution, she was not French but a subject of the emperor Leopold. She was therefore beholden to Austrian law. Théroigne was well aware of this fact, and asked to be tried by 'her' emperor.

In a letter to her brother Pierre-Joseph, she recounted her unhappy adventures with the French aristocrats, and expressed her strong suspicions

that the Prince of Liège, Baron Sélys and the village priest had played a part
in her abduction. As far as the last two were concerned, Théroigne was not
wrong:

> The prince of Liège would have played no part in this injustice, had he not
> been brought to it by some lord, whom I had the misfortune, quite
> unawares, to shock by speaking in a lofty and righteous vein. In addition, I
> committed some unintentional indiscretion in the company of some persons
> who, wishing to benefit by it, were ignoble enough to exaggerate what was
> said to them without a second thought. It was in fact the village priest who
> denounced me, and no more than that was needed, though the order for my
> arrest may have been false. In the meantime, I am to be confined in con-
> ditions of the strictest security, and my poor health will not hold up for long
> in prison. Well, I shall no doubt die, and an injustice will have been done me.

Théroigne beseeched her brother to go to Vienna and to ask the emperor
to have her interrogated there, so that he might ascertain her innocence
himself. But Pierre-Joseph was concerned less with his sister's fate than with
the pension which she paid him. Instead of going to Vienna, he wrote to
Perregaux to ask him for financial assistance. He informed him, nevertheless, that his aunt had hired two lawyers, who had decided to publish a
report and to seek out a French representative who would be prepared to
write to Mercy-Argenteau protesting the prisoner's innocence.[10]

Prince Kaunitz had little understanding of the situation that he had
acquired. He had acted on the basis of a rumour and a series of phantastical
denunciations, and he plainly believed that Théroigne was a spy hired by the
'leaders' of the Revolution in Paris to foment trouble in Liège and in the
Low Countries. He was therefore delighted to have captured so important a
person, and spared no pains to win over the prisoner. He wished to extract
state secrets from her, as well as precise information respecting the situation
of the royal family and the activities of the Jacobin Club, and he briefed one
of his most diligent civil servants, Aulic councillor François de Blanc, to this
effect. He also wrote him a long letter in order to explain to him why
Théroigne had been abducted, and why a thorough interrogation was of
such crucial importance:

> If you are to learn everything which concerns both the French Revolution
> and the revolutionary party, you will have to spare no efforts. A complete
> and sincere account of the events of 6 October 1789 will be of particular

significance for us. In order to arrive at the whole truth, you will need to know: how central a role the prisoner in fact played in the aforesaid events, how it was possible for her to wield such enormous political influence, which men had served as her patrons, how she first came to Paris and who facilitated her political career. Finally, we will need to know who it was that backed her rise to power and who gave her instructions for her activities in public or for her official actions ... you must try to discover as detailed information as possible on the main leaders of the Revolution, on their personal characters and their ideas, and, finally, on their intentions and their ultimate aims.... You should try to ascertain the role, worth and influence of each of the revolutionary leaders, and seek to know in particular which of them is generally reckoned to enjoy the greatest prestige; you should also elicit clear, accurate and detailed information regarding public opinion's attitudes towards each of the members of the royal family, as well as the attitude of each of the leaders of the Revolution towards the king, the queen, and the king's brothers in particular.... It is more than likely that Théroigne de Méricourt's conscience is laden with grave political crimes, committed in the course of her activities in her homeland and abroad. This being the case, you will probably not succeed in getting her to understand just how harmful her ideas are. On the other hand, even if she does happen to make any confessions, and even if she is full of contrition, these cannot be regarded as having the status of proof, for, in the eyes of the public, confessions obtained in conditions of secrecy are always somewhat suspect.... Our aim is not to punish the delightful person who is in our charge, but our hope is rather that she might supply us with information regarding the political affairs of the court of France.... This lady seems to be an exceedingly enterprising person, possessed of an ardent desire to have some influence upon the masses. This, indeed, would seem to be her ruling passion. She has, moreover, a vanity bordering upon fanaticism. You would therefore do well to make her realize that she must henceforth wholly change her manner of life and thought; that she must abandon all hopes of ever playing any political role again, and that, for the time being, she has but one sole thing to do, namely, to save her present and future existence, by recounting honestly, frankly and sincerely all that she knows.... Nevertheless, you had better warn her that, the moment she strays from the truth, she will lose our trust altogether, and will be ranked with suspect, dangerous and incorrigible individuals, who deserve nothing better than to be under perpetual surveillance; that if, on the other hand, she tells the whole truth, the benefits of an ordinary life will continue to be hers.[11]

Such was the demanding commission which had been entrusted to François de Blanc. He made his way to the fortress of Kufstein, and prepared to make the acquaintance of the imposing character whom the old prince had described. François de Blanc was a rigorous civil servant, methodical almost to the point of obsession, and a man who would therefore treat the task in hand with the utmost seriousness. Convinced of the advantages of the Josephine system, and wholly devoted to the person of Leopold, he shared the ideals of the empire whose zealous servant he was. Reason of state was no joking matter to him, and he would stop at nothing to establish the facts or to arrive at conclusive proofs. He believed that a guilty person should be punished mercilessly, but, by the same token, an innocent one should not be condemned. He was not prepared to tolerate error in the quest for truth. For a civil servant of his stripe, the slightest mistake would be intolerable. The proudest claim of such a councillor was that he was above reproach, and wholly true to his own conscience.

Concerned to follow his master's instructions to the letter, he read to Théroigne in French those passages from Kaunitz's document in which he had demanded a complete confession. He was greatly astonished to see his prisoner's face light up upon hearing these words. Not only was she delighted to meet a man of such severity, the veritable embodiment of the abstract and mystical justice which she had always espoused, but she also declared that her trust in His Majesty's justice was such that she could not imagine how an imperial court could ever condemn an individual for a crime of opinion. When faced with this exemplary judge, a supporter of the Ancien Régime, Théroigne showed herself to be an exemplary militant of the Revolution. The long hours she had spent at the Constituent Assembly, her friendship with Gilbert Romme, her participation in the *Société des amis de la loi,* had taught her one essential thing, namely, that freedom of opinion was an inalienable right and, being a right, it could not be a crime. Théroigne was led by this logic into believing that she had the right to fight the monarchy publicly, but that no judicial system had the right to imprison her for this combat since it was no crime. As for the crimes of which she was accused, she was prepared, by her own testimony, to demonstrate that she had never committed them.

Satisfied with this speech, which did not clash with his own principles, François de Blanc urged Théroigne to proceed. Then, he notified her of the arrival of Simon Georges, a French-speaker who would take the minutes of her interrogation. Upon hearing these words, Théroigne was anxious to

59

know whether this man was one of the French aristocrats who had kidnapped her. With some irritation, de Blanc answered somewhat evasively, claiming that her abductors were Belgian. Théroigne retorted:

> What? You wish me to believe that those people were Belgian? Either you are mistaken, or else you are trying to deceive me. Until my dying breath, I will vouch for the fact that they were officers and French aristocrats. It was not merely because of their appearance that I recognized them to be such, but from their arrogant, hateful and evil demeanour. I warn you, Sir, that if one of these gentlemen should come here to take minutes or simply to attend the interviews, I shall not open my mouth; I would prefer to undergo the direst of punishments, even that of being shut up here for the rest of my life! I am Belgian by birth, and I demand that my case should be heard by the imperial authorities and civil servants, and by no one else. It is only in such circumstances that, as a loyal subject of the house of Austria, I will tell you the whole truth.[12]

De Blanc thus realized that the supposed French spy was in fact an imperial subject, and that it would be easier to pass judgement upon her in Austria. He immediately notified Kaunitz.

In response to her judge's request, the prisoner tried hard to draft an exhaustive account of her life. For the whole month of June, she worked each day in her cell, with a pencil, a pen and paper supplied by the prison administration. Since Théroigne had learned to write only very late in life, she had some difficulty in handling both language and spelling. But the Aulic councillor did not hurry her, and proved to be concerned with accuracy. As the days passed, he began to discern Théroigne's true personality. He took note of what she wrote down, requested further details and alternated interrogations with writing sessions. The text which resulted, the five-part *Confessions de Théroigne de Méricourt*, first published in 1892, is an admirable document.[13] Its author was blessed with a remarkable memory, which enabled her to retrace her past, both public and private, from her childhood at Marcourt up until her abduction at La Boverie. She made no mention of her child, and did not write of her venereal disease. On the other hand, she told the story of her English lover, the only man, according to her, with whom she had had sexual relations. She had loved him, but he had disappointed her, refusing to marry her and remaining a rake. This testimony shows that, although Théroigne very probably told the truth, she still sought to conceal what caused her the most shame, namely, her position as a woman under the Ancien Régime.

The papers which had been seized at the time of Théroigne's abduction enabled the Aulic councillor to fill in some of the gaps in her story. He discovered that she had been a mother, from a receipt signed by a surgeon who had cared for her child. He also learned of her venereal disease from doctors' letters, and discovered some of the names of persons who had played a part in her life but who had not featured in her deposition, by reading various communications, those of the Marquis de Persan in particular. Finally, he became aware of the Châtelet law-suit, and of the activities of the *Société des amis de la loi*. The document drafted by the Chancellery did not mention that Théroigne had been a mother, nor that she suffered from a venereal disease. De Blanc deemed it sufficient to emphasize that her amorous intrigues had damaged her health.

De Blanc was in fact less interested in his prisoner's private life than in the part she had played in the Revolution, and in her contacts with Belgian and Liégois patriots. The inventory of her possessions featured manuscripts, bundles of letters wrapped in waxed canvas, books, official records and pawn tickets. He noted that in March 1788 a maternal uncle had sent Théroigne some information on the political situation in the Low Countries, that in June 1790 someone by the name of Le Tellier had invited her to a ladies' club, or literary and patriotic society, located in Paris at 19 rue Notre-Dame-des-Victoires and, finally, that in August of the same year a certain V.D. Linden had addressed a letter to her at Liège in which he spoke of the authentic principles of Machiavelli. In another letter, written as if to an intimate, a Monsieur Quiriny, from Herve, gave an enthusiastic account of the capture of that town by patriots.[14]

The Aulic councillor gradually came to realize that, far from dealing with a historical figure of the first importance or a dangerous spy, he was in fact in the presence of a strange, somewhat exalted woman, who had been humiliated by her relations with men, and whose proud character earned his profound respect:

> When I compare my own impressions with the prisoner's observations, I cannot bring myself to admit that she could have played as important a role in the events in Paris as has been attributed to her, or that she has had such extensive contacts as has been maintained.[15]

Anxious at all costs to avoid a miscarriage of justice, de Blanc decided to make a methodical comparison of the affidavits of the various persons involved in this adventure.

During the night of 6 to 7 June, the chevalier La Valette arrived in Kufstein. Théroigne was unaware of his presence, and continued to draft her report. The effort involved was such that she fell ill. She was wracked day and night by a dry cough, complained of migraines, suffered from insomnia and spat blood.

De Blanc was in fact mistrustful of La Valette. He found him an over-weening and pretentious braggart, the quintessential French aristocrat, steeped in his own privileges, sure of his own rights and incapable of the least feeling of justice. He was, in short, the very opposite of an enlightened noble. As he wrote to Kaunitz:

> The more time I spend in the chevalier's company, the more readily I can understand the prisoner's vehement protests when she learned that he wished to be present at her interrogation. He is literally swollen up with hatred and fury against the French democrats, and often surpasses himself in his transports of rage towards them.[16]

The chevalier claimed to have in his possession irrefutable proof of Théroigne's crimes. De Blanc lost no time in perusing the documents, which consisted of the *Statements and Admissions* drafted in the course of the journey, and of a declaration made by a civil servant from Marcourt, which claimed that the accused had attempted to win the village priest over to her revolutionary ideas. 'As far as these documents are concerned', wrote de Blanc, 'I have to point out that they were drafted and signed by French aristocrats, that is, by people who are plainly the prisoner's sworn enemies.'[17]

When the Aulic councillor compared these documents with the *Confessions de Théroigne*, he perceived numerous contradictions between them. He therefore divided these contradictions into groups, then divided the groups into specific points, which were themselves rephrased in the form of 132 different questions. Between 27 June and 24 July, de Blanc elicited an answer from Théroigne regarding every single one of these questions. She had to pass comment upon the aristocrats' assertions, and then to give her own account of the journey and detail her true 'confessions'. In spite of the pity which he felt for the prisoner and the distaste aroused in him by the chevalier, de Blanc was determined to preserve his neutrality. He therefore treated Théroigne with merciless severity, forcing her to work without respite in order to supply irrefutable proof of her own innocence.

The *Statements and Admissions*, which had been signed by La Valette and Saint-Malon, was a tissue of lies, but it also contained some accurate information. It painted a picture of Théroigne as an enraged madwoman who had played a prominent role in the Revolution since the storming of the Bastille. It was said that she had exulted at the parade of decapitated heads on pikes, that she had declared that she herself had founded a Club for the Rights of Man, that she had had the exclusive privilege of attending the Jacobin Club and that it was believed in Paris that she would return soon to found a women's club. The document of course claimed that she had been involved in the October Days, that she regretted that the royal family had not been assassinated, that she had stressed that she wished to remain in France and that she had offered to place her abductors in important posts there. She had also asserted that she had played a key role in the uprisings in Liège and Brabant.

The manuscript did not offer the slightest shred of evidence that Théroigne was guilty of any crime against the members of the royal family but, in order to be doubly sure, de Blanc again consulted the legal documents from the Châtelet proceedings. He discovered that the depositions against Théroigne had seemed so superficial to this court, which was itself royalist in sympathy, that no summons had been issued against her. As a consequence, no serious proof existed of the young woman's criminal guilt.

In spite of this new evidence, de Blanc persisted in his scrupulous interrogation of Théroigne, and made her comment, word by word and line by line, on the 132 questions which he had formulated. Some of the information which she proffered helped him get a little closer to the truth. Indeed, his prisoner was not satisfied merely to refute the majority of the assertions contained in the supposed 'confessions', but proceeded to demonstrate that they were both grotesque, incoherent and wholly illogical. Thus, with respect to the charge that she had sought to enlist the village priest for her cause, she observed:

> If what my abductors have said here were true, I would have been not so much guilty as foolish, in seeking to begin the revolution in Brabant through the person of a village priest in a poor village only fifty houses strong, in an area that was bristling with Austrian troops, partly in the surrounding villages and partly in what was reputed to be one of the most heavily fortified strongholds in Europe.[18]

Théroigne accepted that not all of her abductors' claims were false. Some were based upon things that she had actually said, and represented distorted versions of her own utterances. Others were accurate. She admitted to de Blanc that she had given her abductors an exaggerated idea of her own part in the Revolution when she realized that they had deceived her by passing themselves off as patriots. She had therefore wanted to mock them in turn:

> If therefore I said such things, it was so as to make as much fun of my abductors as I could, for they were ready enough to believe the most absurd and nonsensical things, provided only that they accorded with their prejudices.... I may well have said a whole host of things to my abductors which I would perhaps not have been able to recall an hour later, once I had cooled down again, but I know full well that several of the things which I said to them were designed either to make fun of them or to mortify and humiliate them, after having been myself provoked and irritated by them in a thousand different ways, each of which was more degrading and more shocking than the last.... For much of what I said was true, and much false, and where such information is recorded in their statements it is presented in a wholly different light; these are so many examples of bad faith by which they have blackened my reputation in the sight of His Majesty the Emperor, exactly as was done earlier in order to bring about my capture.[19]

By cross-referring between the *Confessions*, the *Statements and Admissions* and the various interrogations, de Blanc realized that La Valette was a liar and that Théroigne was telling the truth. She went even further than that, however, for she showed herself capable of reflecting upon the fragility of human testimony in general. In her *Statements and Admissions*, the chevalier had claimed that Théroigne had said that France should rid herself of the Comte d'Artois and the Prince of Condé. When confronted with this accusation, Théroigne told de Blanc that she had said that these two noblemen were vicious persons who aroused a sense of horror in all honest folk,

> but I was far from having said that it was necessary to be rid of them. This is a proposal that could have been ascribed to me only by people of the most ignoble sentiment, people, it suffices to say, who were capable of stepping down from the carriage near to Koblenz simply in order to beat up a wretched postilion and then to say, once they had resumed their seats, and in order to humiliate me, that such were your Rights of Man, and who, finally,

having spoken to me ineffectually of love, told me that I would pay them a higher price in the market–place.[20]

At first, de Blanc had not attached much weight to the phrase 'speaking ineffectually of love'. But the prisoner's testimony made it clear that her abductors were perfectly capable of committing an actual crime. Their anti-patriotic fury had been such that they had shown no hesitation in raining blows upon a poor coachman, simply in order to make fun of the 'Rights of Man'. For a civil servant such as de Blanc, who was convinced of the superiority of the monarchical system, such behaviour was wholly contemptible, for it represented a perversion of the very principles for which he stood.

However, the judge did not show any preference for Théroigne, but rather pursued his inquiry with increased severity. He sought out the third confederate, one Augustin Lechoux, who had witnessed the drubbing to which the coachman had been subjected, and who had overheard the conversations between Théroigne and the two aristocrats. De Blanc hoped that this fresh testimony would enable him to arrive at a just conclusion. While awaiting Lechoux's arrival, he acquainted the chevalier with Théroigne's refutations of passages in the *Statements and Admissions*, and called upon him to comment upon what she had written. La Valette of course stood by his earlier testimony and therefore signed it, denying in the haughtiest possible manner that the prisoner had any rights to challenge him in law. As far as the drubbing of the coachman was concerned, La Valette admitted that he had done the deed, his view being that the man deserved a few blows for his faults. 'The postilion merited his punishment', he wrote, 'for an act of carelessness which cost us some trouble. Mademoiselle wept and wished to oppose this punishment, but nevertheless he got his just deserts.'[21] As for the violent remarks that Théroigne claimed he had made regarding the patriots:

> I note that I only made these observations regarding patriots and those on the left side of the National Assembly; let me add that, if I had a whip in my hand, I would make the whole of the left side of the National Assembly jump, and M. the abbé Sieyès at their head.[22]

This admirable civil servant thus learnt that an abyss lay between himself and these barbaric emigrés from Koblenz. Not only had La Valette been prepared to accuse a loyal woman of imaginary crimes but, without the slightest scruple, he had voiced genuinely criminal intentions towards his political adversaries.

Théroigne was still not aware that her abductor had arrived in Kufstein. The Aulic councillor hoped to get closer to the truth by using the surprise effect of a physical confrontation between the two witnesses. He therefore brought the chevalier brusquely into the room in which Théroigne was being interrogated. For Théroigne, this aristocrat was the embodiment of the hateful regime which the Revolution wished to sweep away. Brought face to face with him, she showed no compunction in admitting what she had up until then preferred to conceal, namely, that he had tried to rape her.

De Blanc was astonished. La Valette, caught off his guard, lost his head and used the title of Marquis when signing the minutes.[23]

The confrontation between the two witnesses had not brought all the facts to light. For further clarification, de Blanc awaited the arrival of Lechoux. But it was now clear that the real Théroigne de Méricourt was neither a spy, nor a high-ranking revolutionary nor a dangerous agitator. The most that she was guilty of, under Austrian law, was a delict of opinion. But, if this were so, her case could be matched by that of thousands of men who had rebelled in the Brabant or the pays Liégois, and whose revolt had been crushed. If this woman had committed the same acts as they, why should she be handled with such secrecy, as if her case were a matter of state security? De Blanc realized that, if Théroigne's internment were to continue for much longer, it would become an embarrassment for the Empire. There was some risk that the affair would be exploited in Paris, and that it would become a scandal or a source of ridicule.

But La Valette had another card up his sleeve. While the judge was asking Metternich to dispatch Lechoux to him as quickly as possible, the French aristocrat was engineering the arrival in Kufstein of a powdered priest who claimed to have irrefutable proof of Théroigne's guilt. This colourful individual was a baron named Mengin-Salabert. No sooner had he arrived at the fortress than he dictated a testimony entitled *Information collected regarding the Pythia of the century*, which rehearsed the prisoner's life, and which, like the *Précis historique*, would subsequently be used as the basis for the legend of a Théroigne who was bloodthirsty, vengeful, libertine and debauched.[24]

Mengin-Salabert's testimony was a remarkable concoction, a skilful mixture of gossip, rumour and gutter-press investigation, which built up the sort of imaginary picture of Théroigne which would accord best with the emigré aristocrats' ideology. This narrative also featured the notion of the Revolution, which was central to royalist discourse.

Mengin-Salabert had learned something about the prisoner's adolescence, and he therefore knew that she had been a cowherd, that she had had an English lover and that she had wished at one stage to be a singer. But he presented her in the guise of a sorceress turning the heads of the men and then abandoning them cruelly. Thus she was initially the unscrupulous mistress of a poor lawyer from Liège, then the fashionable lover of an Englishman, who managed nevertheless to leave her. Finally, she launched herself into the patriotic struggle, seducing four famous men — Barnave, Mirabeau, Robespierre and Sieyès — who were corrupted as she herself was, and who became her lovers. Mengin-Salabert was of course unaware of the existence of either Gilbert Romme or the *Société des amis de la loi*, but he showed not the slightest hesitation in arguing that Théroigne was venerated like a goddess in Paris and that it had been upon her advice that the revolutionaries had drafted the constitution and established the Jacobin Club. He described the October Days as if they were an Orléanist plot, and portrayed Théroigne as the head of the conspirators and a bloodthirsty rabble-rouser:

Everyone knows that it was in the house of this Pythia that the plan for the debauchment of the French guards was conceived, and the most effective way of winning them over to the rebel cause was discussed. Dressed as a man, this woman went from one end of Paris to the other, inveigled her way into all the barracks and made subversive speeches there. At the same time, she distributed money and, by spending over thirty million livres in the space of a fortnight, she succeeded in winning over the whole of the garrison of Paris. It is absolutely certain that the plot of 5 and 6 October was hatched in her residence. With this purpose, Prince Philip of Orléans and several friends devoted both to his person and to his house often visited the Pythia's house by night. There is also the clearest possible proof that she was at the head of the seven or eight thousand women who invaded the Palace of Versailles, it was she who, at the very moment that the massacre of the bodyguard was beginning, yelled at the top of her voice that *one should use the queen's guts to make cockades.* Everyone also knows that it was she and some of her fellows who instigated the defection of the Flanders regiment. Since at this time the National Assembly had decided, amid some uproar, to go and occupy the salon of Hercules, it was she who dissuaded the deputies from pursuing this plan. Haranguing them with passionate and inflammatory speeches, she explained in no uncertain terms that the representatives of the people had no right to hold their sessions in the palace of a tyrant.[25]

After he had reeled off this improbable litany, Mengin-Salabert explained that the court at the Châtelet had issued a warrant for Théroigne's arrest. In order to flesh out these phantasmagorias, he invented a day on 7 October 1789, in the course of which Théroigne, disguised as a man, was supposed to have met Louis XVI in the Tuileries:

> Seeing that the king was alone, somewhat sad and deep in thought, she approached him. The king noticed her and, knowing of the warrant which the Châtelet had taken out against her, he put his hand on her shoulder and said: 'How can you still be here?' — 'Indeed I am, Sire', she replied, in a dis-respectful tone, 'for I did not wish to leave Paris without having seen you again and without urging you to stay here from now on and to respect unconditionally the wishes of the representatives of the people at the National Assembly'.[26]

Although the Aulic councillor was plainly flabbergasted, the baron proceeded with his testimony. When the conspirators heard of Théroigne's impending arrest, they made plans for their 'priestess''s return to her native village. Entrusted with huge sums of money by the National Assembly, she came to Liège and Brabant in order to organize the Revolution. Everywhere she dispensed money and valuables, encouraging the peasants to get drunk. Mengin-Salabert was aware that Théroigne owned a fine necklace. He therefore embroidered the rumour by claiming that in Belgium she was wearing a part of the famous diamond necklace which had belonged to Marie-Antoinette. Mengin-Salabert further added that the people were deaf to her vociferations, and took her for a madwoman.

Finally, he claimed that the only way to make this 'sinister regicide' talk would be to use torture upon her:

> It would be an easy matter to show that Mlle Théroigne is in no way justified in protesting against the injustice of her arrest. Has she not every-where preached the doctrines of false liberty and of insubordination? Has she not stirred up the people against legitimate authority? The fact that, as no one would dispute, she has been in contact with the revolutionary leaders justifies the use of all available forms of constraint. Her avowals must be wrung from her bit by bit. It will require time and patience, but it is the only

way of learning a large part of the truth. Some notorious criminals actually never confessed at all.[27]

In order to shed light on this deposition, the Aulic councillor made Théroigne answer a further round of questions, this time touching upon the Duc d'Orléans, the Palais-Royal, the National Assembly and the October Days. He then adopted the same procedure for Mengin-Salabert's testimony as he had employed with regard to the *Statements and Admissions*. He divided and subdivided until he was left with sixty-seven questions. On 15 July, he arranged for someone to read aloud to Théroigne, in his presence, the baron's deposition, with a view to proceeding with an interrogation, but upon this occasion the prisoner rebelled and refused to be subjected to any further accusations. Théroigne emphasized that, if the judge were to lend an ear to such horrors, he would run the risk of compromising the dignity of imperial justice.

De Blanc did not proceed any further with the interrogation, for the previous day he had noticed that Théroigne was depressed and increasingly ill. He therefore decided to summon the chief doctor of the town of Freibourg, Doctor von Mederer, to her bedside. He arrived at Kufstein on 23 July, examined Théroigne and recommended, in his official report, that she be released as soon as possible:

I have found her physical condition to be precarious, although her life is not itself in danger. On the other hand, her moral condition is such as to prompt the deepest anxieties. If the circumstances which have given rise to this situation are not altered, it is more than likely that the patient's general condition will shortly take a decided turn for the worse. I therefore feel it to be my bounden duty as a doctor to draw the attention of the Imperial Commission to the moral health of the imprisoned person. Let me reiterate that, without further delay, she must be reassured. Otherwise, there is reason to fear a highly troubling deterioration in her condition from one day to the next.[28]

Mederer did not advance any precise diagnosis of Théroigne's 'moral state'. He seemed to ascribe it to the conditions of her incarceration, which she deemed unjust and which led her to try to demonstrate her own innocence. However, the manuscripts found in her portfolio suggest that this 'moral state' indicated a form of derangement which predated her imprisonment and which had been exacerbated or revealed by it.

According to the Chancellery report, Théroigne's notebooks contained two different kinds of manuscript notes. On the one hand, there were quotations and perfectly rational discussions on the topic of democracy or justice and, on the other, there were a series of free associations in which their author formulated murderous phantasies of the most startling kind. Théroigne's mental universe seemed thus to be split between a world of clarity, reason and light, derived from books and from her experience of the Revolution, and a world of shadow, madness and confinement, which was unconsciously transmitted through a form of confidential writing, inspired also by the reading of texts.

In the first notebook, which was some twenty-six pages long, Théroigne argued quite coherently, and gave her views upon public opinion and legislation:

> [Public] opinion, as we have already said, ought in its essence to be the judgement of the greatest number. However, among us the greatest number neither know how to nor dare to judge. The measure of public opinion is supplied by the welfare of the city, of the fatherland. Public opinion would simply be public morality. It is therefore not enough to declare that public opinion is corrupted. It is obvious that no such thing exists.... There will be a genuine public opinion in my country only when we are all equal before the law.... The laws should serve to safeguard each person's liberty or property from attacks. The law which is the mother of all the others is the symbol [*sic*]. Do no wrong to others. However, so deplorable has the effect of the long subjugation of minds been that the peoples, far from understanding their genuine social position, far from feeling that they actually have the right to revoke bad laws, have even reached the point of believing that nothing is theirs save whatever a good or bad law grants them. They seem to be unaware that liberty and property are prior to everything.

Théroigne then proceeded to comment upon the nature of those privileges which she termed unjust, hateful and in contradiction with the supreme purpose of every political society.

In a second notebook, which ran to sixteen pages, Théroigne had jotted down some sentences underlined in black, the content of which seemed to be at odds with the coherence of the notes in the first one:

> The house will consist of a façade of bronze, if my funds permit it, and the vault will be wholly in black. In the middle there will be a woman who

tramples tyranny underfoot. This tyranny will be represented by the figure of a man. This woman will reach out her hand to me and will cry out: help me or I shall succumb. I will then take hold of a dagger from nearby and I will strike the man.

Théroigne then harked back to the question of the coherence of patriotic discourse. She explained the origin of the Estates-General, of the Assemblies of Notables and of the *parlements*. She then elaborated upon the notion of rebellion:

A rebel needs chiefly to have discretion, to be energetic and to be skilled in choosing agents.... One must therefore take great pains to put everyone in their place ... in the case of the leaders of the Revolution in the Brabant, their aim must be first of all to abolish the orders, to allow the people their liberty, to establish a representative government like that in France, and to delegate the legislative power in order to exercise it directly [*sic*]. That would change the order of things established at present for a rigorous Republic. One must give the people the freedom to make whatever government they wish. The subjects of a good king are happy, but what is so fragile and fleeting a happiness to society? As far as politics is concerned, the important thing is not to have a good king but to have a good government. The benefits of a gentle reign are merely temporary for, even if one king does not abuse his power, his successor indubitably will. This is what deceives the people. It never sees that the most skilled tyrants drape its chains with silk, by doing some temporary good in order to make it forget how important a right to liberty [*sic*]. Sometimes they even try to lessen or soften their authority in order to consolidate it later.

When de Blanc asked Théroigne what the sentences underlined in black meant, she replied that the image of the conflict between the woman and masculine tyranny had been inspired by a travel book:

I had read somewhere that, in a vault in Rome, a Fury holding a dagger has been discovered on a tomb; this vision came to me because, having always been offended by the tyranny which men exercise over my own sex, I wished to find an emblem for it in this picture, in which the death of this tyranny would mark the downfall of the prejudices under which we groan, and which it was my dearest wish to have been able to destroy.

71

Amongst some of Théroigne's loose papers, consisting for the most part of accounts and lists of expenses, there was another passage in which considered judgements took second place to the elaboration of phantasies:

> However, public affairs.... A thousand things came rushing in at once upon my fevered imagination. It was in vain that my parents tried yet again to keep me. No, I had to leave. Such was the situation of my soul when it was wholly overwhelmed by our crowning misfortunes. You know as well as I do the circumstances in which the darkest betrayal unfolded. It therefore came to pass. Ah, if you only knew all that I have witnessed, the very thought of it would cause you to shiver. I have been in such places, Oh Heavens, I have seen unheard of barbarities. On the one hand, the hatching of betrayals, on the other hand, I have spoken, they wished to ruin me, unfortunate Belgians: Yes, sir, they have put the most ignorant on the wrong scent; they have been won over by fanaticism, corrupted the most cowardly assassins, ill-treated and imprisoned the most honest, finally from the very beginning.

The sentence ended abruptly at this point.

Another manuscript bore the title *Essais sur la langue française*. It shows that Théroigne never stopped trying to learn to write and to speak, both by studying a treatise on rhetoric and by copying out passages from texts and speeches. One page contained a number of laments on the slavery of women, another featured some remarks on Cromwell and the Duc de Guise, and a third was a draft of a letter to the painter David. Finally, on a piece of paper wrapped around some locks of brown hair, was the following declaration by Mirabeau:

> How sluggish you are in certain matters, how you endanger the public good, through failing to use your foresight and to anticipate the unfolding of events. Do you wish to forestall great anxieties? Educate the people, tell them that you have come to shatter their chains. Advance, promise them the advantages of this same liberty, which they cannot love, since they do not know it and since every effort has been to let them believe that they were born to serve.[29]

Théroigne had copied out this passage because she was unsure of the meaning of the word *péricliter* (endanger) and wished to discover it.

We can use these archives to try to reconstitute the central theme around which Théroigne's personality was structured. She had been deprived of a mother, rejected by her stepmother, 'betrayed' by a father who had failed her, and tricked by brothers whom she adored despite their many short-comings; she therefore experienced her situation as a woman under the Ancien Régime as one of the bitterest humiliation. Nor would the events which punctuated her existence diverge from the pattern established in her early years. From a debauched seducer to a jealous and masochistic Marquis, and a music teacher who was ugly and a 'castrato', all the men in her life were highly flawed. Ugly, old, weak or ignoble, they sometimes seemed to be the servile victims of their vices and sometimes persecutors imbued with their own privileges. As for women, in Théroigne's opinion they were condemned to unhappiness or execration. Through carnal love, they suffered the shame of venereal disease, and, in the supposed joys of mother-hood, they brushed against solitude and death.

Embodying this gloomy reality so highly characteristic of the whole period, but which in this case was lived as a *fatum*, the peasant woman from Marcourt seemed to oscillate forever between a melancholia which was ceaselessly returning her to the ennui of her century and a mania which plunged her into dreams of grandeur only to drown her subsequently in a nightmare of disillusionment. In this respect, Théroigne's journeys, her endless displacements and her attachment to figures of 'passage' (garrisoned officer, Italian mountebank or 'Persian' Marquis) all symbolized this oscil-lation. In other words, the perpetual quest for an 'elsewhere' stemmed from her cyclical personality, in which exaltation was followed by ennui, reason by madness, illusion by disappointment, revolt by persecution, wandering by fixity and confinement by liberty.

Théroigne's involvement in the Revolution seemed to 'cure' her of all this. The National Assembly provided her with a 'family' capable of supporting her. But she also learned there a means of theorizing her per-secutory or murderous leanings and was finally able to take her dreams for realities. In short, with the Revolution, Théroigne was finally settled some-where. She lived in a specific geographical site and she made her way each day at the very same hour to a specific spot, namely, the National Assembly.

The National Assembly served her both as a maternal pole and as a symbolic authority. This was why she wished to 'deify' it, and proposed that a monument be raised to it, on the ruins of the Bastille, which would both shelter it and give it the dignity it deserved in the eyes of the nation. Théroigne was also obsessed by a double dream of procreation. She wished to transmit a knowledge to the people and bequeath to posterity some written 'traces' of her passage. Thus, in the *Société des amis de la loi*, she was responsible for the archives, and whenever the opportunity arose she would draft a 'report'. When she donned her 'amazon's costume' — her riding-habit — which distanced her from her own condition as a woman, she was in her own fashion establishing a 'location' for herself, as if she were becoming the 'warrior' of the Revolution, the lover of an 'idea'. In this respect, the royalist press was not mistaken when it represented her as giving birth to the Constitution.

In her notebook, she dreamed of building a house resembling those neo-classical temples which were to be characteristic of revolutionary aesthetics. She added to it a completely dark vault, as if to bury her bad memories in it. Finally, Théroigne represented the Revolution as a woman much like herself, still fragile and trampling the tyranny of men underfoot, and she saw her own role as being that of a valiant soldier who would answer the Revolution's plea for help. She grabs the dagger in order to cut the throat of the masculine dictatorship, thereby subconsciously acting out the events of 10 August. She was thus either doubled or divided. Through the Revolution, she was able to transform her femininity, once fragile and shameful to her, into something virile and triumphant.

Conversely, her confinement at Kufstein enclosed her within a universe of ennui and gloom. Once imprisoned, she fell ill, spat blood, suffered from coughing fits and migraines. In short, she recovered the 'shame' of her sex. But, once the Aulic councillor had appealed to her intelligence by asking her to write, she marshalled the formidable amount of energy which the Revolution had released in her. The manuscript of the *Confessions*, written under stress, bore the marks of the cyclical nature of her personality. Written in both pen and pencil, it is sometimes legible and regular, some-times full of blotches, deletions and mistakes.

By awakening in her the desire to testify and the will to overcome her internal splitting, the councillor also demonstrated to her that imperial justice was prepared to take her seriously. Through a reference to *the Law* he became her 'confessor' and was able to demolish her accusers' arguments. In Théroigne's eyes, the councillor was not so much a man of flesh and blood as an abstract incarnation of justice or a screen on which phantasies could be projected. Thus, it was not long before she forgot him or, more precisely, repressed his human shape and replaced it with another ideal of justice, the emperor himself, a still more value-laden incarnation of *the Law*.

On 25 July, without waiting for Lechoux's deposition, de Blanc sent Kaunitz a report in which he called for Théroigne's immediate release.

When this secret trial had begun, Prince Kaunitz had asked de Blanc to use the prisoner's interrogation to gather accurate information regarding the Revolution in France and the predicament of the royal family. Whereas the interrogation had not yielded the kind of information for which de Blanc had been looking, *les Confessions de Théroigne* and her accusers' declarations were in fact documents of some value for the Austrian state. They contained a mass of information regarding the outlook of the various contending factions and the mentality of the emigrés, as de Blanc was well aware. This is why, in his report, he explained to Kaunitz that one of the causes of the rebellion in Paris had been the utter incapacity of the French monarchy to introduce reforms:

> After a fresh and more searching examination of the information presented by the two Frenchmen, the chevalier La Valette and Baron Mengin, you would scarcely believe just how pitiful, inept and ridiculous it strikes us as being. If one were to compare the outlook of the two Frenchmen and that of the prisoner, from a strictly intellectual point of view, it is impossible to avoid drawing the conclusion that the latter is indubitably superior. Taking everything into account, Théroigne is not merely an enthusiastic and convinced woman but, in addition, she has some understanding, with a luminous and surprising intuition, of what is happening in her country and she criticizes the anger and intellectual weakness which the nobility and clergy have displayed in opposing the necessary reforms. She advances a convincing case for the view that it is the king himself who, by turning a deaf ear to the desires of the people, is strictly speaking the prime cause of the explosion of popular passions. The prisoner had the opportunity to observe, clearly and at first hand, the consequences of such an attitude in Paris, in Versailles and in the provinces.[30]

Sensing that she was soon to be set free, Anne-Josèphe explained to de Blanc that she was prepared to throw herself upon the emperor Leopold's mercy, even to stay in Vienna and devote herself to music. On 2 August, Prince Kaunitz informed the councillor that the emperor had decided to free the prisoner before the end of her trial and to have her stay anonymously, but under surveillance, in Vienna. She thereupon decided to assume her mother's name and to call herself Mlle Lahaye.[31]

Given Théroigne's depressive condition, de Blanc asked Doctor Von

Mederer to accompany him to Vienna. After six days on the road, the three travellers arrived in the imperial capital. Anne-Josèphe concerned herself with the house in which she had been installed, arranged for a wardrobe to be assembled for her, requested some money and a servant, and caught up on the events which had taken place during her detention. She then contacted her uncle Campinado and her banker Perregaux.

Since April 1791, her relations with the Aulic councillor had been extremely cordial. The judge served her as father, mother, protector, 'midwife' of her writing, as therapist and as supplier of remedies. He also assumed responsibility for her clothes, her personal possessions and for all the details of her everyday existence. She wrote to him frequently, informing him of the state of her health, of her reading, and of the composition of her autobiography. She spoke endlessly of liberty, expressed a wish to see family and friends again. She took pleasure in going for walks with him outside the fortress of Kufstein, and it caused her suffering if she could not see him. Each letter began with a 'Good day Monsieur' or with 'I bid you good day', and ended with an 'Adieu' or 'Adieu, Monsieur'.

Although this correspondence continued in much the same vein in Vienna, an incident soon occurred which unleashed a persecutory reaction in Théroigne towards her protector. At the beginning of October, she was received by Prince Kaunitz, who asked her if she intended to leave Vienna. She immediately jumped to the conclusion that de Blanc had wished to deceive her by letting her believe that she was still a prisoner. She wrote to the prince:

> I have been truly enlightened by the kindness with which Your Excellency has deigned to receive me. I am most indebted to you. After the question Your Excellency deigned to ask me as to whether I was about to leave, I saw clearly that I had been deceived and that I am free without knowing it. If such is indeed the case, I accept the generous offers of kindness which Your Excellency has deigned to make me. As a consequence, I make so bold as to beg Your Excellency to establish my liberty beyond all doubt.

Three days later, Théroigne regretted her suspicions and wrote a long letter to the councillor, in which she admitted that she had allowed herself to be carried away:

> I must make a confession to you, Monsieur, which cannot any longer surprise you, and which is accompanied by my most sincere regrets. I

allowed myself to be swayed by a fit of mistrust towards yourself, which was due to a too hasty judgement I had made regarding the indifference I thought to have discerned for some long time in you. All the times that, in my impatience to have you finish my case, I vexed you, I suspected that my enemies had perhaps found some way of turning you against me, and to destroy the impartiality which I had had such good cause to praise at Kufstein, and I was confirmed in this doubt by your decision to write your report on my case in the German language, believing that you had done this in order to keep its content from me, for it seemed only just that, since you had to be the defender of my innocence, I could claim the right to see what you were writing there in order to demonstrate it. So strong a grip did this suspicion have upon me that I even went so far as to betray some intimations of it to Prince Kaunitz. Since, Monsieur, my reason and my sense of equity, combined with my memory of the honourable treatment I enjoyed at Kufstein, have regained the upper hand, and the honest and quasi-paternal way in which you made me feel yesterday the ill-judged nature of what I had communicated to Monseigneur, and since as an effect of this same mistrust it had however had no other end in view but that of receiving some letters from my brothers and from my banker, I beg your pardon, Monsieur, for the wrong that my soul has done you and I sincerely hope that you will grant me the same, all the more willingly indeed since you have shown yourself to be capable of reading to the very depths of my soul, and of convincing yourself that I have, like all mortals, been capable of being deceived by the falsity of appearances, which the liveliness of my imagination does not allow me to exaggerate, I am incapable of persevering in error.[32]

The councillor had not in fact 'deceived' Théroigne, but he refused to allow her to leave the capital before the case was closed. The final witness, Augustin Lechoux, was due to arrive in Vienna in November, and de Blanc wanted to have sufficient time to interrogate him according to the rules. Moreover, however 'paternal' he had seemed in his dealings with Théroigne, he was still a civil servant of the Ancien Régime. Thus, he wished to make the young woman's liberty dependent upon a number of conditions, which would oblige her to renounce all forms of political activity and to submit to the imperial authority. This was why, on 7 October, de Blanc made Théroigne draft a letter in which she pledged herself to undertake nothing without the express authorization of His Majesty. Nevertheless, she would steal a march upon him and 'deceive' him. At the end of October, she obtained an interview with Leopold, at the end of which she was granted permission to return to the Ardennes. A letter written by de Blanc, and dated 7 November, confirms that this meeting took place, and shows just how dissatisfied the civil servant was with the outcome:

> Théroigne may well have regretted the undertaking she has made, since, about two weeks ago, in the course of an audience with the emperor, she asked permission to return home, and His Majesty, in his goodness — or so she has informed me — has granted her request. It would of course be a simple enough matter to make her understand that this imperial authorization — assuming that it actually was granted — was given under false pretences. His Majesty has been knowingly led astray, since Mlle Théroigne made no mention to him of her previous declaration, in which she said that she was prepared to stay here forever.[33]

De Blanc felt that he had been outflanked by Théroigne's decision, which had been taken on the spur of the moment, and he concluded that the emperor must have been deceived. He continued to show unflagging zeal in his prosecution of the inquiry. On 4 and 5 November, he interrogated Lechoux, who confirmed the prisoner's testimony in every detail and wholly refuted La Valette's declarations, the *Statements and Admissions* and the defamatory deposition made by Mengin-Salabert. The sergeant emphasized that Théroigne had indeed been subjected to verbal and physical violence, that, far from having attacked the Austrian monarchy, she had in fact sung the praises of both Joseph and Leopold and that he himself would not have signed the documents which the two aristocrats had written, had it not been for the threats which they had levelled at him. De Blanc wrote:

> Lechoux declares that the courage and stout-heartedness of this woman had filled him with admiration. Neither the most terrible threats nor the most glittering promises could make her renege upon her principles.[34]

Just as the councillor was putting the final full stop to the case, Théroigne received a sum of 600 florins from the Chancellery to cover the expenses of her return journey. At the end of November, she retrieved her wardrobe, said goodbye to her judge and boarded a postchaise, which took her as far as Brussels after a fortnight's exhausting journey through snowbound countryside. During this same period, Kaunitz sent Mercy-Argenteau a detailed report on the whole affair, advising him to mistrust out-of-work aristocrats, who would be more concerned to line their own pockets than to defend the monarchy. Then he warned Metternich that Théroigne was going to Koblenz:

> Would Your Excellency be so kind as to return her documents and letters to Mlle Théroigne and then abandon her to her fate? — taking whatever precautions are deemed necessary! I cannot refrain from remarking that the chevalier Maynard de La Valette and his companion, while making declarations which threw precious little light upon the whole affair, also demanded enormous advances of money. The minutes of the interrogation at Kufstein make it perfectly plain that these messieurs' testimonies are in no way accurate or truthful.[35]

Towards the end of December, Marie-Christine sent a curious message to her brother Leopold. She reported that Théroigne de Méricourt, in her guise as revolutionary amazon, was causing a terrible commotion in Brussels: 'She boasts of having seen the emperor and of having converted him to her principles and to her sentiments.'[36] This claim would seem to be yet another product of rumour, distorting reality after the fashion of the royalist press. Nevertheless, it is highly probable that Théroigne, in resuming her activities as a militant of the Revolution, had boasted not so much that she had converted the emperor to her ideas but rather that he had listened to her. On various subjects, the sovereign and the young woman had certainly had a quite fruitful dialogue.

Her chief preoccupation, upon arriving in Brussels was the state of her finances. Throughout the period of her incarceration, her brother, Pierre-Joseph, had behaved in a despicable, servile and self-interested manner. He had harassed Baron de Sélys, so as to obtain the right to withdraw jewels belonging to his sister, the famous necklace in particular, from pawnshops in Liège and Paris. When the baron proved noncommittal, he accused him — rightly, as it so happened — of being responsible, through his intrigues, for the abduction of February 1791. Théroigne, however, showed herself to be both naive and generous. She told the baron of her interview with Leopold, and he in his turn passed this information to emigré spies. She then settled some of her debts with him, and gave the famous necklace to her brother.[37]

We know, from a letter which she wrote to the banker Perregaux, dated 5 January 1792, that she was impartial in her assessment of the sequence of events in which she had participated. She did not say that she had 'converted the emperor to her cause' but paid tribute to his justice. The Aulic councillor had been suppressed from her account and replaced by an abstract entity, 'the-justice-of-the-emperor':

> Since I am at present free and can go wheresoever I wish, I am satisfied with the justice of the emperor, and I ought also to say that, during the entire period of my unjust detention, I was treated gently. As for your aristocrats, they have resorted to the lowest means and to the most infamous intrigues in a bid to take my liberty from me forever. I assure you that, if I had had to deal with them alone, I would still be in the fortress of Kufstein, for such indeed is the nature of French chevaliers.[38]

The French press was not slow to respond to the news of Théroigne's release. In a bulletin dated 29 October, dispatched from Vienna and published by the *Moniteur* on 16 November, *La Gazette nationale* gave a fairly objective account of the sequence of events:

> Monsieur de Plank [*sic*], entrusted with the task of proceeding against the famous Mlle Théroigne de Méricourt, who is still imprisoned at Kufstein on the grounds that she had carried out some attacks upon the queen of France, has just arrived in Vienna. He has delivered the record of his interrogations and procedures to the emperor; it turns out that the arrest of this demoiselle was undertaken upon altogether too flimsy a pretext and that the accusations levelled at her are wholly unfounded.[39]

A month later, *le Petit Gautier*'s comments upon this episode employed the habitual language of the royalist press:

> The crapulous creature who goes by the name of Théroigne de Méricourt is now in Brussels. She has appeared before the respectable minister Metternich. Her audacious barbarity has not been lessened by her time in prison, from which she has just emerged. Every honest person in the country must feel outraged at the appearance of this walking carrion. She lodges beneath the sign of *l'Homme sauvage*, who can never have been as bloodthirsty as she herself is.[40]

Several reasons may account for Leopold II's display of clemency towards Théroigne, and for the speed with which he had arrived at a decision. Admittedly, the authorities' realization of the real nature of her personality may have played a part, but a political factor was also involved. Since the 'Flight to Varennes' in June 1791, the monarchical powers' position regarding the Revolution had changed. Since the moderates were now claiming, in an attempt to re-establish Louis XVI on the throne, that he had in reality been 'abducted', Leopold was obliged to pursue policies of detente in two different respects. Given the rise of a republican movement, he could not turn a deaf ear to the incessant demands of the court and of Marie-Antoinette to intervene against France. On the other hand, he had at least to make some show of accepting the notion that Louis XVI had become a constitutional king. Through his botched flight, which had been a desertion of the throne, and his subsequent endorsement of the fiction of his abduction, the French sovereign had rendered the symbols of monarchy ridiculous. The Declaration of Pillnitz of 27 August, made jointly by the Emperor of Austria and by the King of Prussia, reflected very accurately the ambivalent attitude of the enlightened despots towards the court of France. The powers declared that the king's predicament was an object of common interest to all the sovereigns of Europe. They called upon their combined efforts to help Louis XVI to establish 'the bases of a monarchical government in accord with both the rights of sovereigns and the well-being of the French nation',[41] which meant in effect that this declaration made the king's situation still more uncomfortable. Its threatening nature helped to reinforce in the patriots the notion of a counter-revolutionary plot, while its intangibility failed to give much succour to the court.

Seven weeks before Théroigne and the emperor had met, the Constitution of 1791 had been officially proclaimed. At the beginning of October, the Constituent Assembly was replaced by the Legislative Assembly, which was composed of young men with as yet no experience of parliamentary life. It was agreed, on the basis of a motion advanced by Robespierre, that the representatives of the earlier Assembly would not be eligible for re-election. As Jacqueline Chaumie has written:

> In the autumn of 1791, new men entered the political arena. This new generation of revolutionaries, consisting of future Girondins and Montagnards, were possessed by the same ideal, that of carrying the Revolution forward; they admired the same men, namely, Robespierre and Pétion, who had been the most advanced leaders of the Constituent Assembly; and they had the same enemies — emigrés, non-juring priests and, above all, the *Constitutionnels*, men such as Lameth, Barnave and Duport. As is well known,

these two groupings, who composed the second wave of revolutionaries, were to become the bitterest of enemies.[42]

At this date, one would have had no reason to suppose that these two formations within the revolutionary movement would later become such bitter foes. The new arrivals all had the same social origin. They were mainly the sons or grandsons of peasants and had become lawyers, advocates or merchants. But they belonged to different lines of descent and were imbued with a different sensibility. The future Gironde was in the main descended intellectually from Voltaire and the *Encyclopédistes*, and this was where the allegiance of Condorcet, the last of the *philosophes*, lay. This explains both the more obvious feminism of the Girondins, and their liberalism and elitism. The Gironde was republican, and its passion for liberty was such that it was prepared to die for it. It wished also to liberate women from their servile condition. The future Mountain was more Rousseauist in temper, with a voluntarist conception of politics and a greater awareness of social egalitarianism. The Montagnards' vision of women was therefore character-ized by a greater degree of political realism. If women were regarded as first and foremost companions, wives and mothers rather than as free, thinking beings, it was because they were suspected of still being under the influence of priests and of the Ancien Régime. In order, therefore, to rescue women from their condition, one would have to force them to merge with the ideal of the Revolution. Of course, not all the deputies of the future Mountain were anti-feminist, any more than all those of the future Gironde were feminist – the divisions were frequently more subtle than that. Neverthe-less, the anti-feminism of the Mountain was exacerbated by its struggle with the Gironde and, more particularly, by the ill-fated attitude of Madame Roland, who was invariably playing a divisive game. In the autumn of 1792, she showed only disdain towards Danton when he was trying to defend the Girondins against Robespierre's ostracism.[43]

On 5 October 1791, Georges Couthon tabled a motion under five headings for the opening ceremony of the Legislative Assembly, which would place the executive and the legislature on the same footing, and thus strike a blow at the dignity of the crown. From now on, Louis XVI would bear the title of 'King of the French' and would be seated on a chair identical to that occupied by the president. As the diarist of the *Révolutions de Paris* observed:

When the people learns that the king is merely a civil servant, that Majesty is the preserve of God and the nations; when it sees the National Assembly enjoying that superiority which is vested in it by the laws of nature, it will appreciate the worth of a king, and kings appreciated at their true worth are little to be feared.[44]

Even though this decree was revoked on 6 October, the king's dethronement had effectively begun, and it was to lead to the founding of the Republic. In the meantime, the Feuillants, being 360 in number, enjoyed an overwhelming majority in the new Assembly. These men belonged to a club which had been formed through a split with the Jacobins; they were constitutional and thought that the Revolution had ended. The left of the Legislative Assembly consisted of 130 deputies of the future Gironde and of the future Mountain, most of whom belonged to the Jacobin Club. Brissot and Robespierre held a dominant position in each of these groupings. The Plain occupied the centre.

From the perspective of Austria, the French monarchy therefore looked considerably weakened. The only way in which support could be offered, or so it seemed, would be to accept the reality of a constitutional monarchy, even if only to delay the outbreak of war. Among the members of the coalition, the Emperor Leopold II was most opposed to a swift intervention against France. He had not much liked the spirit of Koblenz, and he had little confidence in his sister, Marie-Antoinette. He believed that the Revolution would die down of its own accord. Then and only then would be the moment to crush the rebels and re-establish the dignity of the monarchy. Given such a context, he did not see it as in his interests to hold a prisoner who had been the victim of an idiotic plot. Théroigne's only enemies, as far as Leopold could tell, were emigré ultras who had been goaded into action by the royalist press around the *Amis du roi*, and who were responsible, through their own conservatism, for the actual success of the Revolution.

Furthermore, since the amnesty law of 15 September 1791, all cases bearing upon events occurring during the Revolution, together with all the relevant judgements, had been annulled. Thus, Théroigne de Méricourt was no longer 'guilty of crimes against the queen', for the Châtelet no longer existed. Since the Austrian state no longer had any grievance against her, it seemed preferable to send her back to the Ardennes, if she so wished, or even to Paris, if she still desired to involve herself again in the Revolution.

François de Blanc, who had a greater respect for the rules of procedure than his emperor, was thus overruled by the decisions of his superior.

When Théroigne was living at Vienna, under the watchful eye of her protector, she may have intended to return to Xhoris or Marcourt. However, upon her arrival at Brussels, she changed her mind. She was probably attracted by the second generation of revolutionaries, of whom the Brabançon patriots had spoken. Besides, she had no good reason to stay in Brussels, in Liège or in Luxembourg. Since the revolution had been crushed in the Low Countries, they had little to offer her. She may perhaps have wished to use her notoriety to draw the attention of French patriots to the fate of their foreign brothers. Since she no longer had anything to fear from the court of the Châtelet, Théroigne crossed the frontier in mid-January and decided to take up residence on the left bank, at 8 rue de Tournon, in a town-house belonging to the Archbishop of Arles, who was a deputy in the Constituent Assembly. Ten days later, she made a triumphal entry to the gallery of the Jacobin Club.

THE RIGHTS OF WOMEN

Théroigne had taken leave of the Revolution in the autumn of 1790. When she returned to Paris, in the winter of 1792, much had changed. Our heroine had known the glorious period of the Constituent Assembly, in which the spirit of the Enlightenment had seemed to be sheltered from the harsh winds of discord. At that time, it was as if all had risen up unanimously against tyranny, with the aim of abolishing prejudices and overcoming oppression. In January 1792, however, the face of the Revolution had visibly altered; the patriots were in a state of disarray, the vibrant sense of unity had been destroyed and the factions were tearing each other apart. Jacobin fought against Jacobin, Robespierrist against Brissotin, and Feuillant against republican. The fatherland seemed in danger of civil war.

Opinions were still divided. The court was very much in favour of war, in the hope that the enemy's victory would re-establish hereditary monarchy. La Fayette also wanted military engagement, but for quite opposite reasons. His ambitions lay with the army, supreme command of which might make him a Caesar. The *Constitutionnels* were divided. Barnave and Lameth, the king's advisers, did not favour conflict for, if France were to be victorious, the patriots would seize power and, if France lost, the aristocrats would drive them from the court. In the patriots' camp, Brissot advocated a struggle beyond the country's frontiers. In his view, such a war would serve to unmask the king's treachery, rid France of the monarchy, and spread the spirit of the Revolution to all the peoples of Europe. On 16 December, he declared, with a rhetorical flourish:

A people that has won its liberty after ten centuries of slavery has need of war. The people needs war for consolidation, for purging the vices of despotism, and for expelling from its midst those men who would otherwise be liable to corrupt it.[45]

The only man clear-sighted enough to speak out against the war was Robespierre, and he was fiercely opposed to it. He predicted fatal consequences in every respect. Victory would result in Caesarism, whereas defeat would mean the return of the Ancien Régime. In either case, the Revolution would be crushed. Rather than fighting the external enemy, Robespierre advised a struggle against whatever domestic forces were hostile to the revolutionary cause. On three separate occasions, on 2, 11 and 25 January, he took the floor at the Jacobin Club, delivering lengthy answers to Brissot. Referring to the example of the Brabant, he reminded his audience that a revolution can never be established through a foreign invasion:

> Despotism itself degrades the spirit of men to such a degree that it causes them to adore it and to experience liberty as initially suspect and terrifying. In political questions, there can be nothing more far-fetched than to believe that it is sufficient for one people to invade another by force of arms for it to make it adopt its laws and its constitution.... The movements which have been heard of in Leopold's domains, and in the Brabant in particular, in no way vitiate my argument ... there is a century between the Austrian Low Countries and ourselves, just as there is a century between the people living on the frontiers of your northern provinces and the people of the capital. If you were to propose your civil organization of the clergy, together with the whole of your Constitution, as a model for the Brabançons to copy, you would simply be reinforcing Leopold's authority.[46]

Since war with Austria was the focus for debate in the new year, Théroigne found herself pushed to the centre of the political stage. Where previously she had been an advocate of legality, with an almost mystical belief in right and in the Constitution, she had now become a warmonger, quite prepared to represent her imprisonment at Kufstein as the deed of a despotism which was hateful and should be destroyed. The Aulic councillor, to whom she had been so attached, had been erased from her memory and, although she invariably sought to exempt the figure of the Emperor Leopold, who was the veritable embodiment of *the Law*, she adopted a Brissotin position. Her hatred of the aristocrats, and her wish to see the Low Countries liberated, aligned her with the war party.

Not only did she espouse Brissot's arguments but, in addition, she became involved in the struggle for feminism. Her purpose was not, however, to demand political equality, as Etta Palm and Condorcet were doing, but to claim the right of women to bear arms against the enemy abroad. Before Pauline Léon and Claire Lacombe, who wanted to raise regiments of women against the enemy within, Théroigne was thus the first to advocate 'legions of amazons'. She was therefore responsible for inaugurating the second phase in the history of original feminism — 'warrior' feminism.

Throughout 1791, the fight for political equality continued. Condorcet's arguments were debated, the clubs played an active part in discussions and Etta Palm was increasingly militant. She made several political interventions and, in March, she founded the *Société des amies de la vérité*, which was the first exclusively feminine club of the revolutionary period.[47] Madame Robert-Kéralio also played an important role during that same year. It was in her boudoir, in the winter of 1790, that the discussion of republican principles was held which resulted in the drafting of the petition of 16 July 1791. This leaflet, which was distributed in the Champs-de-Mars, called upon the people to 'acknowledge neither Louis XVI nor any other king'. As Michelet wrote:

> The diminutive Madame Robert who was, according to Madame Roland, both accomplished, witty, proud and, above all, ambitious, and therefore tired of the long years she had spent in obscurity as a woman trying to earn her living with her pen, seized her opportunity with both hands. I have no doubt whatsoever that it was she who dictated [the text of the petition], and big Robert who wrote.[48]

At the same time as the struggle in the clubs for women's equality was gaining ground, early feminism became the target for patriotic attacks, which were Rousseauist in inspiration. The most extreme position was that of Louis Prudhomme, the founder of *Les Révolutions de Paris*, one of the best-selling patriotic papers between July 1789 and February 1794. After the death of Elysée Loustalot, the post of editor-in-chief went to Pierre Chaumette, who was to be *procureur* after 10 August, and whose campaign against women was to prove as harsh as that of Prudhomme. Sometimes he was demagogic and open to persuasion, sometimes he was an ardent revolutionary, and he tried, from his position of responsibility within the Commune, to alleviate the wretchedness of the people. But he invariably presented himself as an apostle of virtue, laying down the law on morality and hounding prostitutes so savagely that the Convention was to reproach him for going too far. On 5 February 1791, the usual anonymous reporter (who may have been Prudhomme) launched the paper's crusade against feminism, in an article entitled 'On the influence of the Revolution upon women'. All Condorcet's arguments were rejected. The author of the article reminded his readers that women had always played a fatal role in politics, as the examples of Madame du Barry or Marie-Antoinette had proved. Then, he reproached the 'bourgeois women' for having found the sight of the severed heads brandished on the ends of pikes, in July and October 1789, hard to stomach, by contrast with the women of the people, who were genuine citizens of the motherland:

> The others [the bourgeois women] fled this virile and impressive spectacle; their frail systems were unable to cope; fainting fits, nervous conditions and premature childbirth made it quite plain what part these little women would subsequently play in this great political crisis.

Having put forward such arguments, the author was willing to acknowledge that women had 'political' rights. They should help men to repulse the enemy, if France were to be invaded:

> Just as the dishevelled bacchantes are represented brandishing their thyrsuses in their hands, use whatever weapons you can find to drive back the conquering slave, and let him pay dearly for his first laurels. Use all your resources, bravery and cunning, steel and poison; pollute fountains and victuals; let the atmosphere itself condemn the enemy to death.

The article ended with an exhortation to the women to stay at home and take responsibility for the hearths of brave patriots.[49] Thus, Prudhomme was asking women to be murderers when they took to the streets and slaves when they stayed at home. An article which adopted a very similar tone, appearing in November 1791, seemed to favour the second option:

> As regards everything which happens outside her own house, a woman should only know as much as her relatives or her husband deem fitting. We do not venture to come and teach you how to love your children, spare us the trouble then of coming to our clubs and expounding our duties as citizens to us.[50]

The most spectacular event of the autumn, as far as women were concerned, was the publication by Olympe de Gouges of the famous Declaration of the Rights of Woman and of the Citizen. The preamble to the text was addressed to Marie-Antoinette:

When the whole Empire accused you and held you responsible for its calamities, I was the sole person, at a time of storm and stress, to have the strength to take up your defence.... It will never be seen as a crime if you strive to restore morality, and to give your sex all the credit it deserves. This would not be the work of a single day, which is unfortunate for the new régime. This revolution will be implemented only when all women have been imbued with a sense of their deplorable lot, and with those rights which they have lost in society. Lend your support, Madame, to this noble cause; defend this unfortunate sex and you will soon have on your side one half of the kingdom and a third at least of the other half.[51]

Born at Montauban in 1748, Marie Gouze may perhaps have been the natural daughter of the Marquis Le Franc de Pompignan, a paltry versifier, whose resemblance to herself she liked to emphasize. Rumour, however, favoured the more prestigious notion that she was a bastard of Louis XV. She took malicious pleasure in correcting this error. 'I am not', she declared, 'the daughter of a king, but rather of a head crowned with laurels.' In any case, she inherited the mediocre talent of her presumed father. At the age of seventeen, she married Louis Aubry, mess officer of messire de Gourgues, the intendant of the town. Two years later, she bore him a son, whom she adored but who was to treat her shabbily. At the age of twenty, she fled the conjugal home. This extravagant woman, who was both sublime and proud, and who seems a kind of Madame Bovary *avant la lettre*, was bored to death by the role of provincial, bourgeois wife. She was fascinated by titles and dreamed of fame. Once at Paris, she became a courtesan, and then an untalented literary figure. The Revolution changed her utterly, and gave her existence a meaning. She was already known as Olympe de Gouges, having borrowed the Christian name from her mother and derived her surname from a combination of 'Gouze' and 'Gourgues'. She launched herself into the struggle for equal rights, and discovered, for the first time, that she had a remarkable visionary talent as a writer. Her love for animals was such that she lived with a veritable menagerie, which consisted of dogs, cats and monkeys. Being a follower of the Enlightenment, she fetishized science and was enthusiastic about zoology, a form of inquiry which fuelled her passion for animals. She therefore spurned an orthodox assessment of the sensibility of animals, for she was a firm believer in the doctrine of reincarnation.

Up until the Flight to Varennes, she declared herself to be a royalist. She then changed her mind, reverting to her former position at the time of the king's trial. Olympe was thoroughly imbued with the way of life of the Ancien Régime, but, never having had access to its privileges, she suffered from the gamut of persecutions, both real and imaginary, which hampered her freedom to act and to create. When the Assembly unveiled a constitution in which women had no rights, however, she drafted an admirable text which is a milestone in the annals of original feminism.[52]

The Declaration of the Rights of Woman and the Citizen pursues much the same line of argument as Condorcet, but whereas the philosopher wished to change the law, Olympe adopted a more militant approach. In addressing herself to the queen and to all women, she called upon them to take their fate into their own hands. Hence the notion that women should be responsible for the struggle for equality, and that they should steer men in the right direction, so as to convince them of the validity of their claims.

The actual form chosen by Olympe for the drafting of this work is of considerable importance. It was in fact a pastiche based point by point upon the famous Declaration of Rights of Man and the Citizen, with an identical number of articles, the very same vocabulary, etc. The only exception was article X, which contained the following astonishing and prophetic sentence: 'A woman has the right to climb the scaffold, and she should therefore also have the right to climb the rostrum.'[53]

This text served to highlight contradictions which had not been evident in the Declaration of August 1789. By failing to grant equal rights to women, although such rights had been given to Protestants and Jews, the representatives had in fact 'betrayed' the Declaration of Rights of Man, since the latter was universal and was addressed to all human beings irrespective of their colour, their sex or their race. However, in September 1791, women had neither civil nor political rights, and it was not until the victory of Valmy, on 20 September 1792, that the Convention granted them the former (although not the latter).

In this respect, the Constitution of 1791 reflected neither the position adopted by the representatives nor the principles affirmed in the Declaration. It was less universalist than the Declaration, since it denied political rights to passive citizens, but it was more universalist than the Assembly, since it nowhere stipulated that women were deprived of such rights. This deprivation was implied by their status as passive citizens, but it was not written into the constitution. The interest of Olympe de Gouges's text therefore lies in the way it highlights the aberrations and juridical contradictions in the Revolution's treatment of women.

AMAZONS

On 26 January 1792, Dufourny announced Théroigne de Méricourt's presence upon the women's platform of the Jacobin Club. He lauded her civic sense and deplored the persecutions to which she had been subjected. She was carried in triumph to the centre of the chamber, and was then invited to give an account of her history at the following session. The session took place on 1 February, and was presided over by Élie Guadet, a Girondin lawyer and representative in the Legislative Assembly, who yielded his place to his comrade, François-Xavier Lanthenas. The latter then offered his congratulations to 'la belle Liégoise'. In the course of her speech, Théroigne explained that the patriots in the Low Countries were very much in favour of French military intervention. She called for the formation of phalanxes of amazons, who might participate in the war. Pierre Manuel, who was Attorney for the Commune, went one better:

> There was a time when a society [composed] of men questioned whether women had a soul. In truth, this society consisted of those two-faced men, priests, who have always pretended to curse women in order to seem not to love them.... If our forefathers had so dim a view of women, it was because they were not free; for liberty would have taught them, just as it has taught us, that it is as easy for nature to create Porcias as Scaevolas. You have just heard one of the first Amazons of liberty. She has been a martyr of the Constitution. I move that, as the president of her sex, seated today alongside our president, she enjoy the honours of the session.[54]

On the following day, Théroigne de Méricourt became officially aligned with Brissot's party. The latter in fact used her testimony in his polemic against Robespierre in favour of war. As *Le Patriote français* wrote:

> The Jacobins have expressed indignation at the infamous treatment
> Théroigne received at the hands of her persecutors, and the deepest admir-
> ation for the fortitude she has shown. This friend of liberty has pointed out
> to us the sole means by which we may consolidate our own, namely, to take
> the war to the rebels and the despots who are threatening to wage war upon
> us, and who fear it more than we do. She has declared that the French
> Revolution has numerous supporters in the Low Countries, in Germany and
> even in the emperor's own palace.[55]

On 18 February, Théroigne was lampooned by the *Révolutions de Paris*,
which took issue with her warrior feminism, but this attack did not check
her fight for the creation of legions of amazons. War was in the air, and the
faubourgs were in uproar. Théroigne continued to be attacked on both
flanks, by Prudhomme's paper on the one hand, which was on the side of
Robespierre and hostile to women, and by the ever turbulent royalist press.
On 1 March, Leopold died, and was succeeded by his son, Francis II. The
new emperor, who was a fanatical enemy of the Revolution, would no
longer hold back before military intervention. According to Michelet:

> He acted promptly and ruthlessly, like the statue of the *Commendatore* or
> Banquo's ghost. What terrifies me is that beneath its remorseless gaze this
> mask is fresh-faced and pink. Such a being would never feel any remorse,
> and would commit crimes with a clear conscience.[56]

On 7 March, the Duke of Brunswick was appointed commander-in-chief of
the joint armies of Prussia and Austria. A further step had been taken in the
inexorable drift towards war.

Although there is no solid evidence for the claim, it could be ventured
that Leopold's death exacerbated Théroigne's military ardour and her
commitment to warrior feminism, as from now on she felt herself to be
'liberated' from all attachments to anything that might still embody in her
eyes an image of clemency and protection. Once the emperor had gone,
there was nothing left to link her to the Kufstein episode and to the stay in
Vienna. Austria, which was an asylum for her worst enemies, the French
aristocrats, could now become a locus for the projection of all possible
persecutions. As the population of Paris brandished its weapons against the

external threat, Théroigne was about to launch herself into the people's conquest.

At the beginning of this same month, *Le Journal général* resumed its attack with the announcement that it was going to sell playing cards for patriots. It showed Théroigne dressed as the Queen of Spades (*dame de pique*) and flanked by the Duc d'Orléans, disguised as the King, and Antoine Santerre, dressed as a Jack. Prior to the Revolution, this wealthy brewer from the faubourg Saint-Antoine had been addicted to the races, and he prided himself upon his horsemanship, which he reckoned to be second only to that of the Duc d'Orléans. This caricature linked Théroigne to two seducers and, through a pun (*dame de pique*) referred both to the legions of amazons armed with pikes (*piques*) and to death. The newspaper also contained obscene caricatures of the 'molls'. Thus, Théroigne was surrounded by Madame de Staël, Sophie de Condorcet and Madame de Lameth, who was known by the nickname of 'Dumpy Picot':

> These ladies are showing themselves to the emperor's troops in order that they may break ranks.... Mademoiselle Théroigne is showing them her *réplique*, Mesdames de Staël, Dondon, Sillers and Condorcet are showing them their *Vilette*.... the army is routed. The soldiers drop their rifles and swords; the flags yield; general Bender drops one of his boots; chaos ensues.[37]

On 11 March, Théroigne, who was still trying to raise her women's regiments, summoned the women citizens to the Champ-de-Mars. *Le Journal général*'s only comment upon this episode was to link her name to that of Claude Basire:

> The martial fire which the Jacobins' strumpet, Mademoiselle Théroigne, had shown on Sunday in her drilling of the ladies of La Halle was such that the demoiselle's moustaches came unstuck. A handsome reward for anyone restoring them to this demoiselle or to Monsieur Basire, her present champion.[58]

At twenty-eight, Basire was the youngest of the deputies in the Legislative Assembly. Together with the ex-Capuchin François Chabot and the lawyer Merlin de Thionville, he formed part of a triumvirate known as the 'Austrian committee', which was renowned for its extremely vehement attacks on the court. At this time, Basire was Etta Palm's lover. Thus,

Théroigne was mistaken here for another feminist.[59] In reality, she was on friendly terms with the Brissotins, the Robespierrists and with members of the Cordeliers club. She was often in the company of Basire, Collot d'Herbois, Marie-Joseph Chénier and Camille Desmoulins, and therefore found herself caught up in all the factional disputes of the period, at a time when each party was beginning to accuse the other of being in the pay of the court. Thus, while Robespierre was making speeches in the Jacobin Club denouncing the alliance between the Gironde and La Fayette, Brissot smelled intrigue in every speech his adversaries delivered.

Anne-Josèphe Théroigne was not the only person to be calling for the formation of women's regiments in March 1792. On 6 March, a petition sent by the *Société fraternelle des Minimes*, with 300 signatures, that of Pauline Léon among them, was read out to the Legislative Assembly:

> All the signs are that we are about to suffer a violent shock. Our fathers, husbands and sons may perhaps be the victims of our enemies' fury. Could we be forbidden the sweetness of avenging them or of dying at their sides.... Do not think, however, that we propose to abandon our domestic duties, which are ever dear to our hearts, to our families and to our homes. No, Messieurs! We wish only to be allowed to defend ourselves. You cannot refuse us, and society cannot deny us, this right, which is given us by nature, unless it is claimed that the Declaration of Rights does not apply to women.[60]

Those who had signed the petition asked permission to learn how to use weapons, and to serve under the former French guards.

This address, which marks the third phase in the history of original feminism, does not tally with the positions assumed by Théroigne. In fact, its signatories did not support the Girondin party. They did not preach war, but simply demanded that they be constituted as regiments, in accord with the Declaration of Rights of Man. Moreover, they did not challenge the view that women should be at their hearths. This petition may be seen as anticipating the anti-Girondin position that female *sans-culottes* would subsequently adopt.

By the end of March, the Gironde was in office. Roland was at the Ministry of the Interior, Clavière at the Ministry of Finance and Dumouriez at the Ministry of Foreign Affairs. On 25 March, an ultimatum was delivered to Austria. On that same day, Théroigne went to the *Société fraternelle des Minimes* and gave a long speech in support of the legions of amazons.

Although it recommended that women undergo training in war, this speech had a different flavour to the petition of 6 March. It was bellicose, upheld the view that the sexes were equal, rejected the notion that a woman's place was at the hearth and asked no 'permission' of male authority. Here is the speech in its entirety:

Women citizens, let us not forget that we owe ourselves wholly to the Fatherland; that it is our most sacred duty to strengthen between us the bonds of union, of confraternity, and to spread the principles of a calm energy, in order to prepare ourselves with as much wisdom as courage to repulse the attacks of the enemy. Women citizens, we may, through our generous devotion, break the thread of these intrigues. Let us arm ourselves; this is our right, by nature and even by the law; let us show the men that we are not inferior to them, either in virtues or in courage: let us show Europe that French women know their rights, and are capable of rising to the heights of the illuminists of the eighteenth century; let us despise prejudices, which, through the simple fact of being prejudices, are absurd, and often immoral, in that they make even our virtues seem a crime. The attempts that the executive might make subsequently in order to win back the confidence of the public will merely be snares which we should mistrust: for so long as our mores are not in accord with our laws, it will not give up hope of profiting from our vices in order to put us in chains again. It is perfectly simple, and you should even be forewarned against it, they will marshall the carpers and the hired hacks in an attempt to keep us back, using the weapons of ridicule and calumny, and all the ignoble means that base men employ in order to stifle the impulses of patriotism in feeble souls. However, fellow Frenchwomen, now that the spread of Enlightenment calls upon you to reflect, compare what we are in the social order with what we should be. In order to know our rights and duties, we must take reason as our arbiter, and, guided by her, we shall distinguish the just from the unjust. What consideration might then hold us back? ... We shall take up arms, because it is reasonable to take steps to defend our rights and our hearths, and because we would be failing both ourselves and the Fatherland if the pusillanimity which we have suffered in our condition of slavery had still sufficient sway over us to prevent us from redoubling our efforts. In all respects, you surely can have no doubts that the example of our devotion will arouse in the souls of men the public virtues and the all-engulfing passions of the love of glory and of the Fatherland. We shall thus preserve liberty through emulation and through the social perfection arising out of this felicitous rivalry. Fellow Frenchwomen! I would urge you yet again: let us raise ourselves to the height of our destinies; let us break our chains; at last the time is ripe for Women to emerge from their shameful nullity, where the ignorance, pride and injustice of men had kept them enslaved for so long a time; let us return to those times when our Mothers, the Gauls and the proud Germans, debated in the public Assemblies, fought side by side with their husbands and repulsed the enemies of Liberty. Fellow Frenchwomen, the same blood still flows in our veins; what we did at Beauvais, and at Versailles, on 5 and 6 October, and in several other important and crucial circumstances, proves that we are not unfamiliar with generous sentiments. Let us then summon up our energy; for, if we wish to preserve our liberty, we must prepare ourselves to do the most sublime things.... Fellow women citizens, why should we not enter into rivalry with the men? Do they alone lay claim to have rights to glory; no, no.... And we too would wish to earn a civic crown, and court the honour of dying for a liberty which is dearer perhaps to us than it is to them, since the effects of despotism weigh still more heavily upon our heads than upon theirs. Yes ... generous fellow women citizens, all of you who hear me, let us take up arms, let us go and drill two or three times a week on the Champs Elysées, or on the Champ de la Fédération; let us open a list of French Amazons; and let all those who truly love their Fatherland write their names there; we shall then meet and agree as to the means by which we may organize a Regiment, after the fashion of the pupils of the Fatherland, the Old Men or of the sacred Regiment of Thebes. To finish, I hope that I may be allowed to present a *tricolore* flag to the women citizens of the faubourg Saint-Antoine.[61]

Although Théroigne did not actually advocate political equality here, she did at least call for equality between the sexes. In this respect, she was still loyal to Gilbert Romme's teaching, and followed the principles which she had elaborated in her notebooks. But her speech was above all else marked by the traces of her involvement with warrior feminism. In spite of the fact that she detested demagoguery, we find her speaking at the *Société fraternelle des Minimes* of 'We women' and, in her populist fervour, she showed no hesitation in glorifying the October Days. Since de Blanc's interrogation had served to show that she had played no part in these famous Days, it is tempting to ask whether her attribution to herself of some role, even a symbolic one, in the events of October, meant that she was effectively shattering the truth of her story. For two whole years, the royalist press had fabricated a spurious Théroigne. Although an essentially solitary woman, Anne-Josèphe was presented by them in the guise of a rabble-rouser; a new and seemingly noble name was foisted upon her and, by stitching together various fragments of distorted gossip, a chaste and somewhat mystical heroine had been turned into a murderous and debauched amazon. Yet it was now as if the genuine Théroigne was merging with the simulacrum which had been devised to represent her. With her tumultuous entrance into military feminism and her evocation of the October Days, she seemed to have become in truth what rumour had made her, and to adopt the theatrical pseudonym — *Théroigne de Méricourt* — which had been ascribed to her.

However, in becoming an 'amazon', Théroigne had laid claim to an image of femininity which suited herself as a woman. Since the time of her first involvement in the Revolution, she had never abandoned her riding-habit, which clearly served her as a fetish. As she herself had put it, she wore it 'in order to seem to be a man, and thereby to avoid the humiliation of being a woman'. This wounded femininity, which was synonymous with the Ancien Régime, had gradually been ousted by an ideal of woman as warrior, and this had enabled her to disavow all other traces of femininity in herself. It would be hard to conceive of a more perfect embodiment of this virile ideal than the Amazon of classical mythology, who had lived in a tribe with her fellows, had burnt off one of her breasts in order to carry weapons in a sling, had fertilized herself by means of manhunts whose sole purpose was to perpetuate her race, had killed half of all male children at birth and had kept the other half — after a collective emasculation — as slaves. In short, the Amazon of Antiquity was the symbol par excellence of belief in the phallicism of the woman. She could even be said to be the delusional version of this belief, since she turned the penis into a fetish, which was sometimes purely reproductive and sometimes a fallen object. Through this mythology, which was reactivated by the Revolution, Théroigne had therefore transposed her repulsion at the idea of being a woman into a warrior feminism. It was also not by chance that she came to be immortalized wearing a costume which served better than any other to represent this transposition.

The evening after Théroigne had given the speech at the *Société fraternelle des Minimes*, she attended a banquet given for the market porters by the inhabitants of the faubourg Saint-Antoine. For this occasion, she dressed as an amazon. Pétion, Mayor of Paris, was fraternizing with the people that evening, but he too had changed since Théroigne had first met him in the Constituent Assembly. He was now a celebrity, and boasted the nickname of 'King Pétion'. Several women citizens had been invited to the feast, among them Jeanne Leduc, alias Queen Audu, one of the best-known heroines of the October Days.[62]

At the beginning of April, *Les Sabats jacobites*, a mediocre royalist paper and a pale imitation of the *Actes des Apôtres*, set the scene for this banquet. Once again, Théroigne featured as Basire's mistress and as the heroine of the October Days. The skit was entitled 'The boudoir of Mademoiselle Théroigne':

> On a kind of dressing-table, a jar of vegetable rouge, a dagger, a few locks of dishevelled hair, a brace of pistols, the *Almanach du Père Gerard*, a cap, the Declaration of Rights of Man, a cap of red wool, a back comb, a phial of vinegar made up by Monsieur Maille, a badly crumpled neckerchief, *La chronique de Paris* and Gorsas's *Le Courrier*. In the background, a camp bed decorated with a mattress, which serves as a bed of rest for the beautiful patriot and her numerous worshippers. Beside the mattress, an enormous pike, near to which there is a magnificent riding-habit in Utrecht velvet.

Théroigne was dressed in red leather pantaloons, with black wool turn-ups, a skirt of blue damask, a tricolour neckerchief and a cap made of flame-coloured gauze, crowned with a green tassel. Her make-up was tricoloured also. In the course of the skit, Théroigne is suspected by Basire of being Chabot's mistress. She reassures him by telling him that she wishes to have nothing more to do with the latter. But her 'lover's' jealousy is then deflected upon Pétion. So Théroigne retorts:

> I love Monsieur Pétion for his civic virtues, for his patriotism, for his devotion to the public good, for his talent for denunciation, for his assiduous appearances at the Jacobin Club; in a word, it is the nation itself that I love in him, for he is its worthiest representative, but you will nevertheless always be my lover, I swear it by my exploits on 6 October.[63]

Théroigne de Méricourt was now at the height of her fame. She was actively involved in propaganda activities in the faubourg Saint-Antoine, with a view to recruiting women citizens and to levying her battalions. But, on 12 April, an incident occurred which marked the beginning of her decline, and which became public knowledge the following day, at the Jacobin Club, when the chairman for the session described the steps taken by a delegation from the *Société des défenseurs des droits de l'homme* to denounce the Amazon for offences against public order:

> The delegation accused this woman citizen of having fomented trouble in faubourg Saint-Antoine by seeking to arrange for meetings to be held in the

Club three times a week for the women of this quarter, and by promising them a meal or civic banquet, for which purpose she thought it fit to bandy about the names of Messieurs Robespierre, Collot d'Herbois and Santerre, doubtless without their permission. This delegation further accused Mlle Théroigne of having deceived the women of this faubourg by showing them, upon a list of supposed signatures for this civic festival, the signature of Madame Santerre, which the commissioners recognized as being that of Mlle Théroigne herself.

Collot d'Herbois did not respond to this declaration, but Robespierre claimed 'never to have had any kind of personal contact with Mlle Théroigne'. He had in fact never met her. Santerre gave a confused account of the whole episode:

> the truth is, a number of rumours were circulating in the faubourg Saint-Antoine, which Mlle Théroigne certainly did not start, although she would seem to have used them to her own advantage. As far as the supposedly forged signature of Madame Santerre is concerned, it was not a list of signatures but a list of the names of those persons who wished to take part in this festival. As for the rumour spread by the women's club, you should lay the blame on these women, because they had tried to coerce the young girls at the Nunnery of La Pitié into attending their meetings, a thing to which the nuns responsible for their education were opposed, because they had approached them in a manner that was hardly befitting. When the men from these *faubourgs* come home from work, they prefer to find their household in good order rather than to await the return of their women from meetings, for such assemblies rarely inculcate a spirit of docility in them, and they have therefore looked askance at such meetings being held three times a week.... The above considerations have caused me to urge Mlle Théroigne to desist from projects of this nature, and I have no doubt whatsoever that, after reflecting upon the repercussions of her activities, she herself has renounced them, and that she has certainly not sought, as some ill-intentioned people have implied, to stir up such trouble again. In the light of this, I move that we proceed with the agenda.[64]

So it was that, seven days before the declaration of war, Théroigne found herself spurned by the *faubourgs*, ignored by Robespierre, grudgingly defended by Santerre and met with silence by Collot d'Herbois. She was clearly heading for disaster.

The reporter on the *Folies d'un mois*, a small royalist rag edited by the abbé

Bouyon, described the above episode, adding, however, a detail which, though invented, was horribly prophetic. He recorded that Théroigne only just escaped a whipping by the people:

> It is now common knowledge that last Thursday the infamous Théroigne barely escaped punishment at the hands of the people of the faubourg Saint-Antoine. The previous day, she had called upon the women to arm them-selves with the pikes which the men refused to bear; she returned, in the company of a handful of prostitutes. *No sooner was she recognized, than the cry went up: there she is, she should be whipped!* [65]

We know that Théroigne went mad a year after an episode in the course of which she really was whipped in the public square. It was as if Théroigne was moving still closer to the simulacrum which had been devised to repre-sent her. The anticipated announcement of this flagellation assumed an even greater resonance from the fact that already, in May 1790, the Apostles were imagining that Théroigne had been 'appointed guard of La Salpêtrière'.[66]

The day before she was due to deliver her speech at the *Société fraternelle des Minimes*, Théroigne presented a petition to the General Council of the Commune. The text was signed by Marie-Joseph Chénier, by the painter David, by a former officer of the house of Madame du Barry and by a man who was subsequently to be a commissioner of war under the Directory. Upon Théroigne's prompting, the authors of this text had proposed a festival in honour of the Swiss soldiers serving with the regiment of Châteauvieux, who had been released from prison in February 1792 on the orders of the Legislative Assembly. This homage was designed to point the contrast between the people's army and the army of the nobles, and to celebrate a bloody episode during the Revolution, in the course of which patriot soldiers had been drawn up against those supporting the aristocracy. In August 1790, the Swiss had fomented a mutiny at Nancy by refusing to give the marquis de Bouillé accounts of the money which they reckoned was due to them. La Fayette had opted for de Bouillé, but a part of the National Guard had supported the Swiss against their own officers. In order to restore order, de Bouillé had mobilized the other national guards, together with the German regiments in the pay of the king. A majority in the Constituent Assembly approved of the repression which followed, with the survivors being court-martialled and then either executed or sent to the galleys. The signatories to the petition declared:

This moving festival will put fear into the hearts of tyrants everywhere, but will offer hope and consolation to patriots. We will thus prove to Europe that the people are not ungrateful, as despots are, and that a nation that has become free knows how to reward the upholders of its freedom, just as it also knows how to strike conspirators, even when they are on the steps of the throne.[67]

Those who had survived their spell in the galleys were carried in triumph to Brest, and then travelled to the capital, flanked by national guards: 'The men shook their hands', wrote Michelet, 'the women blessed them, and the children touched their clothes. Wherever they passed, their forgiveness was asked, in the name of France.'[68] The festival, which had been Théroigne's own idea, was celebrated in Paris on 15 April, in spite of La Fayette's opposition. The royalist press was outraged, and *Les Révolutions de Paris* was flabbergasted. André Chénier attacked the patriots with a violence that was all the greater for the fact that his own brother figured among the organizers of the festival. David's staging of the spectacle linked the theme of the universality of the Revolution with that of its feminization. The statue of liberty was drawn along on a waggon closed off with the prow of a galley. The victims' chains were carried by young nymphs dressed in white and, in the middle of the procession, two sarcophagi, linked to each other, recalled the event with an inscription: 'Bouillé and his accomplices are the only guilty ones'. On the day itself, the bearing of arms was prohibited. Anne-Josèphe was not present at the meeting. She did not show her face anywhere, and no legion of amazons followed her. Because of the incident which had taken place on 12 April, she had preferred to melt into the crowd.

On 20 April, France declared war upon Austria, to great popular acclaim. No one could then foresee just how long the conflict between the old world and the Revolution was to last. At the very moment that Louis XVI, dressed in violet, was entering the Assembly, in order to present his declaration, Condorcet held the floor. He was expounding the first part of his plan for public education, which involved egalitarian schools for men and women, and for rich and poor. This plan presupposed peace, yet Condorcet voted for war. On the following day, the Legislative Assembly moved that the project be printed. With the help of Gilbert Romme, the philosopher was able to proceed with his work.[69]

At the Jacobin Club, there was a fierce debate between Robespierre and the Girondins. In order to strike a blow at his adversaries, the Incorruptible attacked La Fayette, who was in command of the army and who was concerned to placate the court, while the Girondin ministry was under the covert control of Brissot. Between 21 and 25 April, the Robespierrists did their utmost to catch the Feuillants and the Brissotins in the same net. Tallien criticized Condorcet, who denounced Robespierre's alliance with the court, while Chabot poisoned the debate by accusing the philosopher of being dominated by his wife: 'A man should not let himself be blinded by a female.' On the rostrum, Robespierre called for a purge, although he chose to let this truth sink in for several days before acting.[70]

On 23 April, when the atmosphere was still as venomous, Collot d'Herbois attacked Roederer. At the women's rostrum, large numbers of women citizens rallied to Robespierre in a clamorous display of emotion. They idolized the Incorruptible. 'Robespierre was a born priest', wrote Michelet, 'and the women loved him as such. His moral banalities, which reeked of the sermon, suited them perfectly. They felt themselves to be at church.'[71] Théroigne was seated among these women, whose names are lost to us. During his altercation with Roederer, Collot d'Herbois made a humorous aside about his satisfaction at having heard Théroigne that same morning in the café Hotot, on the pavement which the Feuillants used, withdrawing her confidence from Robespierre. When they heard this, the members of the Assembly burst out laughing. Nothing seemed more absurd to them, at that juncture, than the opinion of a woman. If yesterday Théroigne's patriotism had lent her lustre, today she was little more than a madcap, with neither family nor hearth, distracted by her phantasies of women's battalions and having the audacity to behave as if she were the leader of a party. Horrified at being repudiated in this fashion, and at being laughed at, Théroigne crossed the barrier which separated the chamber from the women's rostrum and hurled herself at the bench. With exalted gestures, she requested the right to speak. In the uproar that ensued, the president suspended the session.[72]

The royalist press reported this episode with its habitual crudity. The reporter for the *Petit Gautier* wrote thus:

> Since it is impossible to find men who are capable of remaining minister for very long, why should we not have recourse to Madames Condorcet and Théroigne? They have sufficient talent to be *public women* [i.e. women of the street].... We would even venture to suggest that, in a war with the Low Countries, no one would be more suited than they to bring the two parties to an agreement.[73]

This is effectively what Dumouriez, after his own defection, would say. In his account of the women of the Revolution, he praised Madame Roland and then went on to write the following lines:

> Several other women have trod the boards of the Revolution, but — with the exception of Madame Necker — in a less decent and less noble manner. All the others, beginning with Mlle Labrousse, the prophetess of the Chartreux Dom Gerle, Madames de Staël, Condorcet, Pastoret, Coigny, Théroigne, etc., have played the vulgar role of intriguers, much like the women of the court, or of madwomen, like the fishwives.[74]

If an award were to be given for the most horrific thing written during the early days of the war, the palm would surely go to François Suleau, who published a text on women and the Revolution which must count as the most deranged of the period. In style and content, this work seems to prefigure the anti-Semitic pamphlets written by Léon Daudet and Louis-Ferdinand Céline a century or so later, which compared the Jew to a sick person, bearing all the blemishes of a subhuman species. In Suleau's case, however, the person who featured as the bearer of the stigmata of a shameful disease was the woman who had become involved in the Revolution:

> After careful checking, I have found that, of the women who have harnessed themselves to the chariot (or, more exactly, to the dung-cart) of the Revolution, not one lies outside this disgusting category (the old, the ugly and the infirm). A handful of old dowagers, dyspeptic and toothless (beginning with the Duchess of Enville), were crazed enough to believe that to hurl themselves into the fray and to embrace each novelty as it arose would serve as an elixir of youth. These women were demented enough to suppose that this famous system of equality, whose first wish is to return all human beings to the childhood of beauteous nature, would necessarily have the virtue to rid them of their wrinkles and to patch up their superannuated attractions. An ever larger number of ugly women, beginning with the *gagui* [*sic*] Staël, have believed that, by bedaubing themselves with the colours of the nation, they would themselves assume a human shape and that, by weighing themselves down with tricoloured flounces, they would succeed in concealing their deformities.
>
> The lazar-house seems to me to be a suitable place to put these tender young shoots (foremost among them, la Condorcet) who, with a veneer of health and an appealing face, have however hurled themselves into the

saucepan of the rights of man. Let there be no mistake. In spite of their frisky appearance and their air of being a proper little madam, these creatures are impotent and covered with ulcers. If you look beyond the pretty little faces of these devotees of demagogy, you will find an attractive display of the itch, scabs, ringworm, *fleurs à la Pompadour*, scurf, yaws, blisters on the nape of the neck, suckers on the breast, ulcers on the thighs, and plasters on all their scars. To add insult to injury, these unfortunates are periodically subject to epileptic fits.... It is clear that these ladies have calculated that, since only a king had the virtue to cure scrofulas by touch on sacred days, nothing less than the inauguration of twenty-four million sovereigns would be needed to heal all their infirmities.[75]

THE SWORD AND THE WORD

For the third time since the beginning of the Revolution, after the capture of the Bastille and the October Days, the king and the court party provided the people with a pretext upon which to vent its anger. Incapable of giving a lead in the war which they had unleashed, the Girondins now experienced all the bitterness of defeat. On 28 April, in Belgium, the offensive against Austria went disastrously wrong. This was a moment of triumph for Robespierre:

> When the orators were urging us on to war and when they were showing us
> the Austrian armies deserting the banners of despotism for the tricolour, and
> when the whole of Brabant tottered and seemed eager to subject itself to our
> laws, we had every right to expect a more auspicious debut, and to suppose
> that they had taken such measures as were necessary to fulfil these magnifi-
> cent predictions.[76]

During this same period, Marie-Antoinette's coded letters to the Comte de Fersen communicated to foreign monarchs any information she had managed to gather regarding the plans of the French general staff. Given the perilous situation, the Assembly was in permanent session. On 7 May, it decreed that any priests who had been denounced should be deported, and on 29 May, fearing a show of force, it dissolved the royal bodyguard. Finally, on 8 June, it resolved to set up a camp outside the walls of Paris, consisting of 20,000 *fédérés* from the departments, which would celebrate the festival of 14 July. Whereas Dumouriez advised the king to give the royal assent to the decrees while awaiting victory at the frontier, Roland called upon him — by means of his wife's pen — not to impede the authority of the legislature.

Roland also took the opportunity covertly to denounce Robespierre's party, which he described as 'demagogic'. The king's response was simply to withdraw ministerial portfolios from Brissot's men and to form a Feuillant ministry instead. With the cooperation of the municipality of Paris, which was in Pétion's control, the Girondins then organized a march on the Tuileries, which was to take place on 20 June. This was designed to mark two different anniversaries, namely, the Tennis-Court Oath and the Flight to Varennes. The Commune's *procureur-syndic*, Manuel, took Danton for his deputy. Jaurès wrote:

> Obviously he had passed judgement upon the Gironde; he knew it to be inconsistent and vain.... And he did not wish to be snared by any clique. He sought to preserve his strength free and unencumbered, so that he might use it to serve the great movements whose day was soon to come, and which would involve a crucial struggle against the monarchy and a struggle to the last against the foreigner. He expected little from the sometimes abstract theories of Robespierre and from the politicking of the Gironde, but much from the spontaneous strength of the people ...[77]

Flanked by Santerre and Saint-Huruge, the demonstrators set out in two columns, one from La Salpêtrière and the other from the Bastille. Once they had arrived at the Manège, they asked to be admitted to the Assembly, invaded the corridors and marched around unchecked for three whole hours. They then made their way to the castle, whose gates were not guarded. The king made an appearance and was both jostled and insulted. When called upon to join in the priest hunt, he refused, but he was prepared to drink a glass of wine with the demonstrators and to wear the red cap. They then withdrew. At Marseilles, two days later, in the course of a patriotic banquet, a Jacobin from Montpellier struck up the 'War song for the Army of the Rhine', which the *fédérés* would subsequently sing in the streets of Paris.[78] The uprising of 20 June served to show that neither the king nor the Assembly were well-defended. From now on, the *sans-culottes* of the *faubourgs* of Saint-Marcel and Saint-Antoine embodied the power of the populace against a monarchy that was in full decline and an Assembly that was too weak to rule.

Théroigne did not march at the head of the procession to the Tuileries, with Santerre and Saint-Huruge on either side. She may have been in the thick of the crowd or she may, on the other hand, have been afraid of showing her face, after the humiliations which she had suffered in the recent past. However, on the nights of 19 and 20 June, she had not been inactive. Indeed, anyone might have heard her making provocative speeches, and lending her support to the movement in the *faubourgs* by urging on the people.[79]

After this uprising, anti-monarchist agitation intensified, spreading to all of the *sections*. In the provinces, on the other hand, a movement in support of the king, whose sacred person had been violated, gathered momentum. The royalist press called for revenge. Du Rozoi wrote:

> This is an uprising after the fashion of 6 October but let the regicides who planned and executed this horrible plot not hope to escape without being tried for this abuse, the epitome of all abuses, like that of the October Days at Versailles.... Europe, armed with all the thunderbolts of revenge, will be responsible for executing this solemn and dreadful sentence. This time, the criminals will have no power to overturn the redoubtable court, to which I shall summon them day and night...[80]

La Fayette, who was hostile to the Jacobins, left his army of the centre on 27 June and went to Paris in order to help the royal family. He hoped to engineer a coup d'état with the support of those elements of public opinion which were still favourably disposed towards the monarchy and with the help of the National Guard. But the queen, because of her hatred for La Fayette, warned Pétion, and thereby let slip the court's last opportunity to salvage the monarchy. The review of the national guards, under La Fayette's command, was cancelled, and he rejoined his troops.

Meanwhile, the situation at the frontier had worsened. The Duke of Brunswick, at the head of the émigré army, had invaded national territory. On 11 July, the Legislative Assembly proclaimed the fatherland in danger. The Girondins, terrified of the consequences of the unrest in the streets which they themselves had provoked, recoiled and decided to defend the court. They hoped for a 'suspension' of the king and for a change of government. At the Jacobin Club, Robespierre insisted that the fate of the monarchy should not be decided by a popular insurrection, but by a Convention elected by universal suffrage. On 29 July, he declared that the king was overthrown. At the same time, the Brunswick Manifesto, whose contents had been made known the previous day, showed that Louis XVI had colluded with the enemies of the nation. The Duke himself threatened to raze Paris to the ground and to torture the rebels if the people did not submit themselves unconditionally to the royal will.[81]

The response of the people of Paris to this threat was to contemplate the most violent revenge. The fear of invasion became intermingled with all the habitual phantasies of imminent insurrection. On 30 July, the *fédérés* from Marseilles paraded, singing the 'War song for the Army of the Rhine'. A Directory of patriots was formed with a view to overthrowing the monarchy. On the Champs-Elysées, the first street battles broke out. On the following day, the Monconseil section declared that the king had been dethroned and its members revoked the oath which they had sworn to him. It then called upon all the other *sections* to embrace the same course of action. In the days that followed, the Assembly was inundated with petitions. Forty-seven out of forty-eight *sections* supported the initiative of the citizens of Monconseil. The debate on dethronement was adjourned until 9 August. On 4 August, the Quinze-Vingt section of the faubourg Saint-Antoine declared that, if the Assembly did not defer to the will of the people, the tocsin would sound from nine until midnight. Concerned for its own safety, the court summoned the Swiss regiments from the barracks of Rueil and Courbevoie to the Tuileries. On the eve of this, the second Revolution, which was to bring about the fall of the monarchy, the Assembly had broken up without being able either to discuss the petition of the forty-seven *sections* or to make a statement respecting the question of dethronement.

As Théroigne de Méricourt, now aged twenty-nine, was preparing to take part in the first street battles, another heroine of original feminism made her debut on the stage of the Revolution: Claire Lacombe, legendarily known as 'Rose'. Three years younger than Théroigne, and a footloose actress, she had recently come to Paris from the provinces, and had as yet played no part in history. On 25 July 1792, dressed in a riding-habit, she read out a war petition at the bar of the Legislative Assembly, in which she called for the formation of women's battalions. Her stance may be compared with that of Pauline Léon, with whom she was later to found the *Club des citoyennes republicaines révolutionnaires*:

A Frenchwoman, and an unemployed *artiste*, that is what I am. However, O Legislators, that which should cause me the deepest despair fills my heart with pure joy. Since I am unable to come to the help of my fatherland, which you have declared in danger, by financial sacrifices, I have simply pledged to it my own person instead.[82]

Claire Lacombe went on to describe La Fayette as a Catiline, and to call for his impeachment. She supported the position of Robespierre, who had also called for La Fayette's arraignment.

Like the majority of figures in the Revolution, Claire Lacombe expressed herself in a highly emphatic manner. She decorated her official speeches with references to Antiquity, evoking the shades of Rome and imitating the heroes of a past she had no real knowledge of. Although her speeches resembled Théroigne's, the backgrounds of the two women were totally dissimilar. Théroigne had had a long experience of the revolutionary life, she had travelled and had spent time with the representatives of the Constituent Assembly, with those of the Legislative Assembly, with emigrés and with nobles at the Austrian court. In short, she did not belong to the same revolutionary generation as the new amazon. By the summer of 1792, Théroigne was already a figure of the past, encrusted with rumours, legends and fame. By contrast, citizeness Lacombe represented the future of the Revolution, its youth and the epic that was still to come. Her involvement in the saga began at the moment when the fall of the monarchy precipitated the birth of the First Republic. The actress was moulded in the image of this vengeful, restless and murderous people, which sang the 'Marseillaise' while trampling underfoot the last emblems of a transformed world. She was imbued with all of its violence, ardour and fanaticism.

From the moment that she had set foot on the historical stage, Claire Lacombe thus appeared to be Théroigne de Méricourt's first great rival. These two women had a common aim, namely, that of arming the female population. But the one had already failed and had played her last card with the Girondins, while the other could still hope to succeed by supporting Jacobin radicalism, which in her view was an expression of the will of the *sans-culottes*. Since both rivals participated in the uprising of 10 August, it was not long before they were mistaken for each other, to the extent that, in typical legendary fashion, Claire Lacombe was even supposed to have played a part in the October Days.

On the morning of 10 August, at around 8.30, François Suleau was arrested on the terrace of the Feuillants. With 'banter on his lips and a sword in his hand',[83] he refused to follow the example of the majority of his royalist friends, and therefore made no attempt to conceal himself. He was wearing a grenadier's uniform of the National Guard, and brandished an official document supposedly authorizing him to patrol the château. But the document was as false as the costume that this outlandish character, much given to assuming disguises, was wearing. Judged to be a suspect, Suleau was taken to the Tuileries section, presided over by Citizen Bonjour. There he encountered several royalist detainees who had been imprisoned in the course of the night. For several hours, a rumour had been circulating in Paris that some conspirators who had planned to massacre the people had been taken prisoner. So it was that, as soon as the struggle against the château began, the insurgents invaded the section to seize hold of the prisoners. Thirteen of them managed to flee, but nine men had to stand and face the fury of the populace. Alongside Suleau there stood the abbé Bouyon, a reporter on the *Folies d'un mois*, together with Solminiac, a janitor who had been in the king's service, and, finally, the handsome Vigier, a former member of the royal bodyguard,

Baron Thiébault, a sergeant in the company of grenadiers and a future General under the Empire, was present and tried his utmost to calm the crowd, swearing that the guilty would be punished with all the rigour of the law. But the people threatened to execute the 'plotters'. At this moment, Théroigne de Méricourt loomed up, dressed in a riding-habit of blue cloth and wearing a felt hat in the Henri IV style, topped with black feathers. In her belt, she carried a brace of pistols and a dagger. Excited by the fighting in the streets, in a fever because of her hope of at last playing a warlike role, she conformed with her legend, calling for revenge, and demanding, so it would seem, that the prisoners be judged on the spot by a people's court. Incapable of checking the rising anger of the crowd, citizen Bonjour allowed the armed band access to the detainees.

Théroigne did not know who these men were. She was unaware that her path had just crossed that of the most famous reporter of the Apostles, one of the confederates who had portrayed her as the raging amazon she would later actually become. She was not acquainted with the abbé Bouyon either — the man who had jubilantly announced, in anticipation of the actual event, that she had been whipped by the people. Suleau himself had never written anything against her, but he was a living symbol of all the royalist lies which had led to her abduction at La Boverie and to her confinement at Kufstein. In January 1791, at Koblenz, he had been fulminating against the patriots of Liège and Brabant, and had called upon a 'brutal and bloody tutelary God' to defend France.[84] In April 1792, he wrote his foul misogynist pamphlet, mentioned earlier. Now, on the morning of 10 August, a woman in the middle of the crowd, once a folder for the *Actes des Apôtres*, recognized him and cried out his name.

The abbé Bouyon was the first to be slaughtered, although he was power-
fully built and defended himself vigorously. Next, Solminiac and Vigier
were cut to pieces. Then came the turn of Suleau. Théroigne had heard his
name and repeated it over and over again, mistaking him for the abbé. She
may well have confused him with the already murdered reporter. At any
rate, she leapt at his throat. But Suleau fought bravely and, having wrested a
sabre from one of the insurgents, he struck out at his opponents, cursing
them roundly as he did so, although without ever lowering his guard. Just as
he was about to run Théroigne through, the crowd felled him. Five men
were killed after him, and then decapitated, with their heads being borne in
triumph on the ends of pikes.

Jean-Gabriel Peltier, the founder of the *Actes des Apôtres*, recounted the
story of the heroic death of Suleau, and described the part played by
Théroigne, in a book entitled *Le Dernier Tableau de Paris*, which was
published in 1793. During the uprising of 10 August, he had stayed in
hiding. He was not present at the events described above, but heard about
them from an eye-witness. He wrote his account when in exile in London,
using a documentary style which contrasted with the method employed in
his newspaper. Although Peltier gave a hate-filled version of the uprising of
10 August, he was concerned to show a degree of accuracy, and he was
therefore careful not to attribute imaginary crimes to Théroigne or to hold
her responsible for the killing of Suleau. He caricatured her 'savagery', but
seemed anxious to bequeath a trustworthy account to posterity. However, in
a venomous note at the bottom of the page, he reverted to the habitually
calumnious tone of the Apostles:

> Although this Théroigne de Méricourt is well enough known, it may be
> worth repeating here that she was a prostitute from Luxembourg, thirty
> years of age, short, sickly, ill-formed and worn out by debauchery. There
> being only one revolution for her to exploit, she ran out of lovers to corrupt
> and therefore fell back upon representatives. She began by admiring
> Barnave, next she honoured Pétion with her attentions. Then she opened a
> club, travelled, was taken prisoner and released by Leopold. Here we find her
> once more in the arena when it was a question of spilling blood. Her intrigue
> with Populus was an invention of the author of the *Actes des Apôtres*, a fiction
> derived from the actual name of her supposed lover.[85]

Thiébault, in his *Mémoires*, described Théroigne as beautiful, made more
beautiful still by her revolutionary 'erethism'. In some respects, his narrative

is only partly to be trusted. For example, he believed her to be twenty years old. He also recounts how Théroigne ran to Robespierre's house just as soon as she had got wind of the riot, how she elbowed her way through the crowd, leaping on to a cannon and inciting the people to massacre. On one particular point, however, he was in agreement with Peltier: Théroigne was not a criminal.[86]

When the people invaded the Tuileries, Suleau was not therefore slain by Théroigne de Méricourt's own hand. She had, however, been one of the crowd, and had participated in the whole episode; indeed, she had incited it to a collective murder committed in the heat of an insurrection which had brought down the French monarchy.

After this bloodbath, Théroigne ran towards the *Marseillais*, who were trying to force the gate of the Carrousel. There, for a brief period, her recent espousal of *sans-culotte* ideals was allied with her former respect for due legal process. Her sword served her not so much to strike as to speak. In an open letter addressed to the Duke of Brunswick, *Le Moniteur* gave an eye-witness account of the uprising in order to emphasize the probity of those whom the nobility described as 'canaille'. This witness did not mention Théroigne by name, but he sketched a portrait of her much as she would have wished to be seen since April 1792 — as an amazon of the word, at the head of her women's battalions:

> Shortly before the fighting began, I glimpsed an attractive young woman, sabre in hand, who had mounted a stone and was haranguing the multitude as follows: 'Citizens, the National Assembly has declared that the fatherland is in danger, that it was unable to save it, and that its safety depended on your arms, your courage and your patriotism; take up arms, then, and run to the château des Tuileries, for your enemies' leaders are there. Exterminate this race of vipers, which for three years has done nothing else but conspire against you. If you are not victorious today, in a week's time you yourselves will be exterminated. Choose between life and death, between liberty and slavery. Show due respect for the National Assembly and for property, justice is in your hands.' Thousands of women immediately threw themselves into the throng, some with sabres, the others with pikes. I myself saw several of them killing Swiss guards. Others urged on their husbands, sons and brothers. Several of these women were killed, but their fate did nothing to intimidate the others. I then heard them yelling: 'Let these Prussians or Austrians come; we'll lose many, but not one of these bastards will return home.'[87]

For her courage during the final assault, the *fédérés* awarded Théroigne a civic crown. Claire Lacombe and Queen Audu were granted the same honour.

Royalist discourse had depicted Théroigne de Méricourt as ugly and deformed, and Peltier was behaving in a similar fashion to Suleau when he used terms such as exhaustion, debauchery and sickly appearance to describe her. As far as the Apostles were concerned, the Revolution of 1789 was already a dangerous illness, which had been further exacerbated by the murderous instincts of the mob of women active during the October Days. However, after the *journée* of 10 August, the illness had become an epidemic. The Revolution of 1792 seemed to advance with such tumultuous fury that it could be compared only to a proliferating infection. The involvement of the crowd, and the habitual use by the revolutionaries of feminine symbolism, made these events appear all the more murderous to the royalists, who therefore likened the Revolution to a fallen woman or to a venereal disease. If woman took to the streets, daring to wear a sabre, her body would have to bear the stigmata of that latent inner corruption which had been awoken by 'the rabble'.

Royalist reporters, the heirs of Suleau and Peltier, would return again and again to the equation between Revolution and Woman, and between the pox and ugliness, and they would transmit to the nineteenth century an image of Théroigne as the bearer of all the crimes of the Revolution. Her madness would therefore come to seem a symptom of a 'revolutionary disease', itself comparable to a venereal disease.

In 1801, François Beaulieu, who had known Théroigne at the time of the *Société des amis de la loi*, sketched a portrait of her as a kind of automaton, and this allowed the legend to take shape. He quite rightly emphasized that the young woman was 'the walking image' of the Revolution but, instead of analysing this in dialectical terms he treated it as the history of a process of degradation culminating inexorably in murder and ugliness:

At the end of her career she had lost all her charms. She was livid, blotchy and emaciated. Finally, she was the walking image of the Revolution. Brilliant at the outset, frenzied as it pursued its course, it presented a disgusting spectacle of muck and blood after 10 August.[88]

In 1802, the *Dictionnaire biographique de tous les hommes morts ou vivants* also focussed upon the notion of 'corruption' and placed Théroigne among the women involved in the October Days:

> Linked to various leaders of the popular party, she rendered them useful service in most of the riots and played an especially important role on 5 October 1789 at Versailles, when she led a number of other girls into the streets and instructed them to distribute money to the soldiers.[89]

Finally, in 1806, Maton de la Varenne went a step further, and represented the heroine of this story as suffering from the pox:

> Although she was but thirty years old this wretched woman seemed to be about fifty. She was wrinkled and dyspeptic.... [she was] no longer able to resort to prostitution, because she had been gnawed by the shameful sicknesses which are a consequence of it.[90]

He was unaware, however, that she had really contracted a venereal disease.

Who would now dare say that metaphors are weaker than realities, or that legends are less tenacious than the truth?

AN AIR OF MADNESS WHICH RECALLS GOYA
Portrait by P. Nicolas Selles, 1793.

MASCULINE/FEMININE: AN ORDINARY THÉROIGNE
Physionotrace portraits by Chrétien (*above*).
Portrait attributed to Louis Lagrenée (*below*).

THE ROMANTIC FABLE: LAMARTINE AND MICHELET
Anonymous portrait (*above*).
Portrait by Auguste Raffet (*below*).

PHANTASIES AND RUMOURS
An image from Épinal, nineteenth-century (*above*).
Louis Léopold Boilly's *Triumph of Marat*, 1794, detail (*below*).

SCENES IN A WOMAN'S LIFE
Théroigne and Madame de Staël side by side in the
gallery of the left (*above*). Théroigne beaten by the
Jacobin 'shrews' (*below*).

je vous demande excuse, messieurs, quand je vous
dis, que votre precaution a couvrir le nom de
celui qui signa le katier que vous venez de me
lire etoit inutile, car, outre la presomption
que je tenive de la mains, dont il est ecrit,
la même qui a Barboullé nous pretendus
dire est aveu, comme quoi ces questions
partent de la même source, ils est aimpossible
s'y meprendre lors que, l'on veut faire
attention, a leur contenus qui est empartie
de que mes conducteurs pretendent avoir été
dit est avoué de moi pendant mon voyage
de liege a fribourg; il est tout fait, bien
indifferant quel en soit l'auteurs, et si ce sont
mes conducteurs comme je ne puis en douter
ils n'en auront fait que grossir le nombre
de leur infamie; je declare donc, que mon
respect pour les ordres de l'empereur et son
commissaire ici present, est absolument
poussé a bout, ou que je ne croyois aindigne
de vivre, si je pouvois, tout de bon mettrai
ten ma confiance au point de l'examiner
sur des faits pour la plupart aussi abominable
et aussi hideux, comme ceux qu'on vient de me
lire, et dont les assertions ne tendent pas
seulement, a couvrir de crimes et d'approuve
mais aussi a en faire autant de plusieurs personne
respectable et digné de l'estime publique auquel
ils pretent entre autres des faits, dont les assertions, seroit rire de pitié toute la france
si elle en etoit ainstraite, icisi le pour exemple
celle que mr neker et des deputés de l'assemblee
nationale oie harangué le peuple au palais
Roiale, priant tout ceux qui connoissent
paris et le palais Roiale de dire si l'absurdité
et l'ineptie peuvent être poussé plus loin
ne vous deplaise donc messieurs que je refuse
absolument de repondre a cette pitoiable farse

THÉROIGNE'S HANDWRITTEN CONFESSIONS

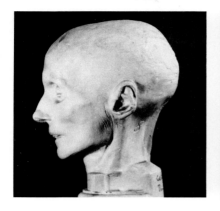
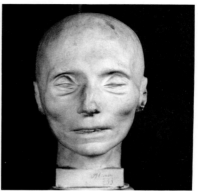

THE ASYLUM AND DEATH
Busts of Théroigne (*above*). Gabriel's portrait of
Théroigne at La Salpêtrière (*below*).

THÉROIGNE AT THE THEATRE:
BETWEEN MELODRAMA AND HYSTERIA
Sarah Bernhardt as Théroigne.

III
History of Madness

SEPTEMBER 1792 TO 1841

SANS-CULOTTE WOMEN

With the insurrection of 10 August, the Revolution became the concern of the Paris *sans-culottes*. The Commune also began to play a dominant role in the election of the future Convention, at a time when the Assembly, though already moribund, was debating a number of revolutionary measures. It decreed that émigrés' property should be sold off in small lots, payable in fifteen annual instalments, and that the peasants should be freed from the compulsory repurchase of feudal rights. It then set about secularizing the state and civil society, a process which would culminate in dechristianization. It voted for the suppression of congregations and religious orders for women, the banning of ecclesiastical dress, save for juring priests, and the compulsory exile of nonjuring priests, on pain of being deported to Guyana.[1] In order to signify the universality of the Revolution, the Assembly next granted the title of French citizen to foreigners who had distinguished themselves in the cause of liberty. Finally, on 30 August, it ratified the principle of divorce. As Condorcet wrote:

> Marriage will no longer be accompanied by bitter regrets, by the lonely tears of those unhappy creatures known by the name of spouse.... After long centuries of servitude ... the holy laws of liberty and equality, which, in the case of women, have for so long gone unrecognized, will flower for them, as for the other half of the human race.[2]

On 27 August, at Robespierre's prompting, the Commune passed a decree compelling the electors of Paris to vote aloud for the elections to the Convention in a public ballot. The choice of representatives would then be subject to the revision of the primary assemblies of the *sections*. This measure effectively placed the elections under the surveillance of the Commune. The Girondins decided to react: Brissot denounced Robespierre, warning that this threatened to produce a despotism that was harsher and more hateful than that of the king. The Assembly dissolved the general council of the Commune and ordered municipal elections to be held within twenty-four hours. But the Commune refused to obey this order, and the Assembly was forced to withdraw.

As these factional disputes grew ever more bitter, the news from the front was itself creating a climate of tension in the streets of the capital. Two Austrian armies were advancing towards Lorraine: one by way of Belgium, the other across the Palatinate. They intended to join up with the Prussian troops, proceed to Châlons and capture Paris. At the end of August, the Duke of Brunswick took Verdun, thus opening a path for the conquest of France.[3]

From 25 August onwards, rumours of plots were rife. It was alleged that the royalists wished to free the criminals arrested on 10 August and arm them against the people. Aristocrats, priests and Swiss soldiers constituted about a third of these detainees: the remainder were common law prisoners. When news came of the fall of Longwy, on 26 August, the threat grew perceptibly worse. With enemies on all sides, the situation seemed desperate. On the morning of Sunday, 2 September, the massacres began. At Le Châtelet, Bicêtre, Saint-Firmain and La Salpêtrière, the most terrible carnage was unleashed. The killing ended a week later.

Théroigne was not in evidence, and yet popular depictions of these events portray her as a murderess, laying about her with her sabre and slaughtering to her heart's content.[4]

The Commune, having failed to check this outburst of collective murder, could not bring itself to repudiate it. The Assembly also refused to take up a position. Robespierre kept his silence, and Roland, who was then Minister of the Interior, advised drawing a veil over the whole episode.[5] Condorcet took a similar line when called upon to formulate the Girondin position:

> We are drawing a curtain over events whose scale and consequences it would be altogether too difficult just now to assess. It is truly an unfortunate and terrible situation that we find ourselves in when the character of a people, though by nature good and generous, is forced to perpetrate such revenge.[6]

While these massacres presented the provinces with a disastrous image of the Parisian Revolution, the conduct of the elections to the Convention was disturbed by faction-fighting. On 1 September, Robespierre denounced his opponents' involvement in a supposed plot, accusing them of wishing to put Brunswick on the French throne. Condorcet was taken to task for having said in April that the Duke and the Prince of Prussia had enlightened opinions. During the night of 2 September, the Watch committee of the Commune, at Marat's instigation, issued a warrant for the arrest of Roland. On the following day, Brissot's house was searched. Danton condemned these acts of violence, on the grounds that a balance should be maintained. But the Girondins were devoting all their energies to the fight against the king and the monarchy.[7]

After 10 August, the distinction between active and passive citizen was abolished. The voting for the elections, which were to give France a new constitution, was to be by means of two-stage universal suffrage. After some hesitation, both domestic servants, who were judged to be still too much enfiefed to the Ancien Régime to think freely, and women were denied political rights. On 20 September, however, women were granted civil rights and, on 19 December, the right to testify. The struggle waged by Condorcet, Etta Palm, Olympe de Gouges and a handful of others had thus ended in virtual failure. The inegalitarian relation between the sexes was no longer masked by the active/passive distinction, so that now it was revealed in its true colours. Women now had rights, but without being full citizens. This change, which was linked to the fall of the monarchy, produced a more egalitarian society, which also presupposed a new definition of the feminine condition.

As soon as they had assembled in the *grand salle des Suisses* in the Tuileries, the representatives of the Convention proceeded to elect the bureau by roll-call. On the following day, they took up their places in the Manège, and officially substituted themselves for the Legislative Assembly. Danton declared that the only legitimate constitution would be one that was 'text-ually and nominally accepted by the majority of the primary assemblies'.[8] He proceeded to announce the placing of persons and property under the safeguard of the nation. Collot d'Herbois then called for a decree abolishing the monarchy. Abbé Grégoire was to declare:

What need is there to discuss this motion when everyone is in agreement? Kings are to the moral order what monsters are to the physical order. Courts are the workshops of crime, the hearths of corruption and the dens of tyrants. The history of kings is the martyrology of the nations.[9]

The vote for the abolition of the monarchy was carried unanimously. The galleries echoed to the cries of 'Long live the nation!' On 22 September, at Billaud-Varenne's request, the Convention ruled that from the following day public records, instead of being dated Year IV of Liberty, would bear the mark of Year I of the Republic.

When the Legislative Assembly had first met, the Girondins had been located on the left side of the chamber, whereas the Montagnards had been seated on the upper tiers. Lower down were the moderates, who constituted the Plain. Avowed supporters of the monarchy no longer had any political existence; the royalist press had disappeared and the aristocrats were in hiding. Participation in elections was very limited, for the notion of universal suffrage had yet to become a habit. Numerous deputies were simply re-elected. Thus, among the former members of the Constituent Assembly could be counted Robespierre, Pétion, Sieyès and abbé Grégoire. The Montagnards now stood for Jacobinism and for the power of Paris, whereas the Girondins, although in a majority, were exhausted by power, and represented the provinces and, subsequently, federalism. As Jaurès was later to write:

> A sombre shadow, and a fatal melancholy had descended upon them and no matter how much they agitated, denounced, accused or proposed motions, it was all in vain, for they had about them an indefinable quality of lassitude and factitiousness. They reminded one of a tree which had been gnawed to the root and which exhausted itself in sprouting a mass of unhealthy foliage.[10]

In the faction-fighting which followed, Madame Roland played a disastrous role. She was jealous of Danton's success with the members of her own circle, and therefore set out to exacerbate the conflict between Girondins and Montagnards, urging the former to call the Commune to account for the September Massacres. Her concern for the welfare of her own clique thus led her to hamper the conciliatory efforts of Danton and Condorcet and to undermine the actual principle of republican legitimacy. The fatal game that she was playing merely served to fuel the Montagnards' anti-feminism.

While the First Republic was being established in Paris, Dumouriez's offensive in the Low Countries was again changing the situation in Argonne. At Valmy, the coalition army retreated before the soldiers of the Republic. At Kellermann's prompting, the patriots waved their hats in the air, to cries of 'Long live the nation!' Michelet wrote:

> The perspicacious and educated general [Brunswick] had been only too well aware that he was facing a phenomenon which had hardly been seen since the Wars of Religion, namely, *an army of fanatics* and, if need be, of martyrs. No matter what the emigrés might claim, he stressed to the king that his view was still that it would prove a difficult business.[11]

In the course of October, Kellermann retook Verdun and Longwy. On 6 November, the battle which had failed to happen at Valmy was fought out beneath the heights of Jemappes. France's victory upon this occasion, which was due to the spontaneous strategy of a mass attack, revealed the true strength of the Republic, just as the outcome of the battle of Bouvines had demonstrated the might of the monarchy. Throughout November, the conquest of the Low Countries continued. Liège was taken but the province of Luxembourg remained under Austrian control. Théroigne's native village was therefore not occupied by the soldiers of the Revolution.

Since Théroigne's return to Paris, the patriots' struggle had taken a more radical form. In January 1792, they had set up a *Comité des Belges et des Liégeois*, which was of a uniformly Jacobin persuasion. In contrast to the former 'Vonckists', whom they viewed as too moderate, the supporters of the pro-Jacobin current wanted to establish a revolution on the French model in their own country. Having definitively rejected enlightened despotism and opted for a general fight for national sovereignty, they annulled the north/south distinction — which had been artificially imposed upon the country by the imperial authorities — and laid the groundwork for a conception which was to come to fruition in 1830, in the form of modern Belgium. They gave the French victory a rapturous welcome.

However, the Jacobins in the Low Countries, who were in favour of annexation, were still in a minority. The dominant force was represented by the 'Estates party', which favoured the creation of a republic of (federated) states. Dumouriez, however, chose not to ally himself with either of these parties, preferring to support the 'Vonckists' instead. A man of high ambition, much given to intrigue, he dreamed of succeeding where La

Fayette had failed and of becoming, in a context in which the Montagnards were growing ever more powerful, a liberal Caesar to the nation. He therefore preached a policy of independence, based upon the construction of a sovereign Belgium, which would not be annexed to France and which would be organized as a republic. However, through his concern to keep several escape routes open, Dumouriez made the mistake of failing accurately to assess the military potential of the Austrians, who would wait until the spring before returning to the field in force.

Although the Convention was opposed to all imperialist policies, it was led by its pragmatism to jettison its own principles and to embark, in spite of all the complications, upon a programme of annexation. On 30 November, four commissioners were sent on a mission to Dumouriez's camp, and expressed their disapproval of his policies. Representatives from Mons, Brussels and Tournai delivered speeches at the bar of the Convention, in which they made impassioned pleas for the independence of their country, but a decree of 15 December ruled in favour of an annexationist policy nevertheless. Various other measures of a similar nature were adopted between February and March 1793, when Liège was retaken by the Austrians and Dumouriez defected.

What was the nature of Théroigne de Méricourt's political involvement after the fall of the monarchy? What was her understanding of the split between Girondins and Montagnards? What did she think of the victories of Valmy and Jemappes, of the capture of Liège by the French, and of Dumouriez's policies? We have no way of knowing.

On 20 October 1792, *La Correspondance littéraire secrète* announced that Théroigne was at last going to publish her memoirs, after which she would 'join Dumouriez's army, which is at present in her native land'. The author added: 'She is not likely to spare the old minister Kaunitz [in her memoirs], for she has a score to settle with him. This, at any rate, is what she told me.'[12] If this testimony can be relied upon, and Théroigne was then indeed trying to write her memoirs, she was never actually to achieve this aim, nor did she ever return to Belgium and join Dumouriez's army. The heroine of our story was never to see the Ardennes again. After her involvement with warrior feminism, and her excitement at the time of the uprising of 10 August, she would seem to have relapsed into a state of apathy, although she did revive her former habit of attending political debates. In the early days of the Revolution, she had followed the proceedings of the Constituent Assembly very closely indeed, and she now approached the sessions of the

Convention in a similar spirit of devotion. She was still close to the Girondins, but she had no public presence as such.

On 9 November, she sent a young woman to Perregaux on a mission of the utmost urgency. In her letter, she asked the banker to advance her a sum of one hundred livres.[13] Théroigne's finances were in a parlous state. In January 1793, she was renting a room at 273 rue Saint-Honoré. Sieyès, who was himself living at this address, may perhaps have helped her to find lodgings near to the Jacobin Club and the Manège. From this date, the historian loses track of Théroigne, although she resurfaces in May 1793. Nor were there any rumours about her, for there was no longer a royalist press to pass comment upon the amazon's adventures.

Théroigne was in fact prey to terrible financial difficulties. The reader will recall that, at the time of her return from Kufstein, she owed money to Baron de Sélys. He had in fact advanced her a sum enabling her to redeem a pair of earrings, a ring and the famous necklace (which was subsequently given to Pierre-Joseph) from pawnshops in Paris and Liège. The baron therefore still had Théroigne's last jewels in his possession, and he had deposited them with the Paris bankers Couteulx et Cie. The bankers would not return these jewels to the young woman until she had reimbursed the baron in cash.

In her dealings with the banker, Théroigne came into contact with the chevalier Jean-Philippe de Limbourg, who represented the bank's interests. This curious character, a native of the Walloon country, was both a doctor and an accomplished financier, and he had helped to spread the fame of the resort city of Spa. On 28 January 1793, Théroigne sent him a letter attesting that a settling of accounts was under way. The matter would seem to have been finally resolved in July 1793.[14]

While Théroigne de Méricourt was disappearing temporarily from Parisian life, Olympe de Gouges made her seminal declaration upon the occasion of the king's trial. She had become a republican after 10 August, and her sympathies lay for the most part with the Girondins. She launched an attack upon Robespierre, treated him as an 'amphibian animal' and accused him of wishing to assassinate Louis XVI in order to prevent him from being judged. On 15 December, she told the Convention that she was willing to help Malesherbes prepare the king's defence. Three days before, Target had stepped down, on the grounds of age and some ill-defined infirmities. Tronchet had agreed to act for the king, but he had shown no great enthusiasm. Malesherbes, although seventy-two years old and long since retired, had let it be known that, if the king were to choose him as his council for the defence, he would be ready to devote himself to the task. Olympe de Gouges thereupon wrote:

> I wish to follow the example of the brave Malesherbes and offer myself as defender of Louis. I beg you to disregard my sex, for heroism and generosity are to be found among women also, as more than one example from the Revolution has shown. I am a frank and loyal republican, with no blot or stain upon my reputation; no one would dispute the fact, not even those who merely feign acknowledgement of my civic virtues. I am therefore in a position to take on this case. I believe Louis to be at fault as a king, but, once stripped of this title and proscribed, he would cease to be guilty in the eyes of the Republic; his ancestors have filled France's cup of woe to the very brim; unfortunately, the cup has shattered in his hands and all the fragments fell on his own head. It may be worth adding that, had it not been for the court's perversity, he would perhaps have been a virtuous king.

By way of conclusion, Olympe affirmed that Louis the Last posed no more of a threat than did his brothers and his sons. She concluded her speech as follows: 'To kill a king, you need to do more than simply remove his head, for, in such circumstances, he will live a long time after his death; he would only really be dead if he were to survive his fall.'[15]

Aside from her heroism, which was to lead her to the scaffold, Olympe de Gouges here displayed yet again a remarkable talent for theoretical speculation, for she was advancing a thesis which was subsequently to be revived by the historian Edgar Quinet, and which supposed that the physical elimination of a sovereign would not necessarily bring about the abolition of the monarchy. Quinet took the argument a step further, and emphasized that regicide has the effect of reviving the monarchy.[16]

Olympe's behaviour upon this occasion pleased neither the king's friends nor his foes. The former reproached her for proclaiming the king's guilt, while the latter accused her of underestimating it. Furthermore, the fact that the proposal had come from a woman made it altogether unacceptable, to the point of being scandalous. The day after she had delivered her speech, Olympe was waylaid by the populace outside her house. Her courage was such that she turned and faced the crowd. But some rogue seized her by the waist and ripped off her famous crumpled gauze head-dress, which served to hide her white hair — she already seemed to be an old woman. With redoubled ferocity, her assailant made as if to auction off her head: 'eighty sous! any takers for eighty sous?' Olympe calmly riposted: 'I bid a thirty sou piece and demand first refusal.' Thanks to the hoots of laughter which greeted this quip, Olympe managed to avoid being whipped by the crowd, which then dispersed.[17]

Théroigne de Méricourt was soon to suffer an equally brutal humiliation but, because she was blessed with neither the sense of humour nor the good health of Olympe de Gouges, she did not escape without a public scourging.

With the advent of the women's *sans-culotte* movement in 1793, the feminism of the time changed its aspect: it no longer produced theoretical texts, it was no longer in evidence among the elites or in the utterances of famous women and, most crucially, it no longer advocated political equality. From February 1793, it was the female element in the popular movement which assumed responsibility for the new claims of women.[18] As a consequence, this female element was affected by each in turn of the conflicts which shook the political currents of the Revolution. It began by siding with the Montagnards against the Girondins, and it then lent its support to the *enragés* in their struggle against the Montagnards, up until the time that it was eliminated politically by the latter.

By the summer of 1793, Marat had become the idol of the *sans-culotte* movement. While he was alive, he was acclaimed from the galleries of the Convention. After he had met his death, stabbed by a woman, the huge crowd of future *tricoteuses*, veritable militants of the guillotine, embalmed him as if he were a god.[19] It is also clear that his madness, his ugliness and his illness, visible in the stigmata of his chronic herpes, which he bore like a blazon upon his body, were a crucial part of this improbable cult. In the speeches of most revolutionaries, Marat was viewed with something approaching horror. His appearance was felt to be repulsive, his manner of speaking extravagant and his imprecations delusional. Nevertheless, he was idealized by the people, and still more so by its wives.

It is hard not to interpret this adoration in terms of the condition of women after the fall of the monarchy. Wholly deprived of rights and humiliated whenever they claimed them, the women of the people were the quintessence of those excluded by the Law. The Revolution had liberated them, but it had not allowed them to be citizens in the full sense of the word. Their existence was therefore symbolized in a strangely hybrid form. Because women seemed to oscillate between opposed poles, being at times tied to the image of the nursing mother, allegory of the Nation and later of

Reason, and at times associated with crime, disorder and instinct, Marat supplied them with all the elements necessary for a far-reaching identification. Through his madness, the 'Friend of the people' seemed to express all the passions of an exacerbated femininity, thereby reminding women of their own exclusion. Once their youth was gone, they too suffered for being judged to be ugly; they too were liable to succumb to a murderous violence, for which Marat seemed to be so repellent a symptom; they too were treated as mad the moment they played some part in public life. But Marat also stood for conjugal happiness and for the simple household. In public, he resembled a hysterical woman, but in private he was a virtuous husband living in common-law marriage with Simone Evrard, who was both mistress, nurse and servant to him. Thus Marat served to represent the feminine ideals of masculine and feminine *sans-culottes*.

At the opposite pole of the collective imagination, the hate aroused by Marie-Antoinette after the king's execution also allowed a remarkable variety of different phantasies to be projected. Debarred from the human community, the queen, like Marat, seemed a hideous figure, in which all the symbols of a femininity reduced to the bare fact of its sexuality were registered. However, whereas the horror which Marat inspired could be transformed into idolatry, since it issued from the entrails of the people, that aroused by Marie-Antoinette could have no redeeming features whatsoever. In the eyes of the *sans-culotte* movement, the provocative remarks and the ravaged face of the friend and idol of the lowly, exposed to all the disturbances of his diseased condition, merely served to demonstrate that he spoke the truth. On the other hand, 'l'Autrichienne', who had formerly enjoyed the status of a goddess, seemed at last to have been unmasked. Her beauty was artificial, powdered, a fiction woven out of gold and false ceremony. Appearances had been deceptive, and her spell in prison had showed, through her illness, her greying hair and the boils from which she now suffered, what depravities she had been guilty of. *Le Père Duchesne* described her as if she were a tigress and a wretched prostitute. It accused her of wallowing in the mire with her footmen, in order to create hunch-backed, crippled and gangrenous monsters. Finally, it likened her entrails to a thrice-wrinkled stomach. When compared with the glorious people, the queen thus represented the vilest perversions of which the fairer sex was capable. Simply to imagine her to be guilty of incest was to condemn her utterly.

The subsistence crisis of February 1793 exacerbated the antagonisms between the various tendencies within the Convention. The price of wheat, sugar and candles rose steadily throughout the winter, even though there had been a good harvest the previous year. Riots broke out at the end of the year, and all the *sections* were now involved in the movement. On 23 February, the laundresses sent a deputation to the Convention to complain at the bar about the price of soap:

> Soon the less well-to-do class of persons will be unable to obtain white linen, which they cannot do without. There is no shortage of foodstuffs, it is hoarding and speculation which are forcing the prices up. We demand the death penalty for hoarders.[20]

Two days later, early in the morning, the grocers' shops were invaded, and the prices were brought down to a level decided upon by the insurgents.[21] The women called for the overthrow of the Girondins, whom they believed to be responsible for rising prices.

The *sans-culotte* women in the Paris of 1793 may be divided into two different categories. Some were active or politicized militants, while others belonged to the base, which consisted of a mixture of 'Jacobin shrews', patriots, *flagellantes* and *tricoteuses* or furies of the guillotine.[22] Claire Lacombe and Pauline Léon led this struggle. They held very similar ideas, and were attached to the same man, Théophile Leclerc. It was Leclerc and Jacques Roux, an ex-priest, who were the driving force behind the *enragés*. Claire Lacombe had been Leclerc's mistress, and Pauline Léon was later to become his wife.[23] Both of these women, like Théroigne, had been advocates of warrior feminism. However, once the subsistence crisis had set in, they became the organizers of a popular feminism in which the social division of the sexes was reproduced. The symmetry was such that, while the militant women saw themselves as the guardians of the hearth, their husbands were supposed to preserve the 'outside' of the country by fighting at the frontier.

The massive presence of these women in the galleries of the Convention, their anti-parliamentary fury, and their excesses of every kind, may perhaps explain why it was that the few representatives still in favour of political equality for women came very soon to abandon this position. In February, when presenting his introductory report on the draft constitution, which had been composed by six members, Condorcet made no mention of the famous right to vote, although he had been a fervent supporter in 1790. However, there had been some discussion within the commission itself, which included among its number Barère, Romme and Lanjuinais. David

Williams, who had become a French citizen after the publication of his *Lettres sur la liberté politique*, had been recalled to Paris by the Girondins in order to participate in the preparatory work for the Constitution. He attended Sophie de Condorcet's salon and, in February, wrote his *Observations sur la dernière constitution de la France avec des vues pour la formulation de la nouvelle constitution*. He advocated giving women a better education, making it possible for them to testify in cases which involved members of their own gender, and granting political rights to all those who were single, whether they were widows or spinsters.[24]

At roughly the same time, Pierre Guyomar, the deputy for Côtes-du-Nord, made a fine plea for political rights which was entitled *le Partisan de l'égalité des droits et de l'inégalité en fait*.[25] He likened prejudice in matters of sex to racial prejudice, and called for its outright abolition. He accused the Declaration of Rights of perpetuating an aristocracy of men, and of thereby maintaining in a covert form the principles of the Ancien Régime. Finally, he proposed granting women a *droit de cité* that would be defined in terms of voting rights. However, in his concern to safeguard women from a hypothetical aristocratic husband or fanatical confessor, Guyomar also suggested that, for a transitional period, the primary assemblies should be divided into two sections, one for women and the other for men. It is also worth quoting from a work by the Montagnard deputy, Lequino, who, in a text which appeared in January 1793, entitled *Les Préjugés détruits*, declared:

> The feminine sex has a sincere desire for liberty, but the force of habit is such that, in spite of its fervent wishes, it does not dare believe itself to be capable of obtaining it, and this new weakness then serves to increase our domination still further. If it truly wishes to be free, it must resolve to muster all its courage and shake off the various yokes which it has had the imprudence to attach itself to, or to suffer itself to be chained to.[26]

After its discussion of Guyomar's text, the commission decided that women would for the time being be denied civil rights. 'The vices of our education', Lanjuinais emphasized, 'still oblige us to perpetuate this exclusion, at any rate for several years to come.'[27] This is how the problem of women's admission to the freedom of the city was resolved in April 1793. Being judged insufficiently educated to participate in the political life of the country, they were referred, much as Lequino wished, to their own desire to shake off the yoke of their own submission. The commission's line of argument was not intrinsically false, but it shows how impossible it was for the legislators of the Convention to impose a principle upon a public opinion that was still incapable of appreciating its virtues. A hundred and fifty years would have to pass, and modern feminism would have to develop, before French women would become citizens in the full sense.

Nevertheless, the activities of Pauline Léon and Claire Lacombe led to the founding of the second of the clubs in the revolutionary period to be the exclusive preserve of women. The Club of the revolutionary women citizens met in the library of the Jacobins, and it aimed to foil the plots of the enemies of the Republic. The president wore the red cap; each member had to prove that her morals were good, and each newly elected member had to swear an oath of allegiance to the republican cause: 'I swear to live for the Republic, or else to die for it.' These women's heirs would be the militants of the socialist movement.[28]

They never advocated political equality, and they did not reject their status as wife and mother, but they refused to be treated as beasts of burden. They considered the Declaration of Rights of Man and the Citizen to be applicable to both sexes:

> The only difference consists in [the respective] duties [of the two sexes]: some are public, and some private.... It is impossible to reconcile what nature imperiously commands and what the love of the public good commands.... After they have carried out the sweet functions of wife and mother, and after they have occupied themselves with those occupations which are basic to them, the women citizens, as vigilant sentinels, will still have a few moments to devote to the fraternal Societies, to surveillance and to education.[29]

This passage shows that the revolutionary women citizens accepted the vision of woman at the hearth, although they appended the claim that she should have a part to play in war, and should therefore have the right to bear arms. Furthermore, instead of casting prostitutes into the hell of vice, they held them to be the victims of libertines and to be susceptible to some sort of moral regeneration. This quite novel perspective was expressed in September 1793.[30]

About the same time as this club was being founded, Théroigne de Méricourt was composing a 'broadsheet' which was undated and which was to serve as her political testament. It was an appeal to the forty-eight *sections* of Paris, printed on grey-blue paper. Here it is in its entirety:

Citizens,

Listen to me. I do not wish to flatter you with fine-sounding phrases, for my sole wish is to tell you the truth, pure and simple.

Where have we got to? We are very nearly at the edge of the precipice, thanks to all the passions which in Paris have been so artfully deployed to waylay and trap us.

Citizens, it is time that we paused a while and reflected. When I returned from Germany, about eighteen months ago, I told you that the Emperor had a prodigious number of spies among us, who would serve to divide us, and to foment civil war from afar, and that the plan was for such a conflict to break out at a time when his satellites were ready to make a concerted effort to invade our territory. This is where we have got to; they are about to implement their plan, and we are all ready to fall into the trap. Already scuffles in various *sections* have served as a premonition of civil war. Let us therefore be on our guard, and calmly examine the situation, so that we may decide just who the *agents provocateurs* are, so that we may learn to recognize our enemies.

Woe betide you, fellow citizens, if you allow similar episodes to recur. If we go so far as to strike each other with our fists, insult each other in a fashion unbecoming to citizens, we shall soon dare to go still further, and I predict that your passions will become so inflamed that it will no longer be in your power to halt the explosion. These intrigues have three aims, namely, civil war, without a doubt, that of justifying the calumnies directed against us by kings and their slaves, who claim that it is not possible for the people to assemble and exercise its sovereignty without abusing it. This is a branch of the great conspiracy against democracy.

Fellow citizens, hold fast to democracy, so that it may never escape you. Your steadfastness, your justice and your wisdom will enable you to foil these intrigues. You will thereby give the lie to those who have heaped calumnies upon you. They are also trying, in so far as it lies within their power, to halt the departure of the contingent of troops which should soon leave Paris to fight the rebels in the Vendée. Instead of coming to the aid of our brothers, they apparently wish to force us to arrive at some agreement. The real aim of the king's agents is to create a diversion, and weaken us by setting us one against the other for, while we are tearing each other to pieces here, the rebels, with the support of the English, who will have no hesitation in raiding our coastline, if Pitt's intrigues continue to hinder us, will prevent us from thinking seriously about our own situation. I warn you that, during this same period, the rebels who, to our shame, are less divided among themselves than we are and more determined to defend despotism and religious prejudices than we are to defend liberty, will make inroads on a scale that we are incapable of imagining, for we have not the same passions as they, because men who are in a situation where it is either death or victory fight with great determination. In alliance with the imperial troops, the Prussians and all the forces of the Coalition, they will advance on all flanks. Our armies and our generals do not know if they are fighting for the Republic or for the parties, or for a tyrant whom they rightly fear to see raise himself up, as at Rome, to put an end to our divisions, and in such circumstances they would therefore be altogether disheartened. And, finally, those weak-willed citizens who are still undecided as to what to do, but who would opt for us if only our union and our strength would give them some strong incentive to do so, being discouraged for these same reasons, and being moreover seduced by perfidious promises, such as those that are contained in the Cobourg proclamation, would remain paralysed. This being so, if we were to fall into the trap that is being laid for us, since the kings have managed to foment civil war among the most energetic of citizens, and to seduce or discourage the rest, what may we oppose to their satellites? How would we check this inundation of hostile forces, who would continue to bear down upon us when we were more than ever at each other's throats? This is so hideous a notion that I cannot bear to develop it any further.

Fellow citizens, let us stop and reflect, or else we are lost. The moment has finally come when the interest of all dictates that we reunite, and sacrifice our hatreds and our passions to the public good. If the voice of the fatherland and the sweet hope of fraternity do not stir our souls, let us consult our private interests. Even once we are all reunited, we are not too strong to repulse our numerous enemies outside and those who have already raised the banner of rebellion. However, I warn you that our enemies will not distinguish between one party or the other and that, if we are defeated, we shall all suffer equally on the day of vengeance. I can assure you that, at the time of my interrogation, I was asked for further information respecting every single patriot involved in the Revolution. All the inhabitants of Paris are proscribed indiscriminately, and I heard those who sought to make me testify against the patriots say a thousand times that it would be necessary to exterminate a good half of all Frenchmen if one wished to subdue the other half.

... Exterminate us, vile slaves! It is we who shall exterminate you. Danger will unify us yet again, and we will show you what men who wish for liberty, and who are working for the cause of humankind, are capable of. We shall march together, both rich and poor, and those who have the requisite strength and yet seek to evade their duty will be spotted with infamy. It is therefore in vain, O tyrant of the earth, that you send your agents here, and that you line pockets with gold. The French are too enlightened to fall into the trap that you have set for them. We want liberty and we will defend it until our last drop of blood is spilt. Eternal justice is on our side, whereas only lies and crime are on yours. Weigh up our cause and your own, and decide for yourself who shall have the victory.

It is from acorns that great oaks grow. Thus, Roman women managed to disarm Coriolanus and to save their fatherland.

Remember, fellow citizens, before 10 August, not one of you had broken the silk ribbon which separated the Feuillants terrace from the Tuileries gardens. The smallest thing may sometimes serve to check a torrent of passions more successfully than any number of larger things one might pit against it.

As a consequence, I propose that each *section* appoint six women citizens, the most virtuous and the most serious for their age, who would have the task of reconciling and uniting the men citizens, of reminding them of the dangers which threaten the fatherland, and who would wear a long scarf, upon which would be written FRIENDSHIP AND FRATERNITY. Each time that there was a general assembly of the *section*, they would gather and call to order any citizen who strayed, who did not respect freedom of opinion, a thing which is so precious to a good public spirit, whereas those whose intentions were good, and who loved their fatherland, would keep silent. But if those who were of bad faith and who had been installed deliber- ately by the aristocrats, by the enemies of democracy and by the kings' agents, with the express purpose of interrupting, trading insults and using their fists, showed no more respect for these women citizens than they did for the voice of the president, this would be one way of knowing just who they were. One would then take note of them, and look more deeply into their case. These women citizens might be changed every six months, although those who displayed the most virtue, determination and patriotism in the glorious ministry of uniting the citizens and of inculcating in them the respect for freedom of opinions could be re-elected for a further year. They would be rewarded by having a place reserved for them in our national festivals and by being entrusted with the task of supervising those houses of education which are for our sex alone.

Such, fellow citizens, is the proposal which I put before you.

THÉROIGNE[31]

This broadsheet contains a virtual summary of France's political situation during April and May, which culminated in the fall of the Gironde.

Théroigne alludes here to the defection of Dumouriez, to the Duke of Saxe-Coburg, the commander-in-chief of the Austrian forces, and to William Pitt, who, as Prime Minister of England, had just established the First Coalition against the French Republic. She also refers to the insurrection in the Vendée and to the danger which the split between Montagnards and Girondins represented.

If Théroigne supported the Girondins, it was because she wished to foster union between all Frenchmen in face of the imminent danger of a further invasion. However, in advocating domestic peace, she was favouring her Girondin friends at the very time when the *sections*, driven forward by the *sans-culotte* movement, were holding them responsible for the rising cost of living and for the defeats on the frontier. Théroigne thus still appeared to be a 'Brissotin'. Moreover, her plan for a female magistracy serving to keep the civil peace was wholly Utopian, and shows how far she had moved towards an idealized form of feminism.

Théroigne's dream of establishing a tribunal of women who were fraternal, virtuous and capable of reconciling warring citizens suggests that she was identifying with a figure of femininity which was the negative image of that of the Amazon. Just as Penthesilea's costume had once enabled her to disavow the signs of her wounded femininity and to defend the integrity of a territory in much the same fashion as one would defend the integrity of a body, so did the allegory of this tribunal of women citizens—goddesses draw Théroigne towards a more maternal pole of femininity. But the latter was also imbued with some of the virile qualities characteristic of the myth of the Amazon. For the goddesses and the Amazons were both a kind of phallic condensation of feminine sexuality. The goddess is a reparatory representation of it, whether fusional or conquering, while the Amazon is a bloody, torn and accursed version.

It is not surprising to find that the only two public speeches delivered by Théroigne which are still extant, the one given at the *Société fraternelle des Minimes* and the other concerned with the magistracy of peace, contain corresponding expressions of a virile omnipotence of femininity: warlike in one case and pacifist in the other. It was as if Anne-Josèphe could appear on the public stage only in circumstances which favoured the exaltation of her personal signifiers, and their fusion with those of the Revolution.

Where previously she had donned the legendary costume of a warrior feminism, she was now presenting herself in the antique garb of a goddess of Justice and Reason. She seemed thereby to recover her law-abiding ideal of

135

1789, after having completed a kind of initiatory trajectory which had taken her from the dawn of 'new times' to the disorder and disunion of the Revolution. The closer the Revolution came to the definitive extinction of the monarchy, the more it conveyed feminine allegories to which Théroigne's identifications might be attached: the Nation and the Law for the period of the Constituent Assembly; warrior liberty for the spring before the fall of the monarchy; Regeneration and Reason for Year II of the Republic and the period of dechristianization; and, finally, Wisdom for the cult of the Supreme Being. As Michel Vovelle has written:

> The far more secret question [remains] open at the level of the creations of the collective imagination of this massive feminization which, against a background of the killing of the father — whether God or king — crystallizes the new religiosity in maternal images.[32]

The festival of the *fédérés* of 10 August 1793, the Festival of Union, of Unity and of the Indivisibility of France was portrayed by Michelet as a story of the Revolution in five acts, narrated to the Parisians in five successive places. On the site where the Bastille had been there was now a fountain of Regeneration, represented by Nature. From her fertile breasts there gushed pure water, with which the representatives of the primary assemblies quenched their thirst. At the Italian Opera, David had built a triumphal arch in honour of the women involved in the October Days. Michelet regretted that Théroigne was not among them:

> If beauty alone was to feature in a representation of this sort, where then was the beautiful Théroigne, the intrepid Liégoise, who, on that memorable day, won over the Flanders regiment and broke the support of the monarchy? She herself was, alas, to be broken! ... whipped, dishonoured in May '93, confined because of her madness in La Salpêtrière! ... This woman, who had once been so adored, had become a foul animal! ... She died there twenty years later, implacable and furious at all the outrages and the ingratitude which she had suffered.[33]

Théroigne was not from Liège, and she had played no part in the October Days. But these details aside, Michelet had understood perfectly well how this woman's commitment might come to be fixed upon certain feminine allegories occasioned by the Revolution. As it happened, her identifications tended to favour pagan and classical figures rather than Rousseauist and Christian representations. She therefore more closely resembled mythical Penthesilea or a Roman goddess than a statue of Regeneration or of a priestess of the Supreme Being.

On 10 May 1793, the Convention left the Manège and installed itself in the Tuileries, in the former machine room, which lay between the Clock pavilion and the Marsan pavilion. The layout of the area was entrusted to an architect by the name of Gisors, and citizen Dupasquier was responsible for creating a plaster statue of liberty draped in an *aube* and a linen cloak. The whole construction was painted in gilt. The room was at once too long and too narrow, so that its many recesses muffled the voices of the less eloquent speakers. It was also too vast for the number of representatives in the Convention, and the benches were too far apart. The bare walls echoed the orators' ringing words back and forth. The ventilation was inadequate.[34]

Théroigne de Méricourt had been given a pass by her Girondin friends, and was therefore able to continue attending the Convention's debates. She used to sit in a gallery reserved by the Girondins for those citizens who supported them. Elsewhere, a throng of women of the people and of republican women citizens acclaimed Marat, and supported the Mountain against the Gironde. According to the *deux amis de la liberté*:

> It was in the café Hotot, on the Feuillants terrace, that people used to plot all those small-scale riots and provocations, which could be observed daily in the Tuileries gardens. It is there that all the revolutionary firebrands, especially the women, who have exerted such a powerful influence on the course of events, receive their instructions.... It was a kind of retrenched camp from which spread out observers and distributors of insults against those whom they were concerned to provoke.[35]

On 13 May, the republican women citizens claimed the right to occupy the galleries which had been kept for the Gironde. They then tried to prevent the spectators from gaining access. Two days later, on Wednesday 15 May, around ten in the morning, Théroigne appeared at the usual time at the entrance to the Convention. She may perhaps have entered into discussion with the habitués of the café Hotot, and have spoken out in defence of the Girondins. She was upbraided, described as a Brissotin and accused of being a moderate. Because she defended herself and threatened her adversaries, she was seized hold of by the Jacobin *mégères*, who lifted up her skirt and whipped her bare flesh in front of the doors of the Convention. The untimely arrival of Marat, the women citizens' god, soon brought this sad scene of flagellation to a halt. Crossing the Feuillants terrace, he took Théroigne under his arm and shielded her from the women's fury.[36] On that same day, a deputy commented upon the new rooms in which the Convention was meeting, and declared: 'I swear that this room will destroy the Mountain, the Republic and the Convention.'[37]

The circumstances surrounding this flagellation are known to us from two police reports and two eye-witness accounts in the press. The first report, dated 15 and 16 May, states that Théroigne was

> whipped today beneath the vestibule of the Convention by women who, for several days past, have been gathering there in large numbers. They took her to the Committee of General Security, and would not have released her at all had not Marat declared that he was taking her under his protection. The women claimed that this woman citizeness was a false patriot.

A second report, filed on the following day, gave another account of the episode:

> The women who mill around the Convention had yesterday stationed a detachment of their number at the doors of the first galleries at nine o'clock in the morning, in order to prevent those women who were in the favour of the representatives from using their passes. Their prosecution of this was effected in as insolent a manner as possible. Citizeness Théroigne, after being whipped by these shrews, told them that she would make them bite the dust sooner or later.... They are probably paid by someone to foment disorder, for they are not at all well-off, and cannot possibly afford to spend whole days without earning a thing.[38]

On 17 May, *Le Courrier des départements* presented a third version of the event:

> A heroine of the Revolution suffered something of a setback the day before yesterday on the Feuillants terrace. Mlle Théroigne, it was said, was recruiting women for the Roland's faction; as luck would have it, she addressed herself to some supporters of Robespierre and Marat, who, having no wish to swell the ranks of the Brissotins, seized hold of the female

recruiter and thrashed her with all due vigour. The police arrived on the scene and wrested the victim from the fury of these shameless furies. Marat himself, who happened to be passing by, took Théroigne under his protection. In this manner she escaped a still more severe whipping from the sisters in the galleries. *Sic transit gloria mundi.*

On 18 May, the reporter for the *Révolutions de Paris* printed a fourth version:

> For the last few days, a number of women have been patrolling the Tuileries gardens and the corridors of the National Convention. They make it their business to inspect cockades and they stop suspicious-looking persons. It was they who, on Wednesday 15 of the present month, charged Théroigne with being a Brissotin and gave her a whipping.[39]

Restif de la Bretonne, who detested Théroigne, gave a thoroughly distorted account of the episode. He believed that she had been given a hiding at Saint-Eustache by royalist women, because she had tried to force them to wear cockades. He thus took her to be a woman citizen from Claire Lacombe's club.[40]

Shortly before, on 12 April, the Girondin majority had issued a warrant for Marat's arrest. He was acquitted by the Revolutionary Tribunal and borne in triumph through the crowd, many of whom were women. Théroigne was not present upon this occasion and yet Louis Boilly, in his famous picture of the episode, places her in the foreground, tall and thin and dressed in the Carmagnole, a form of costume which she never wore.[41]

After the fall of the Gironde and the murder of Marat by Charlotte Corday, republican women citizens' worship of the *Ami du peuple* was taken still further. On 16 July, the day of Marat's funeral, they collected the blood which flowed from his putrefying wound. They then paraded through the streets, bearing the bath and the bloodstained shirt, fetish-objects of the criminal deed which were treated by them as if they were trophies. On the following day, in a sexual rite reminiscent of ancient oriental religions, they turned themselves into posthumous spouses of the embalmed god, swearing an oath before the Convention to engender thousands of sons in Marat's image. Finally, on 28 July, for the celebration of the 'translation of the heart', they surrounded the prophet's remains, wept copiously and threw flowers upon his decomposing body.[42]

There was no place for Anne-Josèphe in a madness of this kind. In spite of her origins, she was no longer in any sense a woman of the people. Her attempt to mobilize the *faubourgs* had failed and, even when she had been swept up by the fury of the populace, she had remained a solitary, a woman apart. Her cult involved ideas, not idols. She was enwrapped in her legend and masquerading under a name which prevented her from either integrating with the crowd of women, which had anyway rejected her, or from rallying to the ideals of the republican women citizens, which she did not share. Even the Convention, which had been her last resort, no longer served to protect her. From this time on, the madness which she bore within her, and which the revolutionary ideal had masked by preventing her from toppling over into delusion, began sporadically to manifest itself in a series of symptoms which were to take her gradually along the path towards her final confinement.

In the summer of 1793, she took her leave of public life altogether, her last action being to resolve her dispute with the Baron de Sélys. In January, she had agreed to pay him the sum of 1,185 livres in *assignats*. Subsequently, however, he had claimed 1,556 livres in cash. On 5 July, she came to a compromise, in order to avoid the courts, and agreed to pay back the higher sum, on condition that it was paid in *assignats*.[43] From this date, she disappears from the historical record. Banker Perregaux had fled Paris, and Théroigne was no longer able to count upon the 'Persian annuity'. She fell silent, very probably devoting herself to the writing of her memoirs. This was the way in which she lived through the Terror.

The women's *sans-culotte* movement, the third stage in the history of original feminism, was officially checked on 30 October 1793, when all women's societies were banned. However, since the beginning of the summer, republican women citizens — plainly directed, in the person of Claire Lacombe, by the *enragés* — had been involved in street battles, the purpose of which was to force women to wear the tricolour cockade. A large number of women from the *sections* were thus brought into their movement, and given their first taste of politics. All of their actions from May onwards earned them the titles of 'bacchantes', 'tigresses', 'cannibals' or 'Medusa's heads'.[44] In short, they were compared to monsters, midway between the animal kingdom and hermaphroditism, as if the discourse concerning 'nature-as-woman' here took the form of the most highly parodic figures of a zoological naturalism. However, the pressure from the streets was such that the Convention was obliged to yield and, on 21 September, it decreed that it was compulsory for women to wear the cockade. The struggle did not end there. The women citizens declared war yet again, rebuking those women who followed only the letter of the decree by wearing the cockade under their headscarfs, ribbons, pompons or surrounding it with tassels, plumes and bouquets.[45]

On 23 September, the *Feuille du Salut public* described Claire Lacombe as a bacchante:

> The woman or girl Lacombe is finally in prison, and out of harm's way; this counter-revolutionary bacchante no longer drinks anything except water, she is known to have been very fond of wine and she was no less fond of food and of men, as the intimate fraternity prevailing between her, Jacques Roux, Leclerc and company testifies.

Two days later, *La Gazette française* announced the arrest of *femme* Lacombe, 'who has played almost as large part in our Revolution as *demoiselle* Théroigne [*sic*].' This information was, however, false, for Claire Lacombe had not been arrested. Nevertheless, the announcement is of some interest, for it shows that, from this time on, Théroigne de Méricourt belonged to the Revolution's past, and that she had been supplanted by Claire Lacombe, the representative of an altogether different kind of feminism. The reporter concerned was moreover aware of such differences, for he drew an implicit contrast between *femme* Lacombe, a popular form of address, and *demoiselle* Théroigne, which was a more elitist title.[46]

The cockade war was followed by the battle of the caps. Republican women citizens had taken to cutting their hair short and wearing the red cap. With the decree of 21 September, it began to be feared that a further decree would make the red cap, short hair and the bearing of arms compulsory for women. No one really favoured such a measure. 'Be careful', warned Fabre d'Eglantine, 'for, once you have passed one decree of this kind, there is no guarantee that things will stop there. You will soon be required to wear a belt, and then you will have to have two pistols in it.'[47]

It was therefore somewhat superficial conflicts that caused the Convention finally to curtail the far more profound debate on women's rights. The Convention's decision, on 30 October, to ban women's societies, and therefore to adopt a negative attitude towards their 'liberation', and to postpone the resolution of the problem to some future date, was not of course merely a response to the fracas over cockades and bonnets, or, indeed, an aspect of the struggle against the *enragés* (with whom the republican women citizens were associated). On this point, representative Amar, the chairman of the Committee of General Security, delivered a notorious speech. He emphasized that women were, by their nature, unsuited to political activity, which should be the preserve of men:

> Each sex is called to the kind of occupation which is suited to it.... What is woman's essential character? Custom and nature have assigned the following functions to her: to begin the education of men, to prepare the hearts and minds of children for the practice of public virtues, to steer them from an early age towards what is good, to raise up their souls and to instruct them in the political cult of liberty; once the household is taken care of, these are their proper functions; a woman's natural destiny is to ensure the love of virtue. When they have fulfilled all these duties, they will have deserved well of the fatherland.... Do you wish that, in the French Republic, they should come to the bar, to the rostrum and to the political assemblies, just as men do? [Do you wish them to] abandon their modesty, which is the source of all the virtues of their sex, and the care of their families?[48]

With the formulation of this credo, which for a whole century was to define the status of bourgeois women, Condorcet's arguments were wholly discredited. Given the violence of the worshippers of Marat, and a public opinion which showed little inclination to think in any other way, Condorcet too had given up the struggle.

As the campaign against popular feminism was entering its closing stages, the guillotine claimed the lives of three women, Marie-Antoinette, Olympe de Gouges and Madame Roland, none of whom were *sans-culottes*. In an anti-feminist tirade of unusual violence, *Le Moniteur* for 19 November 1793 announced the news in such a way as to lend further weight to the Convention's decision:

> In a short space of time, the Revolutionary Tribunal has provided women with a great example, which will no doubt not be lost on them; for justice, which is ever impartial, matches severity with instruction. Marie-Antoinette, who was raised in a perfidious and ambitious court, introduced into France the vices of her family; she sacrificed her husband, her children and her adopted country to the ambitions of the House of Austria, whose plans she furthered, by disposing of the people's blood and money and of government secrets. She was a bad mother, a debauched wife and she died burdened with the curses of those she had sought to ruin. Posterity will forever abhor her

name. Olympe de Gouges, born with an exalted imagination, took her own delusion to be an inspiration of nature. She began by talking nonsense, and she ended up by adopting the scheme of those perfidious persons who wished to divide France; she wished to be a statesman, and the law seems to have punished this conspirator for having forgotten the virtues which best suit her sex. *Femme* Roland, an ambitious wit and small-time philosopher, the queen for a day, surrounded by mercenary writers, to whom she gave dinners, distributed favours, places and money, was in all respects a monster.... She was a mother, but she had sacrificed nature by wishing to raise herself above it; in forgetting such a thing, which is always dangerous, and in wishing to be erudite, she ended up by perishing on the scaffold.[49]

One of these women was seen as a debauchee, the second as a victim of her own delusions, and the third as a monster. They were condemned, it would seem, not so much for what they had actually done as for their 'betrayal' of the nature which had supposedly made them women, that is, exclusively wives and mothers. Pierre Chaumette, a man who shared Prudhomme's pronounced anti-feminism, added the following imprecation:

> Remember this virago, this woman-man, the impudent Olympe de Gouges, who was the first to set up women's assemblies, who wished to indulge in politicking, who neglected her household duties in order to meddle in the Republic's affairs, and whose head has fall [*sic*] beneath the iron avenger of the laws.[50]

By a curious irony of history, Chaumette was himself to perish on the scaffold between two women, namely, Hébert's widow and Lucile Desmoulins.

It is fair to suppose that, had it not been for the ban of 30 October, the violence of the women of the people would have continued throughout the Terror, but it is also feasible to argue that this ban itself led to an exacerbation of that same violence. All observers remarked at the time that, from winter 1793, the women of the people became enthusiastic supporters of the Terror and of the 'holy' guillotine. It was very much as if, given the anti-feminism of the Montagnard Convention, they had transposed the love they had invested in Marat on to the killing machine. As Dominique Godineau has observed, 'the populace, and the women in particular, placed a kind of confidence, which could be described as mystical, in the guillotine, which they saw as the "holy" protector of the Revolution'.[51]

One can also entertain the hypothesis that if, in Year II, the women of the people seemed, in their fascination with the guillotine, to be more blood-thirsty than their male counterparts, this was not because they were in the grip of a more perverse 'instinct', but because their condition as 'quasi-citizens', indeed their 'quasi-animal' status, led them to give vent to their opinions in more extreme ways, through fanaticism, sectarian imprecations and mystical worship.

CONFINEMENT

In spring 1794, Nicolas-Joseph Terwagne, Anne-Josèphe's second brother, who had set up in business as a laundryman in Paris, sent a report to the judge and president of the 1st *arrondissement* notifying them of his sister's madness, and requesting that she be taken into care. She was still living in rue Saint-Honoré, in her fourth-floor room, number 1449. She appeared to be manifesting all the signs of delusions of persecution. However, since she had always been subject to crises of this kind, and since the Terror tended to favour the onset of such delusions, it is hard to decide during this period just who was really being persecuted and who was suffering from delusions. Théroigne herself had in fact 'made suspect remarks' and had been denounced. Thus, shortly after Nicolas-Joseph had drafted his report to the judge, she was arrested by the Revolutionary Committee of the Le Peletier *section*.

This committee, like all the others, had been set up by a decree of 11 March 1793, and it had been initially designed to monitor foreigners and suspects, but subsequently, under the Terror, it served for the arrest of the 'enemies of liberty'. The citizens on the committee searched Théroigne's room and found the famous sabre which she had used at the time of the assault on the Tuileries. In spite of her vigorous protests, they arrested her, confiscated her papers, put seals on the door and filed a report:

Having climbed up to a room on the fourth floor we informed her of the aforesaid order, and after she had made a number of different observations, saying, for example, that she did not recognize any revolutionary committees, but only the Committee of Public Safety and the Committee of Public Security of the Convention, we proceeded nevertheless with a most rigorous inspection of all her papers, which we have deposited in two box-files, bearing the numbers one and two, upon which we have placed our seals, together with those of citizeness Théroigne; we have also put our seals on a case containing some papers, so that all of these things may be taken to our committee and checked in the presence of citizeness Théroigne.

This report demonstrates that, when faced with legal authorities, Théroigne showed no signs of delusion. Upon being arrested against her will, she protested in much the same manner as hundreds of other citizens who had fallen victim to the Terror. She was known as a 'Brissotin', had always been subject to enthusiasms, and was therefore liable at any moment to be denounced for 'suspicious remarks', and to have as a consequence to appear before the Revolutionary Tribunal.

I would advance the hypothesis that, in the spring of 1794, Théroigne presented signs of delusions of persecution which led her brother to fear that she would be arrested as a suspect. He therefore decided to declare her to be mad, for her protection and for his own. He failed, however, to fore-stall a denunciation and an arrest, which occurred quite independently of the measures which he had undertaken.[52]

Three days after the committee had acted, Nicolas-Joseph received permission to have Théroigne taken into care. However, having learned in the meantime of his sister's arrest, he sent a request to the Committee of General Security, which was at the very apex of the police hierarchy, asking that 'citizeness Terwagne's state of *absolute dementia*' be acknowledged. He said that he was convinced that it was her sickness, and the alienation of her mind, which had brought about her arrest. He therefore requested that she be set free, and he asked to be allowed to care for her. By using the phrase *absolute dementia*, rather than simple *dementia*, as in his report, he was clearly emphasizing the extent of his sister's madness in an attempt to win his case. Meanwhile, Théroigne was still confined. The archives record that she was soon transferred to one of those houses used by the Paris sections to hold suspects at a time when state prisons were full. The 'lodgers' at these houses had to pay for their 'shelter'. If they were too poor to raise the sums required, the richer among them were obliged to pay for them. Théroigne was now a prisoner, without money, papers or books; she was judged to be suspect and she had been declared to be in a state of 'absolute dementia'.

One can therefore readily understand how, in such circumstances, she should have decided to write to Saint-Just in order to complain about the sad predicament in which she found herself. She sent a first, unsigned letter, which was never delivered, and a second letter, bearing the date 8 Thermidor Year II, which likewise was never to reach him. The letter was found, still sealed, among the young *Conventionnel*'s papers:

Citizen Saint-Just, I am still under arrest, I have wasted precious time. I wrote to you begging you to send me two hundred livres, and to come and see me, but I have received no answer. I feel none too grateful to the patriots for having left me here wholly bereft. It seems to me that they ought not to be wholly indifferent to my being here, and that they ought to do something. I sent you a letter in which I said that it was I who said that I had friends even in the emperor's palace, that my treatment of citizen Bosque was unjust, but that I was annoyed. People have said that I forgot to sign that letter, that was through not paying attention. I would be truly delighted to see you for a few moments. If you are unable to visit me where I now am, if you simply do not have the time, could I not arrange to be accompanied to your house? I have a thousand things to tell you. We must establish union; I must have the opportunity to develop all my projects, and to continue to write what I was writing. I have great things to say. I can assure you that I have made progress. I have neither paper nor light, in fact I have nothing; even so, I must be free in order to write; it is impossible for me to do anything here. My stay here has taught me something, but if I were to remain here for long, if I were to remain here any longer without doing anything, without publishing anything, I would degrade the patriots and the civic crown. You are aware that both you and I are involved, and that the signs of union require some effects. A quantity of good writings are needed, if a good impetus is to be given. You know my principles. It irks me that I was not able to speak with you prior to my arrest. I called once at your house, but they told me that you had moved. It is to be hoped that the patriots would not let me fall victim to some intrigue. I could still put everything to rights, if you would second me. But I would have to be somewhere where I am respected, for people will stop at nothing in order to degrade me. I have already spoken to you of my plan. While I am waiting for that to be arranged, and while I am waiting to find a house where I would be sheltered from intrigue, and where I would be honourably surrounded by virtue, I demand that I be taken back home.

I would be only too grateful to you if you would lend me two hundred livres.

Adieu

THÉROIGNE[53]

A closer scrutiny of this text makes it plain that it contains two mutually contradictory discourses. On the one hand, it follows a perfectly rational logic; on the other, it is the expression of a genuine delusion. The letter's rationality and coherence may be understood as follows. One assumes that Théroigne wrote to Saint-Just because she had seen him at the Convention, and because he was the author of the decrees of 8 Ventôse, Year II, which were concerned with, among other things, the confiscation of the property of suspects:

> 1. The Committee of General Security is granted the authority to release patriots who have been detained. Any person wishing to reclaim their liberty will have to give an account of their conduct since 1 May 1789. 2. The property of patriots is inviolable and sacred. The possessions of persons acknowledged to be enemies of the Revolution will be confiscated for the benefit of the Republic; these persons will be detained until peacetime, and then banished in perpetuity.[54]

Given these decrees, Saint-Just was therefore the man who could logically free Théroigne, restore her possessions to her and acknowledge her as a genuine patriot. Thus, she acted during summer 1794 in much the same fashion as she had done three years before, at the time of her confinement in Kufstein. Upon that occasion, she had called upon a prince, an emperor and a judge to restore liberty to her. Now, in similar circumstances, she addressed herself to an important figure in the Revolution, who had been responsible for the drafting of some only too real decrees, in order to complain of the injustice which had been done her. Furthermore, this repetition is apparent in the actual text of the letter, for Théroigne's reference to Leopold's palace clearly represents an evocation of her former imprisonment.

Her wish to meet Saint-Just in person was equally logical. Like numerous party leaders, he lived very close to the Jacobin Club, in the United States Hotel. Before her imprisonment, Théroigne was therefore living a short distance away from him. Why should she not have tried to speak to him, and to share with him her long experience of the Revolution and of the need for union? After all, she was not a nobody; she had been famous long before Saint-Just, and he was younger than she was. She had apparently tried to pay him a call, and had been shown the door. She had probably been taken for some Illuminist, out to assassinate a state dignitary.

On the other hand, Théroigne's letter is proof of the onset of a delusion, for, though it was addressed to a real person, Théroigne was behaving as if her confinement in July 1794 was identical to her imprisonment in Kufstein. Not only did the Paris of the Terror not resemble Leopold's Austria but, in addition, in Thermidor Year II there was no legal authority empowered to justify or to dispense justice to such a prisoner. This is why Théroigne's letter gives one the impression that it was written by someone speaking from the rooftops, from some timeless universe which had risen up from within her own imagination. Thus, in speaking to Saint-Just, Théroigne was not so much addressing a real statesman as a pure name. It was to God that Théroigne was writing from the depths of her cell, that is to say, to an essence whose name embodied in her eyes the two primordial virtues of the Revolution. Saint-Just was thus an incarnation of the Mystical (*Saint*) and of Justice (*Just*).

When Théroigne was at Kufstein, she had addressed herself, in the name of a *true* Revolution, to a *genuine* emperor, to a juridical system which was well-established and to an examining magistrate who *really* had the power to have her set free. Even if she at times suffered from delusions, and thus invented false plots alongside the true ones, and even if she was addressing herself less to men than to an abstract incarnation of *the Law*, she was faced with a legalistic discourse which was capable of responding to her imprecations with actual deeds. When faced with such a discourse, she was able to fall back upon the reality of a legally established Revolution. The existence of this twofold reference enabled her, on the one hand, to do justice to it and, on the other, to endow herself with a knowledge which made her a *real* actor in the cause of the Revolution.

Conversely, in July 1794, no authority was empowered to release Théroigne from her mental and physical confinement. Now that she had gone mad, the Revolution no longer served as a guarantee of a reference or of a symbolic law. The Terror was fabricating new suspects daily, and projecting on to them a phantasy woven out of plots and delusions. As for the 'gods' of the nation, they now seemed akin to the last Roman emperors celebrated by Antonin Artaud. Their deaths were merely suspended so that, though they might be kings for a day, they would be overthrown tomorrow. Given a reality of this kind, Anne-Josèphe could not help but topple over into delusion herself, and behave as if her present situation were no different from the one she had known at Kufstein. Imprisoned in a timeless universe, she spoke to phantoms while believing that she was addressing princes.

Théroigne's whole path in life would seem to have corresponded to a dialectic of confinement and liberty, of reason and madness, and of exile and return. Although alienated by her position as a woman of the Ancien Régime, through the Revolution she had won the right to another identity. If her confinement in Austria had failed to precipitate the onset of her madness, it was no doubt because it reminded her of another, more structural confinement, one associated with the humiliation of being a woman. Her 'judge's' willingness to listen and the writing of her autobiography had enabled her to take a further step towards liberty. But the humiliation of being whipped, her failure to make any progress with her writing and then, to make her situation still worse, a more or less solitary confinement set her altogether adrift. Her madness was fully in evidence once she had written her letters to Saint-Just, that is to say, when she had escaped from the justice of the Terror, or from the madness of the Revolution, through having already been declared officially mad by her brother. One can see here that the onset of a legalized madness, which was to be transformed into an asylum madness, put an end to any unregulated expression of lunacy, which the Revolution was able to sustain only when it was itself still a bringer of liberty.

It is no surprise to find that the onset of legalized madness occurred at the very moment when the Revolution was culminating in the Terror, and when the Thermidorean reaction was being set in motion. For so long as it was sustained by the revolutionary ideal, Théroigne's madness could remain masked or else express itself freely in what were very probably oscillations between exhilaration and melancholy. Conversely, with the advent of a new moral order, which no longer sanctioned such a free expression of madness, her insanity tended to assume a legalized form. Then, with the birth of the modern asylum, that is, the definitive confinement of the mad under the medical gaze and in suitable sites, Théroigne's madness became increasingly fixed as a nosological object recognizable by science. If her involvement with original feminism had enabled her to live her life under the banner of liberty, and thereby to express her latent madness in acts of positive revolt, the collapse of the revolutionary ideal plunged her into a state of definitive alienation which then brought out her latent psychosis. In moving from a 'free' and 'travelling' madness to a chronic psychosis, she then lapsed into the repetitive lethargy of asylum dementia. When, under the Restoration, Esquirol wrote his famous observation of Théroigne, he reversed her destiny. Instead of realizing that the Revolution had 'carried' Théroigne's madness to such a degree that it had effectively masked it, he set out to prove that, on the contrary, her involvement in revolutionary politics lay at the root of that madness, and of a madness at large in the world as a whole. However, in order to substantiate such a diagnosis, he was forced to invoke a royalist historiography which, as we shall see below, allowed him to effect his own revision of the inheritance of Pinel.

On 20 September 1794, Théroigne de Méricourt was officially recognized as mad by a health officer from the Le Peletier *section*. A fortnight later, she asked that her papers be returned to her brother. In December, she was set free and lived with him in rue Croulebarbe for a period of several weeks. However, at some point during the first quarter of 1795, he had her committed to the madhouse of the faubourg Saint-Marceau. Once there, she protested endlessly against her fate and asked to be released, claiming that she was the victim of a plot.

During this period, Courtois, who was a deputy in the Convention and a former supporter of Danton, was entrusted with the task of examining the papers of Robespierre and Saint-Just. It was while he was sorting through these that he discovered Théroigne's famous letter to Saint-Just. A year to the day after the letter had been written, Courtois read the Convention a report in the name of the Committees of Public Safety and General Security regarding the events of 9 Thermidor, Year II. On this occasion, he recorded how the Committee of the Le Peletier *section* had intercepted Théroigne's letter and had sent it on 16 Thermidor to the Committee of General Security, who had at first judged it to provide proof of a conspiracy but who had decided in the end that it merely served as evidence for Théroigne's madness. Courtois proceeded to apologize for having described Théroigne as 'famous', and to emphasize her condition of absolute dementia:

> Citizeness Théroigne, whom I have called famous because of the active part which she played in the Revolution, and because of the celebrity which she earned through being the emperor's prisoner and through the role which she has played since, is now in a madhouse in the faubourg Saint-Marceau. In one of her lucid moments, she recently called from her window to a neighbour, begging him to concern himself with her fate, and to help to get her out of that unhappy place. The neighbour, fearing that Théroigne was indeed an innocent victim, as she said, of a perfidious web, took an interest in her fate, and appeared before the Committee of General Security to testify in her favour. But it turned out that her alienated mind was the sole cause of her detention, and the approaches made by the interfering but humane

neighbour to the Committee of General Security, which he found very amenable, were therefore not crowned with success.[55]

This report shows that at this date Théroigne was not prepared to accept her entrance into a state of legalized madness. Indeed, because her demeanour was not at all that of a mad person, and because she seemed rather to be the victim of an injustice, a neighbour was prepared to intervene on her behalf to effect her release.

In 1797, Théroigne was transferred to the great hospice of the Hôtel-Dieu — a huge hell of unreason. When she was there, Pierre Villiers, a former secretary of Robespierre and a chronicler of the revolutionary period, paid her a visit: 'I have seen this revolutionary fury. I chatted with her in 1797, and her reason really was alienated. The words "liberty" and "levelling" were ever upon her lips.'[56] Although this testimony is none too trustworthy, it shows how far legalized madness had gained ground upon real madness. During this period, the dialectic of confinement and liberty, which was to prove so characteristic of Théroigne's life, would seem to have been expressed by pure signifiers. These referred to the universe in which Théroigne seems to have been fixed since her letter to Saint-Just had remained unanswered. The word 'levelling' evokes the 'normalization' underway in her passage from a generalized madness to an asylum madness, but it also indicates a fixation with the vocabulary of Year II. Being deprived of everything which represented her fortune, that is, her knowledge, her notebooks, her books, her clothes, her quotations and her ribbons, Théroigne had been quite literally 'levelled', or reduced to the zero degree of a vegetative existence. But 'levelling' was also a term used by the Thermidoreans to refer to those extremists of the *sans-culotte* movement who cultivated 'holy equality' and who wished to 'level' fortunes. Having identified with Saint-Just and with the Ventôse Decrees, as if with a 'deified' form of the Revolution, Théroigne was now uttering words which had been current during the Terror. In her insanity, she laid claim in a hallucinatory fashion to a kind of egalitarian madness of the Revolution, whereas in fact she herself had been one of its victims, both when she was whipped by the Jacobin women and during her arrest. Thus her own sense of herself converged with the image that the royalist press and the Thermidorean reaction had already created for her, when calling her, as Pierre Villiers had done, a 'revolutionary fury'.

On 9 December 1799, she was transferred to the *Maison des Folles* of La

Salpêtrière, where Philippe Pinel, the founder of alienism, had been head doctor for the previous four years. He had been rejoined there by a warden named Jean-Baptiste Pussin, his best assistant, who had learned from him, while at the men's hospital of Bicêtre, how to care for the insane by removing their chains. At La Salpêtrière, Pinel had made Pussin responsible for the treatment of a quarter of the female inmates so that he might put his reforms into practice. Both Pussin and Pinel may have encountered Théroigne. When Étienne Esquirol had come to this same hospital, a few months previously, to follow the teaching of his master, Pinel, he knew nothing about the woman from the Ardennes. Besides, her first period of internment had not lasted very long. Théroigne had not taken kindly to life in an asylum, and protested endlessly about her confinement. On 11 January 1800, she was sent to the Petites-Maisons hospital, where she was given the first empty bed. There is no trace of her in the archives for the following seven years. However, on 7 December 1807, she was once again interned in La Salpêtrière, where she would remain up until her death on 8 June 1817.[57] In the meantime, Esquirol's gaze was to make her one of the most famous cases in modern alienism.

At the dawn of the nineteenth century, in spite of the abolition of *lettres de cachet* and the closing down of the *Hôpital général*, the situation of madwomen at La Salpêtrière was not greatly altered. In 1785, Jean Colombier and François Doublet had signed the birth certificate of the modern asylum by advocating a radical transformation in places of confinement. They recommended that the inmates be provided with healthy water, pure air, freedom of movement, green spaces and open galleries. A year later, the architect Viel rebuilt La Salpêtrière's quarters for the alienated along lines laid down in the two men's directives.[58] However, in spite of the work of the Constituent Assembly, in spite of the hierarchization of the universe of unreason and the transformation of the insane into the alienated, that is to say, into the sick, the places of confinement remained in a pitiable state. Thus, La Salpêtrière in the early 1800s was still very much as it had been when La Rochefoucault-Liancourt had presented his first report to the Mendicity Committee established by the Constituent Assembly.

Shut up forever in the asylum, the madwomen were dressed in dirty and torn clothes. They lived in the midst of refuse, and were ill-treated by their keepers, who chained them to their cells, which were separated from the visitors by a corridor full of grills. The most demented of the inmates used to eat their own excrement, while others simply pushed it towards the rakes which were used to sweep it up. When they were in the grip of their fits, the inmates would crawl in the gutters or utter horrible plaintive cries. They were fed like animals, and their bread and soup, and the straw which served as their litter, were handed through the bars. Some were fettered to a ring, which was riveted to the wall, making all movement of hands and feet impossible. Air and light penetrated through a grill, and in winter, when the Seine was in flood, the cells were infested with rats and vermin; in the morning, the women's faces would often be marked by animal bites.

In 1818, Esquirol embarked upon a journey across France, visiting hospitals and prisons en route. His purpose was to inquire into the fate of the alienated outside of Paris, and he recorded a truly nightmarish vision:

> I saw them covered in rags, having nothing but straw to protect them from the cold and damp flagstones upon which they lay. I found them to be poorly fed, deprived of air to breathe, of water to quench their thirst, and of those things which are most necessary for life. I saw them delivered up and abandoned to the brutal supervision of people who were really nothing but gaolers. I saw them in narrow, dirty, contaminated, dark and airless hovels, chained up in lairs in which one would hesitate to chain up wild beasts.[59]

Such was the world in which Anne-Josèphe spent the last ten years of her life, while at the same time the criteria of the new mental hygiene were applied to the observation of her madness.

From 1807 onwards, Théroigne de Méricourt's destiny became inextricably entangled with the description given by Esquirol of her case. At the time of her definitive confinement at La Salpêtrière, she was still fixated upon the vocabulary of Year II. She was in a highly agitated state, and would swear, threaten those about her, speak of liberty and of the Committee of Public Safety and accuse anyone who came near of being a royalist or a moderate. A year later, a former party leader visited La Salpêtrière. Théroigne recognized him and rebuked him for being a 'moderate who should soon be done justice by a decree from the Committee of Public Safety'.[60]

On 21 March 1808, Regnaud de Saint-Jean-d'Angely, who had been a representative in the Constituent Assembly and, in later years, hospital administrator for the Italian army, was concerned about Théroigne's fate, and therefore wrote to the Prefect of the Ourthe, asking him to inquire after the whereabouts of her family:

Sir, I beg you to be so kind as to inquire in Méricourt, which is near to Liège, regarding the family of Mlle Théroigne. She has a private fortune and her kin have left her in hospital without any resources and in the most deplorable state. I beg you to seek out the most prompt and precise information possible regarding any possessions which Mlle Théroigne either has or used to have.[61]

After a year of inquiries, the Prefect sent Regnaud a letter written by a notable who had gathered together the responses from the Ardennes:

At the beginning of the Revolution, a female adventurer arrived in Xhoris dressed as an amazon, and answering to the name of Théroigne de Méricourt. She was said to be visiting some of her kin in that commune, and their name was Terwagne. This young lady spent several months in this country, and I seem to recall having seen her myself. Sometimes she would wear men's clothes and cajole the coquettes of the area, and sometimes she would wear those of her own sex and appear on the arm of some whipper-snapper. She disappeared quite suddenly, and it was said that she had returned to Paris, from where she would seem to have come. Her family name must be Terwagne, and she must have been born at Marcourt, as I have had the honour to explain to you. But, being myself some distance from that hamlet, it became impossible for me to give you all the information which you seemed to desire. She may have some kin at some remove from Xhoris, who lead a very regular sort of life and who are of a middling fortune.[62]

This is a curious kind of answer, given that Pierre-Joseph, Théroigne's elder brother, is known to have been living at this period in Liège, where he had married Élisabeth Pirson, the daughter of a confectioner, whose business he had revived. Moreover, Nicolas-Joseph, the former laundryman, did not die until 1850. Théroigne's half-brother, the elder son from their father's second marriage, was also still living. He had become a soldier. All three had therefore forgotten her and left her to languish in the asylum, with no resources whatsoever of her own.

In 1810, Théroigne became much calmer. She lapsed more and more into a state of dementia, which suggests that she had moved definitively into the world of institutionalized madness. Her fixation upon the vocabulary of Year II seemed now to be permanent. For hours at a time, she would speak to herself, in a basic language, acknowledging no other reality save that of her own monologue, which would unfold interminably. She saw herself as occupied with great things, and at times she would smile at those around her and utter in a low voice certain incantatory sentences, which featured a number of by now automatized terms, such as fortune, liberty, committee, revolution, knaves, decree, order. She would sometimes punctuate such speeches, which were composed of pure signifiers, with rituals of self-abasement. Thus, she would immerse herself in refuse or in water that was polluted with excrement. At other times, she would enact purificatory rituals, which involved the sprinkling of icy water over her body, as if to wash away some imaginary defilement or to erase all traces of the humili-ations which she had previously inflicted upon herself. After twenty years of confinement, Théroigne had become something very like a wild beast which, being trapped in the circular universe of the asylum, was condemned to alternate between delusions of self-punishment and a cannibalistic devouring of the lost ideal. She would bite, crawl, eat straw and feathers, walk about naked without the least shame, no longer had any motivation and no longer knew how to write. Once her health had been fragile and she had forever been complaining of migraines, but now she was armed with an unbelievable resistance to every kind of physical illness or the harshest weather. The closer her melancholy came to autism, to loss of a sense of self, to chronicity or to an incurable schizophrenia, the more her body took on the appearance of a fortress that was wholly impermeable to external aggression.

When death finally came, it looked very much as if it had been the outcome of the ultimate form of unconscious self-punishment. A rash covered the whole of her body, which was then calmed through a ritual application of iced water and drenched straw. But Théroigne immediately took to her bed, drank only water and refused to eat until stricken with extreme catechia. At the end of a fortnight, oedema manifested itself. The death certificate indicated that 'chronic double pneumonia' was the cause of death. After an autopsy had been performed and a cast taken of her skull and face, what remained of her corpse was thrown into the ditch of the hospital cemetery, which today lies beneath one of the central buildings.

For twenty-three years, Théroigne de Méricourt had been in mourning for the Revolution. Her death under the Restoration is a reflection of her destiny as a melancholic woman, in which nothing was able to fill the place left empty through the irremediable loss of the ideal object.

ESQUIROL'S GAZE

In order to grasp the meaning of the gaze directed by Esquirol at Théroigne de Méricourt's melancholy, we need to examine the transformation which occurred between the work of Pinel and that of his brilliant disciple. These two alienists did not view the Revolution in the same light, and the part which they themselves had played in it differed markedly. Like Lavoisier, Lamarck, Volney or Cabanis, Pinel belonged to the last generation of Enlightenment *philosophes*, known as the *idéologues*.[63] He had grown up under the Ancien Régime, and he had participated with enthusiasm in the heady events of 1789. He had spent time in the company of Condorcet and the Girondins, attended Madame Helvétius's salon and shifted to a moderate position during the Terror.

Esquirol, on the other hand, belonged to a later generation. He had had no first-hand knowledge of the *Encyclopédistes*, and possessed only bad memories of the Revolution: the Terror, to begin with, then the troubles which had beset the Directory. His elder brother, a diehard royalist whose excesses had been repudiated by his own family, was condemned and then executed in Thermidor, Year VII, for his involvement in the conspiracy in the Haute-Garonne. Esquirol chose to pursue a career in medicine in 1793, and later reforms decided upon by the Convention aided him in his studies. His intellectual formation belonged to the period of the Directory and the Consulate, while his growing notoriety under the Empire was to culminate in glory under the Restoration and the July Monarchy.

As the real founder of the clinical treatment of mental illness, Pinel was the first scientist to bring madness within the domain of medical knowledge. He conceived of madness itself in terms of a 'residue of reason', and sought to link the discourse of the ancient Greeks to the philosophy of the Enlightenment. He was still a theoretician of the soul and of the passions, an advocate of the moral, humanist treatment characteristic of the eighteenth century. Esquirol, on the other hand, was already a modern psychiatrist, a nineteenth-century legislator, a functionary concerned with institutions and with science. It was to be his task to implement the law of 1838 concerning the confinement and the rights of the alienated. The doctrines of master and pupil[64] bore a striking resemblance to each other, but, in spite of appearances, there were profound differences between them.

There were also, nevertheless, numerous parallels. Both were born in the south of France. Both had followed the same course of study with the *doctrinaires* of the college of the Esquille at Toulouse, and, before they had felt the call of medicine, both had been intended for the priesthood. Finally, both were opportunists, who were concerned to consolidate the position of medical knowledge in relation to the political authorities. They therefore espoused the great ideal which had arisen in the course of the Revolution of a 'national' medicine, whose organization would resemble that of a lay clergy, but they likewise rejected the Montagnard illusion that the Revolution, if effectively handled, would lead to a society that had been restored to its original health and that was free from trouble and passion.[65]

On 18 January 1790, at a time when Théroigne de Méricourt was working with Gilbert Romme on various projects for the emancipation of the people, Pinel published an article in which he discussed the Revolution from the viewpoint of the passions. He stigmatized the aristocracy's luxury and softness: faults which in his view were responsible for nervous complaints, for melancholy, and for vapours, which had been a common-place affliction throughout the eighteenth century. He then paid homage to the movement of 1789 for having managed to revive the moral strength of the nation and to infuse new vigour into human energy. But in the same breath he emphasized that the social unrest caused by the Revolution had intensified states of passion and had thereby increased the incidence of mental illness. His view of the Revolution's essence was thus a contradictory one. On the one hand, he saw it as liberatory, on the grounds that it enabled men to escape from their apathy; on the other, he regarded it as harmful, because it intensified psychic disturbances.[66]

Pinel's attitude towards the Revolution not only tells us a great deal about the theory of alienation that he was to develop between 1790 and 1800, but it also foreshadows the opportunist position which he would adopt towards all political authorities of whatever complexion. In the first edition of his *Medico-philosophical treatise on mental alienation*,[67] which was published in October 1800, he delineated a framework for a genuine knowledge of madness. Four different kinds of alienation were defined, namely, *melancholia*, or exclusive delusion, *mania*, with or without delusion, *dementia*, or the abolition of thought, and, finally, *idiocy*, or the obliteration of the affective and intellectual faculties. Since Pinel espoused a materialistic view of the brain, he conceived of madness as a derangement of the cerebral faculties, which he had initially attributed to causes of a physical nature, such as a blow to the skull or a particular typology, but which he later viewed as hereditary in nature. However, Pinel's real innovation lay in the domain of moral causation. According to him, passions and excesses of all kinds were the chief cause of madness. In the majority of cases, therefore, any material impact upon the brain was discounted.[68]

Given a perspective of this kind, madness was a specific form of illness, quite distinct from conditions affecting the organs of the body, which could therefore be cured by appropriate methods. By thus founding a clinical treatment of mental illness, Pinel was subscribing to the doctrine of moral treatment which had already been put into effect by Louis Daquin, William Tuke and a number of others.[69] Since mental alienation was never total, the mind of a deranged man could be restored to rationality by perfecting that residue of reason which remained within him.

Moral treatment entailed subjecting the sick person to a severe discipline, consisting of threats and rewards. Instead of chaining him up like an animal, one had to tame him without resorting to violence, to subdue him and to make him closely dependent upon the doctor, who would thus manage to reason with him and to wean him of his delusional ideas. Sometimes the alienated person was intimidated by a cohort of nurses, and sometimes he had to be manipulated by theatrical techniques, which involved staging his delusions, and thereby eradicating them. Pinel also advocated the use of fear, persuasion, confidence, traumatic shock, a regular routine or rest. In short, the Pinelian asylum operated as a centre of re-education, at which submission to authority was the first step on the path to cure.

This overall conception, as regards both its theoretical aspect and its therapeutic model, resembled Pinel's representation of the Revolution. Just as the latter had proved to be both alienating and liberatory, since, by arousing energies, it had accentuated the passions, so too moral treatment alienated the subject from authority while liberating him from his feudal subjection to madness. As for the clinic itself, it too was informed by the

Pinelian image of the Revolution. Its object was the 'deranged man', that is, a subject who oscillates between a residue of liberty and a state of alienation.

Pinelian theory thus engendered a new social character, namely, the asylum doctor. Serving as a symbol of wisdom, of benevolent neutrality and of moral severity, this figure's lofty gaze held sway over the 'madnesses' of the world, be they revolutionary disorders or mental disturbances. The basic features of the asylum doctor are clearly delineated in the letter which Pinel wrote to his brother on the evening of 21 January 1793. As a member of the National Guard, he had just been present, bearing arms, at the execution of the king. Horrified by the scene which he had witnessed, Pinel expressed a profound distaste for all forms of political involvement. By the same token, he praised almost to the point of apotheosis his position as a doctor 'observer', who was capable of raising himself above the passions:

> As a doctor and a philosopher and as one accustomed to meditate upon ancient and modern forms of government and upon the nature of man, I foresee only anarchy, factions, and a war that will prove disastrous, even for the victors.... You may count yourself as fortunate indeed that you are in the country and that your soul has not been overwhelmed by bitterness at the spectacle of factions and dumb intrigues and by the blackest and most melancholy presentiments for the future.[70]

It was through increasingly assuming the role of such an observer that Pinel was to play a crucial part in the Revolution, even though, after the execution of the king, he was able to perceive only its harmful aspects.

If, after the fall of the monarchy, Pinel lived in fear of being arrested, it was with good reason. For he had in his care some well-to-do clients at the Maison Belhomme, where suspect aristocrats were held in large numbers. This is why he requested Jacques Thouret to have him appointed head-doctor at the asylum of Bicêtre. In September 1793, the Convention ruled in his favour, and he was able to take up his appointment there, his chief aim being to lie low. At the asylum, however, he met the warden Pussin, who, without having consulted anyone, was experimenting on his own initiative with a form of moral treatment by removing the chains from the insane in order to calm them down and to prevent them from screaming.

The Revolution had therefore impinged upon Pinel in every conceivable manner. At the theoretical level, it bore witness to a dialectic of alienation and liberty and, as far as moral treatment was concerned, it referred to the idea of the curability and perfectibility of the human mind. The event itself had affected Pinel through a decree of the Montagnard Convention, which had enabled him to meet Pussin, and which had given rise to the myth of the 'liberation of the mad'. But the Revolution also affected Pinel's actual relations with the alienated. At Bicêtre, he treated men who resembled himself, to the extent that they had also been actors in the revolutionary saga. Through observing them, he constructed his own theory, and renewed contact with his own phantasies. Much like a reporter, he recounted the many individual destinies of an anonymous crowd which had been swept up in the Revolution.

On one page of his *Treatise*, Pinel recounts how he tried to cure a melancholic whose delusion turned upon the question of regicide. The man in question was a tailor who had let slip a number of hostile remarks regarding the condemnation of the king. His fear of being named a suspect was such that he exaggerated his danger, lost all appetite and was unable to sleep until, finally, he became convinced that he would have to die upon the scaffold. His mind soon began to wander. At Bicêtre, Pinel set him to work repairing the garments of the other inmates, and paid him a wage. At the end of six months of assiduous work, he seemed to be cured. However, a short time later, he relapsed into a state of melancholy. When Pinel left the asylum, he did not forsake his patient, but asked Pussin to give the tailor's delusion a theatrical form. A spurious law-court was convoked, in which three doctors, dressed in black, played the parts of people's commissioners. After a long interrogation, they passed judgement upon the tailor in the name of the National Assembly, absolving 'the accused' of all suspicions and reintegrating him into a sentiment of pure patriotism. The tailor was purged of his melancholy and was able to resume his work. However, as soon as he learned of the deception, he was plunged a second time into a state of madness. Pinel thereupon pronounced him incurable.[71]

This narrative shows that it was from his own experience that Pinel had drawn a teaching which enabled him to invent the conditions for moral treatment. Although he sought to be a neutral observer, he was really in the same boat as his own patients, with whom he clearly identified. He too was afraid of being branded a suspect, and he too had criticized the condemnation of the king. On the basis of this example, one can imagine how such an *idéologue* would have tried to treat Théroigne de Méricourt if he had encountered her at the time of her first confinement, that is to say, before she had sunk into a chronic psychosis. He would very probably have used

the moral treatment to try and rid her of her 'exclusive delusion', represented by her fixation with the vocabulary of the Terror. In the guise of the
Aulic councillor, he could have embodied *the Law* and served as a support
for her phantasies. Where Saint-Just had remained dumb, he could have
answered her demand. But he would have been able to act thus in so far as his
own involvement in the Revolution would have made him a valid inter-
locutor, who was himself capable of understanding the meaning of such a
vocabulary, such a fixation and such a demand.

Although Esquirol was Pinel's heir, he did not treat Théroigne de
Méricourt as his master would have done. We shall shortly see why. In 1811,
at the age of thirty-seven, he succeeded Pussin as warden in the *division des
folles*. The following year, he was appointed *médecin ordinaire* alongside Pinel,
who was still at La Salpêtrière, but vested with purely honorific functions.
His observations of Théroigne took place between 1812 and 1817. She was
exactly ten years older than him. The alienist did not know who she really
was, and he made no real attempt to find out. He was confronted with a
creature of the asylums, a phantom of the past, enveloped in a sulphurous
legend, who incarnated all the horrors of a Revolution whose history was
reduced in his eyes to the 'excesses' of the Terror and of the Thermidorean
Reaction.

In the two volumes of his *Des maladies mentales*, written between 1816 and
1838, Esquirol seemed to preserve Pinel's inheritance while updating it. He
separated *congenital idiocy* from *acquired idiocy*, divided *dementia* into an acute,
but curable, form and a chronic, incurable form, described the symptoms of
general paralysis, abandoned the notion of *mania* without delusions and,
finally, created the large class of *monomanias*. *Mania* and *melancholia* were
included within this latter category, but, to break with a terminology judged
to be too literary, he called the latter *lypemania* or *folie de la tristesse*. In this
way he hoped to supply the famous condition of 'black bile' with a scientific
nomenclature — the term was to become obsolete. Esquirol drew up a
catalogue of causes in terms of climates, seasons, age, sex, typology and
temperament. He observed that melancholics have thin and slender bodies,
black hair, a pale complexion, a darkish, scaly skin and a dark red nose. He
then emphasized that those who lived in mountain areas were less prone to
the condition than were those from marshlands. Finally, he observed that
the majority of lypemaniacs succumb to pulmonary infections.[72]

Nevertheless, in order to mark his continuing attachment to the ancient
tradition, he observed that melancholics possessed powerful, profound and

wide-ranging intellects, and it was for this reason that Aristotle, he emphasized, had judged the great legislators to be, as a rule, melancholic. Esquirol
then mentioned in passing, almost with regret, the names of Mahommed,
Cato, Pascal and Rousseau, as if one had completely to forget so many
outworn literary ideas. Melancholy was to have a medical basis or to be
discounted entirely.

The modernization of Pinelian nosology was accompanied here by a
technical improvement in clinical description. As the organizer of the
nineteenth-century asylum, Esquirol understood madness in terms of architectural space. From this perspective, the relation of patient to doctor was
replaced by a function of wardenship, in which the institution played the
role of the caring person. Thus, the alienist simply observed the movements,
contortions and rituals of the alienated, without seeking to perceive in them
that residue of reason which would make moral treatment possible. Having
retreated to the fortress of his scientific discourse, he would then refer the
mad person to a classification which was so immense as to transcend him
altogether. Works by Bichat and Cuvier clearly had had a part to play in this
transformation of the Pinelian heritage. The asylum as Esquirol conceived of
it was meant to resemble a zoological garden, a veritable paradise of fixity, in
which species would parade, completely classified and without consciousness. Moreover, within this space, the living body already had the dead body
as its homologue. Pinel had seen that the opening up of corpses would not
increase one's understanding of madness, since the latter was almost wholly
due to moral causes. His *Treatise* contained no description of organs after
death. Esquirol, on the other hand, systematized the practice of autopsy. As
an advocate of an anatomo-pathology that was just then in full expansion,
he completed each observation of a living subject with a description of the
corpse, even though he was fully aware that the examination of the dead
added nothing to one's knowledge of madness. At best, he believed that he
had discovered that melancholics were more constipated than maniacs, and
that their intestines descended almost as far as the pubis.

Pinel's inheritance was transformed in yet another way by the spread of
iconography. There had been only one plate in the *Treatise*, on which were
reproduced faces and brain-pans. Pinel had had these drawn in order to
establish correspondences between anatomical flaws and cognitive functions. Nevertheless, the faces remained anonymous and did not refer to any
model in particular. Conversely, in Esquirol's clinical practice, iconography
was as important as autopsy. Georges-François Gabriel was responsible for

drawing the mad, who were invariably caught in passionate poses, and Ambroise Tardieu engraved the drawings that were to be published. Esquirol wrote:

> The study of the physiognomy of the alienated is not merely a matter for idle curiosity. This study helps us to identify the nature of the ideas and affections which underlie the sick person's delusions. With this purpose in mind, I have commissioned over two hundred drawings. One day I will perhaps publish my observations on this interesting subject.[73]

It was no accident that Gabriel had been chosen to perform this task. Born in 1775, this draughtsman was a veritable necrophiliac. Under the Terror, he had followed behind the condemned and had taken up his position at the foot of the scaffold in order to represent them at the moment that they were about to die. He drew them in full or three-quarter profile, adding sometimes a touch of grey and white to the gouache. His pencil thus conjures up Brissot, Carrier, Couthon and many others at the moment at which they were drawing their last breath. The gaze which Gabriel directed at them testifies to the most astonishing sadism. On the faces of these heroes, who were now being likened to sedition-mongers, he painted neither smiles, nor tears nor distress, as if he wished to reduce them to bits of organs taken from an anatomy plate. As far as he was concerned, the Revolution was wholly contained within the blade of the guillotine. Just as his political portraits resembled still lifes, so do the criminals and the alienated whose features he drew twenty years later seem to be the living replicas of persons caught by the killing machine.

In 1816, Gabriel was asked by Esquirol to draw Théroigne. He drew her right profile, with her eye staring fixedly ahead, her neck extended, her hair straggly and her face altogether dehumanized. A year before her death, fixed in her melancholic eternity, she seemed to be listening to the silences of a history that had no further connection with the world of the living.[74]

Esquirol's transformation of Pinel's thought thus involved a new representation of the Revolution. In the opening chapter of his treatise *Des maladies mentales*, which was written in 1816, Esquirol had emphasized that shifts in regime, that is, excesses of all kinds, featured among the major causes of alienation. Thus, nascent Christianity had engendered religious melancholias, whereas the spirit of chivalry, the outcome of the crusades, had led to a proliferation of erotic melancholias. By the same token, the

French Revolution had caused mental derangement:

> The ideas of liberty and reforms have turned many heads in France, and it is
> remarkable that the madnesses which have exploded in the last thirty years
> have taken their defining features from the storms which have troubled our
> fatherland.[75]

Whereas Pinel had conceived of the Revolution as a dialectic between
derangement and liberty, his pupil reduced it to a bad object. We are now in
a position to appreciate how far the disciple had travelled from his original
'loyalty' to his master's doctrine. Where the reference to the Revolution had
served as a lynchpin, it now led to the need for an elimination, a repression.
Pinel's theory was, like most of the work of the *idéologues*, essentially
'Girondin' in nature. It therefore presupposed a kind of cult of elites, a
horror of extremes, admiration for a federalist structure of knowledge and
power, notions of progress and perfectibility, etc. In the case of Esquirol,
however, the model of constitutional monarchy had become increasingly
dominant. The space of the asylum was thus conceived as a fictitious kingdom, but it was inspired by the institutional reality of the Empire, of the
Restoration, and then of the July Monarchy. This arrangement featured a
king, a people, a religion and a state apparatus. 'Each house of the mad',
wrote the doctor, 'has its gods, its priests, its faithful and its fanatics. It has its
emperors, its kings, its ministers, its courtesans, its rich men, its generals, its
soldiers and a people who obeys.'[76]

To liken the Revolution to a bad object was clearly to revise Pinel's
doctrine, if not to obliterate it. Jacques Postel and Gladys Swain have shown
quite convincingly how this was achieved through the myth of the liberation of the mad. Around 1805, Esquirol fabricated a legend about Pinel,
who appeared not so much as the founder of the clinical treatment of
mental illness as a heroic philanthropist who had for the first time broken
the chains which bound the insane. In 1816, the *Traité medico-philosophique*
was reduced to nothing more than a guide to moral treatment. Two years
later, in an article in the *Dictionnaire des sciences medicales*, Esquirol was still
comparing Pinel to a philanthropist, but his legendary deed was described in
such a way as to imply that it had been co-opted by agitators. 'The ideas
which were then current', he wrote, 'made this release of the mad chained
up at Bicêtre appear an event of the utmost importance. The success of this
erudite doctor, the friend of misfortune, became a trophy for agitators.'[77] In

other words, having first invented a myth in order to eliminate Pinel's actual doctrine, Esquirol then proceeded to denounce the use to which it had supposedly been put by the revolutionaries and by their heirs. Finally, in 1838, he reinforced his rejection by emphasizing that the act of deliverance had been 'denatured' by the 'ideas of the time', that is, by revolutionary extremism.[78] It was therefore necessary to condemn the Revolution in order to save the myth, which had itself been fabricated in order to destroy the clinical 'revolution' which Pinel had introduced.

In the meantime, the myth had assumed its canonical form, in an article written by Scipio Pinel, the son of the alienist, and published in 1836 in the *Traité complet du régime sanitaire des aliénés*. The abolition of the chains was now presented as an anti-revolutionary act, the Revolution itself being reduced to a huge system of Terror. The author tells the story of how, shortly after his appointment to his position at Bicêtre, Pinel received a visit from Couthon, who was searching for suspects among the mad. Everyone trembled at the sight of this curious figure, a paralytic who had abandoned his wheelchair and was carried by men. Pinel took Couthon to the section of the hospital where the cells were. The sight of the disturbed inmates terri-fied him, and, upon being greeted with a volley of insults, Couthon turned to the alienist and exclaimed: 'Citizen, you yourself must be mad to wish to set free such animals as these!' The doctor answered calmly that the insane were all the more difficult to treat for being deprived of air and of liberty. Couthon was therefore forced to agree to the chains being struck off, but he warned Pinel about his presumption. He was borne away in his carriage, and the great philanthropist, once rid of this horrifying vision, set about his work of liberation.[79]

The myth, thus sanctified, serves as much to obliterate Pinel's actual doctrine as to mask the fact that the doctor owed his appointment to a decree of the Montagnard Convention, that is, to those 'extremists' who were supposed to have been eliminated. But it also serves to counter one of the dreams of Montagnard thought, as voiced by Barère in Messidor Year II, namely, that the asylum presupposed its own end, inasmuch as every successful revolution should bring the unhappiness of men to an end and eradicate madness definitively. This was also how the heirs of Jacobinism — the 'agitators' mentioned by Esquirol — would view, if not Pinel's famous deed, at any rate the question of the relation between madness and the Revolution. From Lenin to Mao Zedong, and from libertarian thought to anti-psychiatry, the definition of the asylum encompasses the end of the asylum, and therefore its suppression; which is why the idea of abolition is part of the great utopias of the revolutionary movement.

In the mythical version formulated by Scipio Pinel in 1836, this crucial element of the discourse of the Revolution was eliminated. It was replaced, however, by another of its elements, namely, a national medicine, which was something which both the Constituent Assembly and the Convention had consistently called for. This was to be organized in much the same way as the clergy, and would be based upon the omnipotence of medical observation. It was as if the asylum was designed to serve, in opposition to the Jacobin Terror, as an end in itself, an immutable paradise of administered madness. The myth therefore preserved the idea of the omnipotence of medical observation, but at the price of dispensing with its other aim, which was now deemed too 'extremist', of bringing about the end of the asylum. This is why Couthon, a Montagnard, did not feature in the myth as a utopian wishing to abolish the asylum, but rather as a tyrant who was terrified by the mad and was altogether in favour of keeping them in chains. When compared with this embodiment of revolutionary 'deformity', Pinel seemed to be some Saint Michael liberating France from its Jacobin dragon. Moreover, the role of philanthropist ascribed to him was the very same one that the Constituent Assembly, and after it the Convention, had assigned to the medical profession by inventing the asylum.

It was not until the Freudian discovery of the unconscious and the achievements of dynamic psychiatry that the utopian notion of the end of the asylum was once again to be subsumed within the definition of the institution. But, if utopia then became reality, the price to be paid was that it was achieved under the aegis of medical discourse. Thus, the Montagnard dream of abolition was to be realized in community psychiatry, which was to dispense with the asylum in the name of the Pinelian myth, without ever comprehending that the myth had itself been fabricated in the first place in order to combat that same dream.

Furthermore, the rejection of revolutionary 'extremism', in the form that it took in the myth of 1836, was accompanied by a general abandonment of moral treatment. From the 1820s, in fact, the pressure of anatomopathology was such that madness was seen more in terms of organic disturbances than in relation to moral causes. Moral treatment and the revolutionary ideal were both dismissed out of hand, for both presupposed a notion of the progress of the human mind which could not be reconciled with the prevailing organicism, in which diagnosis primarily referred to incurability. The myth of Pinel was informed by the tropes of royalist historiography, and it therefore reflected the new ordering of medical knowledge which had been established under the Restoration. By reducing to a single heroic gesture a doctrine which had effected a 'revolution' in the clinical treatment of mental illnesses, the myth confined the subject within a strictly deterministic notion of insanity. Thus, in social terms, every attempt to change the established order was now regarded as a symptom of derangement, while, as far·as the asylum was concerned, all hope of moral curability seemed doomed to failure.

If we keep the above considerations in mind, we may more readily understand the meaning of the gaze which Esquirol directed at Théroigne de Méricourt's melancholia. It was as if the observation written in 1820 and published in 1838 served to illustrate the shift from Pinel's work to that of his pupil.

In the first part of his exposition, Esquirol recounted both the history of the Revolution and that of his patient, each being presented as a diversion: the Revolution had diverted the values of civilization, and Théroigne was an agitator who, when the opportunity arose, diverted the Revolution to her own advantage. Esquirol took the clichés of royalist historiography at face value, and therefore began by presenting Théroigne as a curious sort of creature, of possible interest to those who enjoyed strong sensations or who felt nostalgic about a bygone epoch. He then likened her to a fury of the people, buying off soldiers and prostituting herself to faction leaders. Forgetting that she had in fact been a Girondin, Esquirol merely noted her 'moderantisme', so as to enable him better to attack her as an unbridled Jacobin who wore the red cap. The episode of the flagellation would plainly have undermined this view of Théroigne, and Esquirol made no mention of it, either because of his ignorance of it, or because, though aware of it, he set little store by it. Finally, he emphasized that Théroigne had taken advantage of the September Massacres to cut off the head of a former lover. Esquirol thus believed that her madness had originally been caused by her situation as a courtesan, and that it had been exacerbated by her involvement in a revolutionary debauch, which had unhinged her mind. The Revolution did not feature here as the *initial cause* of her madness, but as the *crucial catalyst* for her entrance into this total, chronic and incurable insanity. The Revolution was therefore characterized as a bad object, a representation of a radical elsewhere — a great shipwreck of reason.

Esquirol's gaze allowed neither content nor history to Théroigne's specific melancholia. Being now a condition that was wholly medicalized, bearing the barbaric name of lypemania, it referred neither to the madness of Hercules, nor to the ennui of the pre-revolutionary period, nor to the possible 'déclassement' of this peasant woman from the Ardennes, nor even to the languor from which women suffered under the Restoration — a phenomenon which the alienist was able to observe daily. The meaning of melancholia was now merely zoographic. The condition had nothing to do with spleen, with blackness, with genius or with structural invariants of any kind, for now it was connected only with a climate, with the colour of an organ or with a statistical configuration.

The second part of the text contains a superb description of Théroigne's asylum psychosis, which shows how Esquirol had abandoned Pinel's clinical theories, which had been based upon moral treatment and upon the notion of a residue of reason, and replaced them with an exclusively visual identification of the signs of madness. These signs, now detached from their subject, had merged with the architecture of a garden of delights, derived from Hieronymus Bosch, corrected by Cuvier and then subordinated to the rules of medical iconography. The lypemaniac Théroigne who existed within this vast purgatory, from which the very notion of cure would seem to have disappeared, therefore calls to mind Gabriel's sketch. When one considers that this portrait is the only one which was definitely taken from life, vertigo strikes, for it portrays Théroigne as a model of Esquirolean nosology. This impression is further reinforced by Ambroise Tardieu's engraving, which fixes her features still more, and thus transforms her into an even purer representation of asylum morphology. This is indeed a curious palimpsest.

Consider, however, another portrait of Théroigne, which used the physionotrace method, and which was executed by Louis Chrétien. This was based on a drawing by Jean Fouquet, presumably also taken from life, and features the same nose, the same mouth, the same look, the same right profile, sometimes as a man, sometimes as a woman, which are evident in Gabriel's sketch. The difference is simply that, in Chrétien's portrait, Théroigne is thirty years younger and has curly hair. There is also a carved wooden medallion which shows Théroigne's left profile, and represents her with the same features that Fouquet had drawn. We cannot be certain that one of these profiles is 'truer' than the others. In one case, we have an 'ordinary' Théroigne, dressed according to eighteenth-century fashion; in the Salpêtrière drawing, on the other hand, history is abolished and is replaced by the stasis of insanity. These portraits are situated at either end of our heroine's life, as if to testify that, beneath the apparently continuous nature of a physiognomy, a rupture had occurred between two hetero- geneous moments of history: a time 'before' madness, when the young woman was still an anonymous figure of her period, and one 'after', when she was simply a still life of her ruined ideal.[80]

The third part of Esquirol's exposition concerns the opening up of the corpse, undertaken, in the presence of the master, by three pupils, namely, Descuret, Amussat and Rostan, a future resident professor of clinical medicine in the faculty of medicine. This post-mortem established that Théroigne's earlier venereal disease had not led to syphilitic complications and, ultimately, to general paralysis. In short, it was not the pox which had driven her mad, and no organic trace could account for her dementia, whose origin had therefore to be sought for in the confrontation between a personal destiny and the history of an epoch. By the same token, the pneumonia which had caused her death did not derive from an earlier tuberculosis which might be diagnosed on the basis of her spitting of blood at Kufstein. Modern nosology would tend to regard Théroigne's melan- cholia as schizophrenia or as manic–depressive psychosis.[81]

Here is Esquirol's description in full:

Téroenne, or Théroigne de Méricourt, was a famous courtesan, born in the country of Luxembourg. She was of medium height, with chestnut hair, large blue eyes, mobile features, a lively, relaxed and even elegant manner.

Some said that this girl came from a good family, while others claimed that she rose from the ranks of the courtesans. Be this as it may, she played a thoroughly deplorable role during the early years of the Revolution. She was twenty-eight to thirty years old.

She gave herself to various leaders of the party, for whom she did useful service during most of the riots, and she played a particularly important part, on 5 and 6 October 1789, in corrupting the Flanders regiment, by intro- ducing streetwalkers into the ranks, and by distributing money to the soldiers.

In 1790, she was sent to the country of Liège, to foment rebellion among the people. She held military rank there. She stood out amidst the unbridled populace which was sent to Versailles on 5 and 6 October 1790. The Austrians arrested her in January 1791. She was taken to Vienna, and shut up in a fortress; the Emperor Leopold expressed a wish to see her, conversed with her, and set her free in December of that same year; she returned to

Paris, and again showed her face on the revolutionary stage. She was prominent on the Tuileries terraces, on the rostrums, boldly haranguing the
people, and seeking to return them to *modérantisme* and to the Constitution.
This role was not likely to suit her for long. Soon the Jacobins got hold of
Téroenne, and she was to be seen with a red cap on her head, a sabre at her
side, a pike in her hand, commanding an army of women. She played a key
part in the events of September 1792. Although there is no proof that she
actually participated in the massacres, nevertheless it is said that she went to
the courtyard of the abbey, and that there she used her sabre to cut off the
head of a poor wretch who was just then being taken to the court in that
prison. We are assured that this man was one of her former lovers.

When the Directory was constituted, the popular societies were closed
down, and Téroenne lost her reason. She was taken to a house in the
faubourg Saint-Marceau. One of her letters was found in Saint-Just's correspondence, dated 26 July 1794, which already betrays some signs that she was
losing her wits.

In November 1800, she was sent to La Salpêtrière; the following month,
she was transferred to the Petites-Maisons, where she was to be for the next
seven years. When the asylum administration had all the insane evacuated
from the Petites-Maisons, Téroenne returned to La Salpêtrière, on 7
September 1807. She was about forty-seven years old.

Upon her arrival, she was very agitated, cursed and threatened everyone,
spoke of nothing but liberty, committees of public safety, revolutionary
committees, etc., accusing all those who came near her of being moderates,
royalists, etc.

In 1808, an important person, who had been a party leader during the
Revolution, visited La Salpêtrière. Téroenne recognized him, raised herself
up from the straw upon her bed, upon which she was lying, and heaped
insults upon the visitor, accusing him of having abandoned the popular
party, of being a moderate, and said that *a decree from the committee of public
safety would soon see justice done.*

In 1810, she became calmer, and lapsed into a state of dementia, which
revealed the traces of her first dominant ideas.

Téroenne was reluctant to wear any clothes at all, even a shirt. Every day,
morning and evening, and in fact several times a day, she would drench her
bed, or rather the straw on her bed, with several pails of water, and she
would then lie down and cover herself with her sheet, if it were summer, or
with her sheet and her coverlet, if it were winter. She took pleasure in
walking barefoot in her cell, which was paved with stone and flooded with
water.

The severe cold had no impact upon this regime. She could never be persuaded to wear a nightshirt, nor to add a second coverlet. In the last three years of her life, she was given a very large dressing-gown, but she hardly ever used it. When everything had iced over, and it was impossible to have much water, she would break the ice and scoop up the water and sprinkle it over her body, especially her feet.

Although in a small, dark, very damp, unfurnished cell, she seemed very comfortable; she acted as if she were involved in very important matters; she smiled at the persons around her; sometimes she answered brusquely: 'I do not know you', and wrapped herself up in her coverlet. It was rare for her to answer a question in an appropriate manner. She often said: 'I don't know' or 'I've forgotten'. If one insisted, she grew impatient and spoke to herself in a low voice, using disjointed sentences composed of words such as 'fortune', 'liberty', 'committee', 'revolution', 'wretches', 'decree', 'ruling', etc. She had a real grievance against the moderates.

She grew irked and flew into a temper if she was crossed, especially when people tried to stop her using water. Once she bit one of her companions with such fury that she removed a piece of flesh. This woman's essential character had therefore survived, even when her intelligence had gone.

She almost never left her cell, and usually stayed lying down. When she did go out, she would be naked, or wearing a chemise. She would take only a few steps, and generally she would walk on all fours, stretching her body out on the ground; with staring eyes, she would pick up any morsels which she found on the floor and eat them. I myself have seen her pick up and devour straw, feathers, dried leaves, and pieces of meat which had been dropped in the mud, etc. She drank water from the gutters, while the courtyards were being cleaned, although this water was polluted and full of excrement, preferring this drink to any other.

I wished her to write something. She outlined a few words, but she never managed to form a whole sentence. She never gave any signs of hysteria. All feelings of shame seemed to have been extinguished in her, and she was habitually naked, though in full view of men, without blushing.

Since drawings had been made of her in 1816, she was quite accustomed to this sort of activity; she seemed to attach no importance at all to what the draughtsman was doing.

In spite of this regime, which Téroenne had maintained for ten whole years, she menstruated regularly; she ate a great deal, she was not ill and she had not contracted any infirmity.

A few days before her admission to the infirmary, a rash broke out all over her body; Téroenne washed herself as usual with cold water and lay down on her waterlogged bed, and the spots disappeared; from then on she kept to her bed, eating nothing, and drinking only water.

On 1 May 1817, Téroenne was admitted to the infirmary in an extremely weak condition, refusing all food, drinking water, remaining supine, speaking often to herself, but in a very low voice. 15 [May], thinness, an extremely pallid face, fixed, lustreless eyes, a few convulsive movements in the face, a very weak pulse, a slight swelling of the hands, oedema in the feet; finally, on 9 June, she expired, at the age of fifty-seven, without having recovered the use of her reason, even for a moment.

The autopsy was held at ten in the morning.

Dura mater adhering to the skull, skull broad at the posterior, very low median line.

Very soft, discoloured brain, the membrane lining the ventricles had thickened, the underlying cerebral substance, a line thick, was of a vitreous appearance and greyish white.

The Plexus choroids discoloured, displaying small serous cysts.

Carotids adjacent to the spongy sinuses having acquired the diameter of a very large feather.

Pituitary gland containing a brownish fluid. Serosity in the two pleurae, also in the pericardium.

Heart flaccid.

Stomach distended with a greenish fluid.

Perpendicular transverse colon precipitated behind the pubis.

Small, greenish liver; its tissue very soft; its own envelope being detached with the greatest of ease. Gall-bladder distended with thick, clotted, black bile. Soft spleen, greenish like the liver.

Bladder highly contracted, its walls very thick.

Envelope of the ovaries thick, and even cartilaginous at various points.

In the [original] observation of Téroenne, as in the succeeding ones, the transverse colon had changed direction and had descended behind the pubis.[82]

In the aftermath of 8 June 1817, it was not only medical experts who took an interest in Théroigne's corpse. It also became an object of study for doctor Pierre Dumoutier, a disciple of Gall and the founder in Paris of a Phrenological Museum which was just then remarkably fashionable. This 'science of localizations' aimed to prove that there were connections between character, intelligence and the form of the skull. Thus, the moment he had learned of the death of the famous heroine of the Revolution, Dumoutier went to La Salpêtrière to take a cast of her skull and of her face. He then gave an erudite phrenological description:

Théroigne de Méricourt's head is remarkable for the degree of development of the lateral parts, where the instincts are located; and the most developed organs of this region are those of courage, of destruction and of cunning. If we compare the upper region, where the moral sentiments are located, with the base, which is the site of the instincts, we shall see that the upper area is flattened from top to bottom and narrow in its middle region, from which we may conclude that the former had not had sufficient power to resist the activity of the latter. She was endowed with affection and the organ corresponding to this faculty is sufficiently developed to suggest a high degree of activity there. The [organ of] philogeniture is also large and could lead one to suppose that she loved children, but we lack any information on this topic. She was loyal and impressionable, and there is a fairly good development of the organs of kindness and idealism. Everything in this organization must have been felt with vigour and enthusiasm. The intellectual faculties, although displaying a fine development, have served only to perform acts determined by the instincts.[83]

While this outmoded gloss holds little interest for a modern reader, the cast itself, which may still be viewed today, is astonishing. Like Gabriel's drawing, it too is a 'portrait' of Théroigne, and one obviously also taken from life. Mummified for all eternity, this creature of the museums resembles a fetish object of the kind to be found among so-called primitive cultures. Nevertheless, it is possible to discern in this cast the outline of a face which reminds us of those depicted by Louis Chrétien and Georges Gabriel. As for the cachexy of the skeleton, it serves merely to remind us, if there were any need for it, of how death had occurred through a slow extinction of the organs, arising from the depths of melancholia.

Two years before the publication of the treatise *Des maladies mentales*, there appeared a two-volume work entitled *La Jolie Liégoise, correspondance par le vicomte de V... Y...*.[84] This pseudonym was that of the Baron Lamothe-Langon, former Auditor General of the Council of State. The first part of this work contains an imaginary biography of Théroigne, which is an epitome of all the clichés of royalist historiography. The author's heroine is born at Liège in 1759, is called Lambertine and described as a courtesan in contact with shadowy powers and subject to nauseating hallucinations. The second volume contains thirty-one apocryphal letters, supposedly written by her at La Salpêtrière and addressed to Rose (*sic*) Lacombe. Théroigne recounts her liaison with a colonel in the Austrian army, her early involvement in the Revolution, motivated by hatred of the aristocracy, her journey to England and her amorous relations with the Prince of Wales. Composed in purple prose, the narrative combines a pseudo-erotic style with the most grotesque imaginable counter-revolutionary argument. When republished in 1837, this work met with considerable success, and helped to popularize the myth of 'Lambertine, courtesan and bloodthirsty amazon'.

However, the real interest of the book lies in the fact that, in some passages at least, it was inspired by the Esquirolean theory of monomania and by the concept of the asylum which was reflected in it. When this work appeared, a major debate was in progress regarding the isolation of the insane, and this would lead to the famous law of 1838. As the juridical culmination of the principles of alienism, this law gave a concrete form to the separation of asylum and prison, defined the rules for confinement and shielded the insane from criminal justice, in conformity with article 64 of the Penal Code, which had been in force since 1810: 'There is neither crime nor delict when the accused was in a state of dementia at the time of the deed.'

This rescue of the criminally insane from penal justice involved a definition of responsibility based upon reason. If the deed was committed in a state of dementia, it was not rational, and the responsibility of the criminal was not involved, since the latter presupposes reason. Now, the discussion concerning the notion of monomania, introduced by Esquirol to designate a form of mania in which the madness was fixed upon a single theme, provoked a lively polemic in 1835. The supporters of the 'school of La Salpêtrière', being in favour of a complete medicalization of madness, considered the lunatic as a sick person who needed protection, care and isolation, whether he or she were criminal or not. The advocates of the punitive tradition, on the other hand, being committed to the omnipotence of the penal apparatus, denied the notion of irresponsibility, their aim being to prove that it led to increasing numbers of accused persons simulating insanity. In order to escape the death penalty, a criminal could always 'pretend to be mad' and thus avoid being condemned.

Esquirol and his pupils had thus fought hard to establish the asylum on a sound footing, and to shield madness from repression. This struggle was a direct continuation of Pinel's intellectual inheritance and, in this respect, although Esquirol's approach to the clinic was an internal revision of the master's work, it was a continuation of it as far as the 'progressive' representation of madness and a therapeutic organization of confinement were concerned. Hence the paradox that the myth of the abolition of chains, which had been fabricated in a negative spirit in order to obliterate a doctrine and to exorcize a revolution, could be transformed into its opposite and serve as a torch in a 'revolutionary' combat in favour of the caring institution. Seen from this perspective, the great Esquirolean slogan of the 1830s — caring, not punishing — was inspired by the Declaration of Rights of Man and therefore by a positive image of the Revolution. Michel Foucault has shown very clearly the revolutionary value introduced into the history of the foundation of the asylum by the myth of abolition.[85]

In the second volume of his work, Lamothe-Langon has Théroigne talk in the first person. In a letter, she draws a portrait of Marat which was directly inspired by the debates of the period concerning monomania. The 'Friend of the People' is depicted as a raging madman, combining in his person the typical characteristics and symptoms of Esquirolean monomania:

> Marat, the friend of the people, was mad. This was his sole shortcoming. If he had been in his right mind, he would have rendered his country immense services. The French nation was his idol; any act that harmed his fatherland should be met in his view by a sacrifice, even by capital punishment if need be. 'The end justifies the means', he used to say; and since he wished to see his fatherland at liberty he lost count of the number of heads which had to fall for this great emancipation to be realized; he would have had no hesitation in adding his own if his head would have served to complete the construction of the building. He has been rebuked for his patently hallucinatory actions, and he is held responsible for the weakness of his brain. Can one fairly reproach a man in full enjoyment of his reason for the violence he did when in a drunken state? Clearly, one cannot; but why does he drink? To that, there are those who could answer: but why am I being forced to drink? This was Marat's own situation exactly. Nature had made him a maniac, he suffered from delusions, certainly, in spite of himself and, in his delusion, he printed and uttered some horrific things, I'll grant you; but once he was restored to the tribunal of his wisdom, he was a warm friend, an incorruptible patriot, etc.[86]

In this text, as can be seen, Lamothe-Langon was not content merely to draw without acknowledgement upon Esquirolean nosology. He also has Théroigne deliver an encomium of Marat, in which, echoing the principles of article 64, she declares him to be not responsible for deeds which he had committed in a state of dementia (drunkenness). However, in order to make it perfectly clear that he did not subscribe to the arguments of the heroine whose letters he was claiming to publish, Lamothe-Langon added the following comment at the foot of the page: 'Théroigne and the mad of today are the sole persons in a position to praise him [Marat], for he was their father.'[87]

This argument was cunning indeed, for not only did it criminalize the Revolution, by representing one of its leaders as an 'irresponsible mono-maniac', but in addition it ridiculed the struggle in which Esquirol and his pupils were engaged, by implying that this fight justified the mad in claiming kinship with a criminal whom one could pass off as a madman. In other words, the underlying message of the work could be summarized as follows. Confined in La Salpêtrière, a heroine of the Revolution was cared for by Esquirol, the leader of a liberatory movement on behalf of the criminally insane. From the depths of her madness, she writes a number of letters to another woman of the Revolution, who is not mad, but *enragée* or 'Jacobin', that is, in her own image. In her letters, she adopts the Esquirolean terminology and delivers an encomium of a famous member of the Convention, whose crime she acknowledges (he cuts off people's heads) but who, she insists, is not responsible for his actions. In order to differentiate the authorial voice from that of his characters, the 'commentator' then emphasizes that only the mad of today, that is, those in favour of the Esquirolean asylum, would be capable of praising Marat, their idol. It can be deduced, on the other hand, that men endowed with reason, such as Lamothe-Langon, reject the new clinical vocabulary, which enables the mad to claim kinship with a criminal revolution by passing off Marat as a madman.

We are now in a position to appreciate the link between Esquirol's obser-vation of Théroigne and Lamothe-Langon's *feuilleton*. In either case, the Revolution was presented as being all the more harmful for being Jacobin or *enragé*. Théroigne's entrance into madness is therefore seen in terms of her adherence to Jacobinism: either she wears a red cap, or she writes to an *enragé*. But the distance between the two arguments is equally clear. In Esquirol's observation, the Revolution is seen as a form of social disorder, whereas in Lamothe-Langon's *feuilleton*, it is compared to a criminal syndicate. This thoroughly mediocre writer uses, throughout his book, the vocabulary of mental pathology, thus effecting a synthesis between the old clichés of royalist discourse and the formulations of modern science.

In 1841, Théroigne's madness was once again the object of a commentary by J.B. Descuret, in a book entitled *La Médecine des passions*.[88] The medical expert, who had performed the post-mortem on the heroine's body, composed a sequel to Esquirol's observation, in which the category 'political fanaticism' was applied to the Revolution. After derangement and criminalization, this therefore resembled the third volet in a triptych through which alienism had triumphed over the judicial apparatus. By this date, the asylum had become the legal domain for the administration of madness. And, in this context, the Revolution could be decriminalized, just as madness had been. This was both because, being less and less trammelled by royalist discourse, it had become the object of a serious and objective historiography, and because medical science was now able to annex it in an equally positive way, no longer as a bad object, but through a distinction between norm and deviance, reason and excess. Hence the label 'political fanaticism' applied by the doctor to Théroigne's case. The use of such a term made it possible to differentiate between good 'politics' and revolutionary illusion, and to plead indulgence, on the part of the tribunal of the nation, for the lost sheep who had now been committed to the asylum.

The word 'revolution' thus occupied a curiously ambivalent place in clinical discourse, just as the word 'madness' had odd connotations within the vocabulary of the Revolution. From the Constituent Assembly to the Convention, from Enlightenment philosophy to the Montagnard utopia, two different conceptions of liberty dominated the dreams of the nation's representatives. One entailed using the asylum to humanize madness, while the other rested upon the dream of abolishing the asylum in order to restore the mad to reason. These two conceptions involved an alternation between hierarchy and egalitarian certainty, between the power of science and a belief in happiness, and between rationality and illusion. It was the first conception, however, which was to triumph, while the second was pushed ever further towards the shores of deviance. Théroigne de Méricourt was to pay the price for this triumph and, until Michelet rehabilitated her, she remained the phantasmal embodiment of a Jacobinism reduced to its purest expression and which, after having dreamed of abolishing the asylum and overcoming madness, would not have been able to sustain the illusions of one of the most melancholic heroines of the Revolution. If Théroigne had been able to 'keep pace with the times', she would have become a character in Balzac's *Comédie humaine*, either a courtesan besotted with some Rubempré, or a Countess d'Aiglemont, prey to all the mirages of ennui.

IV

The Historiography of Théroigne

1844 TO 1988

BETWEEN LEGEND AND HISTORY

If we consider the first great wave of historians who, running from Thiers to Quinet by way of Tocqueville, undertook to study the French Revolution seriously, only four of their number paused at the name of Théroigne de Méricourt. Each of these writers had particular reasons for doing so, as we shall see below. In Lamartine's history, Théroigne was a flamboyant female adventurer, in accord with the legend. Louis Blanc, on the other hand, displayed a scrupulous concern for accuracy, and gave a proper account of her story, when and where his narrative called for it. Finally, in Edgar Quinet's work, her case was merely anecdotal. By contrast with these other historians, Michelet devoted a detailed study to her, which was in effect a 'rehabilitation'. He was in fact the only historian of his generation to ascribe a specific place to women at the very heart of the Revolution. He was not content simply to integrate them, whether as individuals or as parts of a collective movement, in his *Histoire de la Révolution française*, but also chose to write an original work on the theme, entitled *Les Femmes de la Révolution*, in which he sought to give a theoretical account of their historical role. He was therefore the first historian to open up a new area to historical research, by taking as his object Woman in all her aspects, as witch, wife, mother, initiator, blood, instinct, the crowd, etc.[1]

However, it is not until the turn of the century, when we come to the third generation of historians of the Revolution — the one after Taine — and to the works of Alphonse Aulard in particular, that, in place of woman as object, the history of feminism is studied in relation to the individual or collective involvement of women in the revolutionary process. It was during this period that a number of biographies or occasional works were written describing the role of such women in what from then on would be called, in a retrospective spirit, original feminism.[2]

Three perspectives were to be explored in relation to Théroigne de Méricourt. The first took its inspiration, either in a negative or in a positive fashion, from royalist or republican historiography, and therefore simply reinforced the legend. This perspective continued to thrive in both France and Belgium until around 1885, and it involved a wholly mythical account of the heroine. As Minerva, Penthesilea, Mimalone, Virgin, Pythia, priestess of the Gauls, riff-raff, regicide, or necklace-stealer, Théroigne exerted an enduring fascination upon poets, journalists and literary types of every sort, from Auguste Barthélemy to Emmanuel des Essarts. She would be represented as dishevelled, dressed as an amazon, straddling cannons or brandishing a sabre. From this tradition, I shall concentrate upon a superb sonnet by Baudelaire, which reverses all the clichés of the legend, a curious portrait by the Goncourt brothers, which seems to cast the heroine back into the eighteenth century and, finally, a few lines by Taine, which treat her as emblematic of a pathological essence of the crowd.[3]

The second perspective represented an extension of Esquirol's observation. It flourished towards the end of the nineteenth century, at a time when the theory of degenerationism was making inroads into psychiatric discourse. This theory made it possible to apply to the Revolution, and to its leading figures, a nosology based upon taints, anomalies, deviances and perversions. Théroigne was therefore seen as a superior sort of degenerate, placed midway between crime and genius.

Finally, the third approach is represented by an immense and heterogeneous body of work, ranging from biographical studies, a novelistic version of the Kufstein confessions, a novel and various plays. This corpus began to grow around 1886 with the publication of a first biography by Marcellin Pellet. Up until the Second World War, a new image of Théroigne was gradually consolidated, one which rested upon the history of feminism, upon some Belgian documents, and, above all, upon the Viennese archives, the contents of which began to be known from 1892 onwards with the publication of various works by Ferdinand Strobl von Ravelsberg. These texts all served to promote a myth which was the polar opposite of the one fostered by earlier historiography.[4] Having been transformed into a salon suffragette, the heroine then became the interpreter of the divided consciousness of women of the Belle Époque. Sometimes emancipated, as when she triumphed over the tyranny of men, sometimes the victim of her own actions, as when she tried to break the chains of her anatomical destiny, she summoned up, from the depths of her own melodrama, the spectacle of a fallen monarchy and of a victorious Revolution, now reunited under the crozier of the great national reconciliation. To each their own martyrs, their own excesses, their own dreams, since the motherland, having become republican, knew how to accommodate things: neither Henri V, nor the Commune, but a gloriously happy medium, the symbol of all hopes.

In the aftermath of the Revolution of 1848, Michelet conceived the idea of the *Légende d'or*, which would appear in both *feuilleton* and book form, and which would acquaint the people with the heroes of the republican faith.[5] At this date, his *Histoire de la Révolution française*, the publication of which had begun the previous year, was nowhere near completion. In March 1849, he married Athénaïs Mialaret, who was thirty years his junior and was frigid. She served as his muse and his inspiration. After his death, she was to abuse her position as his widow, even going so far as to forge unpublished texts in order to create doubtful posthumous works. The historian's published diary provides many details of this devouring relationship. Love was a source of regeneration, and, for Michelet, uniting oneself with a woman was a sacred and a religious act:

> Once I had penetrated her chaste and holy person, when I had brought my storm there and drawn upon her serenity, I emerged in a highly inventive frame of mind, with complete possession of my lucidity.[6]

Like a voyeur, he contemplated the body of the venerated lover, on the look-out for blood and body fluids, even recounting, with a wealth of detail, the digestive functions. He observed 'the crisis of love which makes woman what she is, this divine rhythm which, month by month, measures out time for her.'

Such was the source of Michelet's last lectures at the Collège de France. For his theme he chose love, the education of the people and that of women. As an heir to the Jacobin tradition, he was quite willing to admit that, if women were enfranchised, they would surrender their votes to the priests and thus deprive the Republic of them. He therefore rejected the notion of political equality, replacing it with the romantic notion of woman as inspiration. However, although he espoused this ideal, he did not accept the notion that women were intellectually or physiologically inferior. Instead, he adopted the thesis of complementarity, and saw the relation between the sexes as a matter of fusion. Her spiritual and anatomical destiny meant that woman was dedicated to love, instinct, fecundity and the heart. She was to serve as the new religion of man and, just as the Revolution had replaced Christianity, which had been corrupted by priests and by the Church, so too was woman the Messiah of modern times. Michelet was not so far removed in this respect from the French Saint-Simonians, and from Fourier.

Roland Barthes has shown how this 'feminary', apparently based upon the difference between the two sexes, belongs more to an erotics of voyeurism and of bisexuality than to a cult of orgasm and of otherness. If Michelet preferred 'the crisis of love' to beauty, and looking to possessing, it was because nothing was more sublime to him than a woman who was humiliated and apprehended at the very moment when she was undergoing her convulsions and her weaknesses. And so, in order to spy upon her, he became woman, wife and sister, thereby penetrating the intimate world which was usually the exclusive preserve of housemaids.[7]

The coup d'état of 2 December set Michelet on the road to exile. In April 1852, he was deprived of his post at the Collège de France for having refused to swear an oath of loyalty to Badinguet. He also forfeited his position as head of department at the Archives Nationales, and went to live near Nantes. In August 1853, he bid farewell to his great work, the *Histoire de la Révolution française*, but, through his history of the women of the Revolution, the *Légende d'or* was still taking shape. The work consisted of excerpting those passages which had been devoted to women in his great work and refashioning them to make a fresh book, in which their role would be theorized. In October 1853, in a state of exhaustion, Michelet fell ill. He left with Arthénaïs for Italy in order to restore his health, taking with him the documents which would be required for the further development of his book. The couple found a place to stay at Nervi, a small Mediterranean port, but their baggage was still held up at the station. Deprived of his archives and still sick, Michelet drank nothing but milk. In December, he slowly began to recover. At the beginning of January, the boxes of documents finally arrived. On 6 January, the historian set to work and, on 8 January, he wrote his portrait of Théroigne. On 25 January, he completed the text and entrusted it to Athénaïs, who travelled to Genoa, placing it in the hands of a trustworthy traveller who took it to Paris. Michelet subsequently added various corrections to the manuscript. In the space of nineteen days, he had given birth to the *Femmes de la Révolution*, beside the sea, with his lover close by, and after having swallowed mugfuls of milk. The feminine fluid had led to his regeneration.

At a time when the Revolution of 1848 had relaunched the women's clubs and the fight for equal rights, which was shortly to give birth to radical feminism, Michelet invoked the shades of the past in order to remind the women of his own time of their duties and their destiny. He rebuked them for having accepted the tyranny of the Empire and of the Restoration, a 'long reaction which had lasted for half a century'. In order to educate them, he paraded before their eyes the glories of a revolutionary heroism of a feminine 'nature'.

The book began with a stirring encomium to the women of the 1770s, who had given birth to men of genius. Here, the names of Bonaparte, Saint-Simon, Cuvier, Fourier and Bichat tumbled out, almost at random. Michelet then proceeded to evoke the mothers of the previous period, who had been just as heroic, and who had given to the world the armies of Year II, the Girondins and the Montagnards. All glory to them, for they had given birth to the genius of the Revolution.

The position which Michelet ascribed to the women of the revolutionary period, however, was somewhat contradictory. Up until 1791, they were collectively heroines, imbued with a great 'pity for the world'. Then, once the subsistence crises had struck, and events had taken their course, they became more violent than the men. Finally, after Thermidor, they launched themselves into reaction. According to this argument, women were seen in terms of a dualism of regeneration and destruction. In addition, Michelet maintained that each party had perished through its women. The downfall of La Fayette had been caused by his worshippers, as had been that of Robespierre; Madame Roland had been the ruin of the Girondins; Danton had been damaged by his two wives, as had Louis XVI by Marie-Antoinette, and the rebels of the Vendée by their womenfolk. Nevertheless, women might also be muses, as the case of Sophie de Condorcet, the metaphysician with the noble countenance, proved, or they might be figures with whom people could identify, such as Madame Roland, a virtuous symbol of revolutionary heroism, and Charlotte Corday, the inspiration for a 'religion of the dagger'.

Michelet was especially concerned with women in crowds, with women in salons, with women in couples, with women in relation to priests, as well as with various heroic deeds, whether famous or anonymous. On the other hand, he seemed to be ill at ease with 'anomaly', marginality, excess or with certain extreme situations. Whenever he mentioned Olympe de Gouges, an altogether extravagant figure, he would describe her in some humiliating circumstance, and he barely referred to Claire Lacombe, who had been an *énragée*. Finally, he was not at all inspired by the women who had worshipped Marat. Michelet's 'feminary' thus consisted of woman-as-people, woman-as-wife, woman-as-muse, woman-in-crisis, and woman-as-enlightened, to the detriment of those women he saw as bizarre, deluded, extreme, deviant or hysterical. It was as if Michelet, through what was in a way a kind of bestiary, had taken a snapshot of the feminine condition during a crucial period of transition. This was the moment at which women, who had been transfigured by the Revolution, wavered between the art of the salon, which would lead them to their ruin around the time of the Restoration, and the love of the people, which was a redeeming force and which could draw them towards the bourgeois ideal of fecundity.

But this feminary did not serve simply to express an oscillation of this kind. Michelet invariably represents the women of the Revolution as being *acted upon by something other than themselves*. They are either in the shadow of men or of parties, or caught up by their love of the people and their pity for the world. In other words, the only means available to them of expressing their otherness was to remain masked. And, since Michelet thought of this otherness in terms of nature and physiology, without basing it, first of all, as Condorcet had done, on an acknowledgement of political equality, he ultimately reversed the myth of woman's inferiority and glorified her, thereby making the feminine sex an object that was all the more dominating and tyrannical for being referred to an alienation, that is to say, to an illusion of complementarity.

It is therefore clear just why Théroigne de Méricourt should have proved so fascinating a figure to Michelet. At first glance, this crisis-ridden woman, a mystical lover of liberty, would seem to be the perfect specimen for Michelet's feminary. But the historian was too well acquainted with the women of the Revolution to be able to overlook the fact that she was in fact a 'borderline case' which could not be contained within his theory. She was not the muse of any salon, the wife of any man, the servant of any priest or the demon of any party. She was not even a woman such as Charlotte Corday, whose loneliness had spurred her into action. In order to grasp the true nature of Théroigne's history, one had therefore to invoke her status as a 'foreigner'. The country of Liège would have one day to account for the enigma of this 'foreignness'. Michelet therefore evoked 'race', roots and the

geography of childhood. He admitted that he did not understand everything, but he rehabilitated Théroigne in the name of her revolutionary faith
and forgave her her 'crime' against Suleau. However, since he seemed to
want to reserve for men the power of humiliating women, in order the
better to watch their humiliation and to compound it by becoming himself
the defender of an always wounded sex, he 'forgot' that Théroigne had in
fact been whipped by women, and attributed this deed to men. Michelet's
text reads as follows:

> There is a very fine, engraved portrait of the beautiful, courageous but ill-
> fated woman from Liège, who, on 3 October, had the great presence of mind
> to win over the Flanders regiment, to shatter the support of the monarchy
> and who, on 10 August, among the first combatants, entered the château
> sword in hand, and was awarded a [civic] crown by the conquerors. Unfortu-
> nately this portrait, which was drawn at La Salpêtrière, when she had gone
> mad, gives only a very faint notion of the heroic beauty which ravished the
> hearts of our fathers and caused them to see in a woman the actual image of
> liberty.
>
> Her round and strongly-shaped head (characteristic of the Liégois), with
> its dark eyes, somewhat large and somewhat hard, has not lost its flame.
> There is still passion there, and a trace of the violent love for which this girl
> lived and died. Strange though it may seem in the context of such a life, her
> love was not for a man, but for an idea, for Liberty and for the Revolution.
>
> The poor girl's eyes are, however, not haggard; they are full of bitterness,
> of pain and of reproach towards a world that had treated her with such
> terrible ingratitude! … At any rate, time too, no less than misfortune, has
> taken its toll. The swollen features have coarsened. Save for the black hair
> bound in a neckerchief, everything has an air of abandon; her bare breast, the
> last vestige of her beauty, a breast preserving something of pure, firm and
> virginal forms, seems to testify that the unfortunate woman, having been
> squandered on the passions of others, had herself taken very little from life.
>
> If we are to understand who this woman was, we need to know some-
> thing of her country, of Walloon country, from Tournai as far as Liège, and
> we need above all to know Liège, an ardent little France on the Meuse, a
> wedge running deep into the German populations of the Low Countries. I
> have recounted its valiant history during the fifteenth century when, shat-
> tered countless times but still undefeated, this heroic population of a town
> fought a whole empire, when one night three hundred Liégois raided a camp
> of forty thousand men in order to kill Charles the Bold (*Histoire de France*, vol.
> 6). I have told how, in the wars of '93, a Walloon labourer, an iron-beater

from Tournai, the tinker Meuris, with a devotion to match that of the three hundred, saved the town of Nantes, and how the Vendée was broken into pieces in order to save France (*Histoire de la Révolution*).

In order to know Théroigne better, we would also need to know something of the fate of the town of Liège, which was a martyr to liberty at the very beginning of the Revolution. A serf to the worst of tyrannies, a serf to priests, it freed itself for the space of two years, only to fall to its bishop once more, who was restored by Austria. Having taken refuge in great numbers among us, the Liégois shone in our armies through their ardent courage, and they were no less distinguished in our clubs for their choleric eloquence. They were our brothers or our children. The most affecting festival of the Revolution was perhaps the one in which the Commune, solemnly adopting them, paraded the Liège archives through Paris, before receiving them in its bosom in the Hôtel de Ville.

Théroigne was the daughter of a well-to-do farmer, who had given her some sort of education, and she had a lively mind and a high degree of natural eloquence, for this northern race has much of the south in it. Seduced by a German gentleman, then abandoned by him, much admired in England and surrounded by lovers, she spurned them all, choosing instead an Italian singer, a castrato, who was ugly and old, and who fleeced her, and sold her diamonds. She was known at that time as the comtesse de Campinados, in memory of her own country (la Campine). In France, too, she always became enamoured of men who knew nothing of love. She averred that Mirabeau's immorality was detestable to her; she loved only the dry and cold Sieyès, a born enemy of women. She singled out another austere man, one of those who would later found the cult of Reason, the author of the republican calendar, the mathematician Romme, whose face was as ugly as his heart was pure and lofty; he stabbed himself through that same heart the day he judged the Republic to be dead. In 1789, Romme arrived from Russia; he was tutor to the young prince Strogonoff, and showed no scruple in taking his pupil to the salons of the beautiful *Liégoise*, which were attended by men such as Sieyès and Pétion. It is sufficient to say that Théroigne, unclear though her situation in the world was, was in no sense a girl.

She spent whole days at the Assembly, and hung on every syllable. One of the most frequently repeated jokes of the royalists who edited the *Actes des Apôtres* was to marry off Théroigne to the representative Populus, who had never even met her.

Even at a time when Théroigne had done nothing, she was immortalized in a wonderful piece by Camille Desmoulins on a session at the Cordeliers. Here is the extract in question, which I have quoted upon another occasion:

'The orator was interrupted. There was a noise at the door, and a pleasing murmur of approbation.... A young woman entered and asked to speak.... Heavens! it was no less a person than mademoiselle Théroigne, the beautiful amazon from Liège! Here was her red silk overcoat, and her great sword of 5 October. The enthusiasm of the gathering knew no bounds. "It is the Queen of Sheba", exclaimed Desmoulins, "come to visit the Solomon of the districts."

'She swiftly crossed the Assembly floor, with a step as light as a panther, and mounted the tribune. She was like one inspired and her pretty head seemed to gleam amidst the sombre, apocalyptic figures of Danton and Marat.

'"If you are truly Solomons," said Théroigne, "you will prove it by building the Temple, the temple of liberty, the palace of the National Assembly.... And you will build it on the square where the Bastille stood.

'"How can it be that, while the executive is lodged in the most beautiful palace in the universe, the *pavillon de Flore* and the colonnades of the Louvre, the legislature is still camped beneath tents, in the Tennis Court, in the Menus, in the Manège ... like Noah's dove, which has nowhere to put its foot!

'"This state of affairs cannot be allowed to continue. The peoples ought to be able, simply by looking at the buildings in which the two powers live, to tell where the true sovereign resides. What is a sovereign without a palace? A god without an altar. Who would recognize his cult?

'"Let us build this altar. Let everyone make a contribution, let everyone bring their gold and their precious stones; here then are mine. Let us build the only true temple. No other is worthy of God save that in which the Declaration of Rights of Man was pronounced. Paris, being the guardian of this temple, will be not so much a city as a common fatherland to all, the meeting-place of the tribes, and their Jerusalem!"'

When Liège, having been crushed by the Austrians, was handed back to its ecclesiastical tyrant in 1791, Théroigne did not fail her fatherland. But she was followed from Paris to Liège, arrested upon her arrival, the main charge against her being that she had been guilty on 6 October of an assault upon the queen of France, the sister of emperor Leopold. She was escorted to Vienna, released for want of any concrete evidence, and returned to Paris in a kind of fury, angry above all with the queen's agents, who had followed her and then delivered her up to the Austrian authorities. She wrote an account of her adventure and wished to print it; she is said to have read some pages from this document at the Jacobin Club, when the *journée* of 10 August erupted.

One of the men she hated most was the journalist Suleau, one of the most rabid agents of the Counter-Revolution. If she had a grudge against him, it was not solely because of the jokes he had aimed at her, but also because, in Brussels, in Austrian territory, he had published one of the papers which had helped to crush the Revolution in Liège, the *Tocsin des rois*. Suleau was dangerous not so much through his pen, as through his courage, and through his extraordinarily wide network of connections, both in his native province and elsewhere. Montlosier records that Suleau had said to him, when he was in danger: 'If the need arises, I shall send all my Picardy to your rescue.' So extraordinarily active was Suleau that he seemed to proliferate; one often came across him in disguise. Lafayette tells of encountering him thus, in 1790, coming out of the town-house of the Archbishop of Bordeaux. On the morning of 10 August, when the fury of the populace was at its height, Suleau was likewise in disguise. The crowd, seemingly drunk at the very idea of the coming struggle, sought but one enemy. No sooner was Suleau taken than he was as good as dead. When arrested, he was in a spurious royalist patrol, armed with blunderbusses, which was effecting a reconnoitre around the Tuileries.

Théroigne was out walking with a French guard on the terrace of the Feuillants when Suleau was arrested. If he perished, it was not she at any rate who could put him to death. The very jokes which he had uttered at her expense should have protected him. From the point of view of chivalry, she should have protected him; from the point of view which then prevailed, the unfettered imitation of the republicans of Antiquity, she should strike the public enemy, even though he were her own enemy also. A commissioner, having mounted a trestle, tried to pacify the crowd; Théroigne overturned it, took the man's place, and denounced Suleau. Two hundred national guards were defending the prisoners; an order from the *section* instructed them to offer no resistance to the crowd. Called one by one, the prisoners were slaughtered. It is said that Suleau displayed great courage, seizing a sabre from his attackers and trying to break free. In order to embroider the tale, some have claimed that the virago — who was small and slight, in spite of her passionate energy — cut down this man herself, though he was tall, and though despair must have unleashed great vigour and strength in him. Others say that it was the French guard accompanying Théroigne who dealt the first blow.

Her participation in 10 August, and the crown bestowed upon her by the conquering *Marseillais*, had strengthened her links with the Girondins, who were friends of these same *Marseillais*, and who had summoned them. She grew still closer to them through their shared horror at the September Massacres, which she had fiercely criticized. From April 1792, she broke violently with Robespierre, saying proudly in a café that, if he slandered without proof, 'she would cease to respect him.' This episode, recounted ironically that same evening in the Jacobins by Collot d'Herbois, roused the amazon to a pitch of fury, amusing to behold. She was in the gallery, surrounded by Robespierre's acolytes. In spite of the efforts they made to restrain her, she vaulted the barrier separating the galleries from the chamber, breached the hostile crowd and asked in vain to be allowed to speak. They shut their ears, for fear of hearing some blasphemy against the god of the temple; Théroigne was ejected without being granted a hearing.

She was still very popular, loved and admired by the crowd for her courage and her beauty. They dreamed up a means of wresting this prestige from her, and of humiliating her, by resorting to one of the most cowardly forms of violence to which a man can subject a woman. She was walking virtually alone on the terrace of the Tuileries; they surrounded her, suddenly closed in on her, seized hold of her, raised her skirts, and, with the crowd jeering, whipped her naked body as if she were a child. Her prayers, cries and shrieks of despair merely caused this cruel and cynical crowd to laugh the louder. When at last she was released, Théroigne went on shrieking; this barbaric insult to her dignity and courage had killed something in her; she had lost her mind. From 1793 up until 1817, for twenty-four long years (effectively half of an adult life), she remained raving mad, screaming as she had done on the first day. It was a heartbreaking spectacle to see this heroic, charming woman, who had descended lower than the beasts, and who was now reduced to beating at the bars of her cell, to tearing at her flesh and to eating her own excrement. The royalists took pleasure in recognizing in her sorry fate God's vengeance upon a woman whose fatal beauty had intoxicated the Revolution in its early days.[8]

For the writing of his *History of the Girondins*, which he completed between 1843 and 1847, Lamartine used a much less extensive documentation than Michelet had done. Being neither an archivist nor a professional historian, Lamartine relied upon oral tradition, narrative accounts by surviving witnesses, memoirs and published correspondence. He also drew upon contemporary sources which were used at the time, such as *Le Moniteur* and Buchez and Roux's *Archives parlementaires*. He had three reasons for wishing to write a saga of the Gironde. First of all, there were his financial motives. Being the heir to a huge landed estate, which was given over to viticulture, Lamartine had to pay exorbitant annual rents to his sisters' families. In 1842, he was on the verge of bankruptcy, and had to find a fresh source of income. The Revolution, being a highly fashionable topic, could prove a bestseller.[9] Secondly, the poet dreamed of expressing himself in prose. Now that the success enjoyed by his *Méditations* and by *Jocelyn* was a thing of the past, he dreamed of writing a *feuilleton*, which would be in the manner of Eugène Suë but would be imbued with a romantic fervour. Thirdly, disillusioned by the legitimist cause and rejected by the conservatives, Lamartine was moving towards the left.[10] The Girondins, magnificent though defeated protagonists of the Revolution, caught between their own moral demands and the ineluctable violence of history, between their courage and their lasting impotence, seemed to him to be sufficiently illustrious to serve as the characters in a new *Aeneid*.

Being more concerned with lyricism than with accuracy, Lamartine had no hesitation in resorting to fables. He invented episodes which had never taken place, but whose emotive value served to illustrate certain especially symbolic episodes in history. He wrote, for example, of the famous banquet of the Girondins, of which there is no record in the archives, but which provided the perfect context for an imaginary funereal oration by his heroes on the eve of their execution.

The poet and novelist had no theory of his own regarding the part played by women in the Revolution. However, they were accorded a prominent place in his narrative. Madame Roland was in fact the central figure in his book. She was represented in the guise of a romantic muse, and was a dazzling source of inspiration for all of the Gironde's dreams. Alongside her stood Charlotte Corday, who seemed an archangel of crime whose mission it was to crush the demon of the Word. Lamartine describes a hand-to-hand conflict between two fanaticisms, 'one under the hideous features of the people's revenge, in Marat, the other under the celestial beauty of the love of the fatherland, in a Joan of Arc of liberty'.[11]

Lamartine depicted Marie-Antoinette, on the other hand, at the hour of her downfall, and accepted all the incidental details which revolutionaries, in their hatred, had embroidered. In this account we see an aristocrat who knew how to die, mustering all the disdain of the caste to which she belonged:

> She climbed the rungs of the platform with great majesty. Upon reaching the scaffold, she chanced to tread upon the executioner's foot. The man cried out in pain. 'Pardon me', she said to the executioner, using much the same tone of voice as she might have used with one of her courtiers.[12]

Lamartine's representation of revolutionary femininity rested upon a hierarchy with three different levels. First of all came the 'true' women, who combined the qualities of heart, mind and virtue; then the fanatics, criminals, courtesans, band-leaders or Illuminists; finally, the furies or idolators, whether in groups or in a mob, a repugnant incarnation of a subhuman species. Each stage was described in terms of a romantic mythology, in which the antagonism between angel and demon again featured. It was as a reformist that Lamartine was depicting the rise of the popular masses and, in order to forestall their excesses, he announced in the Chamber of Representatives, in 1835, that the proletarian question should be resolved by political changes rather than by disturbances in the streets. An identical programme was touched upon in the *History of the Girondins* since, by means of such popular unrest, the poet explained the failure of a revolution for liberty when pitted against a revolution for equality, and then the failure of the latter in turn. It was for the July Monarchy to draw the appropriate conclusions on the eve of a fresh wave of popular uprisings. Moreover, just as Lamartine asserted that the people venerated idols only to punish them later for having seduced them, so too he took pleasure in relating the excesses surrounding the apotheosis of Marat, and, following that, the fall of Robespierre.

In this respect, Théroigne de Méricourt held a key position in his hierarchy. Lamartine knew her to be a Girondin, and yet he placed her in the category of the fanatics, the courtesans and the bloodthirsty, and therefore disregarded her real political alignment, preferring to concoct a fiction derived from Lamothe-Langon's phantasies and the *Mémoires* of the executioner Sanson. Depicted as an impure Joan of Arc clad in purple, Théroigne seemed to resemble the 'furies' who had whipped her. This is why Lamartine depicts her as having participated in the demonstration of 20 June, indeed, as having been a band-leader, immersed in the riff-raff, with Santerre and Saint-Huruge at her side. For his description of the 'crime' of 10 August, he relies upon Peltier's narrative.

Nevertheless, his portrait of Théroigne shows signs of real talent, and owes nothing to the style of royalist historiography, even though it takes its inspiration from that source. As an avowed romantic, Lamartine rejected both the neo-classical aesthetics of the revolutionary period — he described David as a plagiarist of Antiquity — and the official classicism which had been in favour under the Restoration. In this respect, his *History of the Girondins* still bears the traces of Hernani's battle. Not only did he attempt to wrest the Revolution from the metaphors of Antiquity in which it had draped itself, but, in addition, he waged a struggle against the supporters of the academicism of his own period. In their historical writing, such men sought to follow the canons of a classicism which was supposed to be the inheritance of the *grand siècle*. Lamartine himself recounted the history of the Revolution in the lyrical language of romanticism. Given this perspective, his Théroigne seemed less a Sadean libertine or a courtesan from Antiquity than an oriental prostitute. She was no longer Minerva, but Joan of Arc instead. She was not pox-ridden but impure. If she wallowed in blood, it was not so much the sign of a 'debauched nature' as that of a 'voluntary fall from grace'. The *History of the Girondins* was hugely successful, right from the day of publication, and this success was to help to reinforce this new image of Théroigne, which accorded more with the representations of the Counter-Revolution than with Michelet's feminary. Lamartine's portrait reads as follows:

> After Saint-Huruge, marched Théroigne de Méricourt. Théroigne, or Lambertine de Méricourt, who commanded the third corps of the army of the *faubourgs*, was known among the people by the name of *La belle Liégoise*. The French Revolution had drawn her to Paris, as the whirlwind attracts things of no weight. She was the impure Joan of Arc of the public streets. Outraged love had plunged her into disorder, and the vice, at which she herself blushed, only made her thirst for vengeance. In destroying the aristocrats, she fancied she purified her honour, and washed out her shame in blood.
>
> She was born at the village of Méricourt, near Liège, of a family of wealthy farmers, and had received a finished education. At the age of seventeen her singular loveliness had attracted the attention of a young *seigneur*, whose château was close to her residence. Beloved, seduced and deserted, she had fled from her father's home and taken refuge in England, whence, after a residence of some months, she proceeded to France. Introduced to Mirabeau, she knew through him Sieyès, Joseph Chénier, Danton, Brissot and Camille Desmoulins.... Youth, love, revenge and the contact with this furnace of a revolution had turned her head, and she lived in the intoxication of passions, ideas, and pleasures. Connected at first with the great innovators of '89, she had passed from their arms into those of rich voluptuaries, who purchased her charms dearly. Courtesan of opulence, she became the voluntary prostitute of the people; and like her celebrated prototypes of Egypt or of Rome, she lavished upon liberty the wealth she derived from vice.

At the time of the first uprisings, she appeared in the streets, and devoted her beauty to serve as an ensign to the people. Dressed in a riding-habit the colour of blood, a plume of feathers in her hat, a sabre at her side and a brace of pistols in her belt, she hastened to join every insurrection. She was the first of those who burst open the gate of the Invalides and took the cannon from there. She was also one of the first to attack the Bastille; and a sword of honour was voted her on the breach by the victors. During the October Days, she had led the women of Paris to Versailles, on horseback, by the side of the ferocious Jourdan, called 'the man with the long beard'. She had brought back the king to Paris: she had followed, without emotion, the heads of the royal bodyguard, stuck on pikes as trophies. Her language, although marked by a foreign accent, nevertheless had a tumultuous eloquence. She raised her voice at the stormy meetings of the clubs, and publicly rebuked speakers from her position in the galleries. Sometimes she spoke at the Cordeliers. Camille Desmoulins mentions the enthusiasm which her harangues aroused. 'Her similes', he records, 'were drawn from the Bible and Pindar, — it was the eloquence of a Judith.' She proposed to build the palace of the representative body on the site of the Bastille. 'To found and embellish this edifice', she said, 'let us strip ourselves of our ornaments, our gold, our jewels. I will be the first to set the example.' And with these words she tore off her ornaments in the tribune. Her ascendancy during the uprisings was so great that with a single sign she could condemn or acquit a victim; and the royalists trembled when they met her.

During this period, by one of those chances that appear like the pre-meditated vengeances of destiny, she recognized in Paris the young Belgian gentleman who had seduced and abandoned her. Her look told him how great his danger was, and he sought to avert it by begging her pardon. 'My pardon', she said, 'at what price can you purchase it? My innocence gone — my family lost to me — my brothers and sisters pursued in their own country by the jeers and sarcasm of their kindred; the curses of my father — my exile from my native land — my enrolment among the infamous caste of courtesans; the blood with which my hands have been, and will in the future be, stained; my memory execrated by men, that eternal curse attached to my name, instead of that immortal value, which you have taught me to doubt. It is for this that you would purchase my forgiveness! Do you know any price on earth capable of purchasing it?' The young man made no reply. Théroigne had not the generosity to forgive him, and he perished in the September Massacres.

As the Revolution grew bloodier, she plunged deeper into it. She could no longer exist without the feverish excitement of public emotion. However, her early sympathies for Brissot were reawakened by the fall of the

Girondins. She too wished to check the momentum of the Revolution. But there were women whose power was superior even to her own. These women, known as the furies of the guillotine, stripped *La belle Liégoise* of her clothes, and publicly whipped her on the terrace of the Tuileries, on 31 May. This punishment, more terrible than death itself, deranged her, and she was conveyed to a madhouse, where she lived twenty years. These twenty years were one long paroxysm of fury. Shameless and bloodthirsty in her delirium, she refused to wear any garments, in memory of the outrage she had suffered. She dragged herself, with her long white hair as her sole covering, along the flagstones of her cell, or clung with her wasted hands to the bars of her window, and from there she would address an imaginary people, and demand the blood of Suleau....

Whilst the hall was filled, and in this agitated but inactive state of expectation, the people, unrestrained by any force in the rue St Honoré, had penetrated to the very threshold of the Assembly, clamouring for twenty-two prisoners, royalists, arrested during the night in the Champs-Elysées by the National Guard. These prisoners were accused of having formed part of the secret patrol of the palace; and their uniform, arms and card of admission to the Tuileries, found on their persons, proved in fact that they were National Guards, volunteers devoted to the king. As they had been arrested, they were placed in the guardhouse of the Cour des Feuillants. At eight o'clock, they led thither a young man about thirty years old, in the costume of the National Guard. His proud and manly countenance, his martial appearance, and the name of Suleau, hated by the people, had attracted attention to him.

It was Suleau, one of those young royalist writers who, like André Chénier, Roucher, Mallet du Pan, Sérizy and several others, had embraced the cause of the monarchy when it had been abandoned by all the world, and mistook their generous feelings for the conviction of their minds. The freedom of the press was the defensive weapon which they had received from the hands of the Constitution, and which they used courageously to combat the excesses of liberty. But revolutions wish weapons only to be in the hands of their friends. Suleau had harried the popular parties, sometimes through bloodthirsty pamphlets directed at the Duc d'Orléans, sometimes through witty sarcasms aimed at the Jacobins; he had mocked the omnipotence of the people, which does not nurse a grudge but which is merciless in revenge.

The populace hated Suleau, as every tyranny hates its Tacitus. In vain did the young writer produce an order of the municipal commissioners that summoned him to the château; he was cast into the same dungeon as the rest. His name had worked upon and irritated the crowd, which loudly demanded his head. A commissioner mounted upon a table, harangued the crowd, and sought to delay them by promising justice. Théroigne de Méricourt, dressed in a riding-habit and brandishing a naked sabre in her hand, hurled the commissioner from the table and assumed his place. By her language she aroused the people's thirst for blood, and caused commissioners of every *section* to be appointed by acclamation, who ascended with her to the committee of the *section*, to snatch the victims from the slow processes of the law. The president of the *section*, Bonjour, head clerk in the bureau of the minister for naval affairs, who was himself ambitious of the ministry, forbade the National Guard to resist the will of the people. Two hundred armed men obeyed this order, and surrendered the prisoners; eleven escaped by a back window, eleven still remained in the guardhouse; they were summoned one after the other into the courtyard to be immolated. A few National Guards, more humane or less cowardly, wished, in spite of the orders of Bonjour, to rescue these unhappy men. 'No,' cried Suleau, 'let me meet them; I see that today the people must have blood, perhaps that of one victim may suffice. I will pay for all!' He was about to leap out of the window, but they held him.

The abbé Bougon, a dramatist, was the first to be seized. Endowed with prodigious strength, the abbé struggled with the energy of despair, and killed several of his assailants, but was at last overpowered by numbers, and hewn to pieces.

M. de Solimniac, one of the royal guards, was the second, and then two others. Those who awaited their fate in the guardhouse heard the cries and struggles of their friends, and suffered tenfold agony. Suleau was then summoned: he had been deprived of his bear-skin cap, his sabre and bayonet, but his arms were free. A woman pointed him out to Théroigne de Méricourt, who did not know him personally, but who hated him by report, and burned to avenge herself for the derision to which his writings upheld her. Théroigne seized him by the collar. Suleau, however, disengaged himself, and had well nigh cut his way through them when he was thrown down, disarmed and pierced by twenty swords: he expired at the feet of Théroigne. His head was cut off and borne in triumph about the rue St Honoré.[13]

Louis Blanc, a militant socialist, endeavoured to reconstruct a portrait of Théroigne that differed from the versions of both Michelet and Lamartine. He did not accord her a very important role in his *Histoire de la Révolution française*, which was published between 1847 and 1862, but, at several stages in his narrative, he displayed a real concern for accuracy. In his handling of the October Days, he emphasized that the depositions assembled by the court of the Châtelet proved nothing. His treatment of the rising of 10 August was based entirely upon Peltier's testimony, but he was very critical of it. He noted the differences of opinion between Leopold and the emigrés. Finally, in his account of the flagellation, he corrected Michelet, attributed the deed to the Jacobin women and insisted that the Montagnard party had not really been responsible for it. Here are a few extracts from his narrative:

It is said that Théroigne de Méricourt was observed distributing money to the dragoons. This is a royalist calumny, and derives from the embittered testimony, itself very vague, delivered by a priest before the judges of the Châtelet. He claimed that Théroigne had walked in front of the troops carrying a basket from which the soldiers took small packets. The pieces of gold which she used to win over the Flanders regiment were, according to an English historian, 'Her proud looks, her demeanour — which was that of a pagan goddess — her eloquent tongue and the play of her heart'.... The famous Théroigne de Méricourt, driven from Paris to Liège by her desire to propagate revolutionary sentiments, had been arrested, delivered up to Austria and thrown into the fortress of Kulstein [*sic*]: the emperor was tempted out of curiosity to see her, found her pretty and set her free. For this, the emigrés must have harboured no small grievance! To the princes of Condé, in particular, Leopold's waverings must have seemed especially reprehensible. When one of his confidantes said one day in his presence: 'What will the brother do if the sister is murdered?' 'Perhaps', answered the emperor bitterly, 'perhaps he will dare to wear mourning.' ... Suleau, the notorious Suleau, whose pen was dipped in the same gall as Marat, for a different cause, had taken delight in dipping his own, had in turn harassed the Revolution in Paris, in Brussels and in Koblenz. The prisoners, upon seeing death rear up before them, faced it with indomitable courage. At the head of their slaughterers, and the one to deal the first blow, was a woman dressed in a riding-habit with a brace of pistols in her belt and a sabre in her shoulder-strap. It was Théroigne de Méricourt. Everything imaginable that could be said to offend a woman's pride, her coquetry or her sense of shame had been said by Suleau of Théroigne, and now she had to choose whether to have her enemy killed or to humiliate him by sparing him. Of these two methods of avenging herself, she chose the less proud; being unable to climb as high as disdain, she descended as low as murder.... And one's heart is smitten with a sense of disgust at the memory of poor Théroigne de Méricourt being seized in the middle of the Tuileries gardens, by a gang of *mégères*, and, because she was a Brissotin, being pitilessly whipped. The humiliation was so terrible that it drove her mad. However, it is neither honest nor sensible to hold the Jacobin party wholly responsible for such indignities, for this abject violence was not perpetrated by men, as has been claimed, but by women.[14]

In his book, *La Révolution*, which was published in 1865, Edgar Quinet used Marc-Antoine Baudot's unpublished *Notes historiques*, which were edited by his widow and eventually appeared in 1893. Baudot had been a representative at the Legislative Assembly, and subsequently a Montagnard, but he had not been present at the Convention on the day that Robespierre's fate was decided.[15] In his memoirs, he gives a physical portrait of Théroigne which is undoubtedly very accurate, and which is reminiscent of the two physionotrace engravings by Louis Chrétien mentioned earlier. The same countenance also features on another portrait, attributed to Louis Lagrenée, which depicts her as melancholic, with hair dressed in the style of a lioness and with no detail of her clothing linking her precisely to any particular period.[16] But Baudot also describes her in her fetish costume, without however treating this clothing as a legendary garb. He makes no mention of any purple, of any sabre or dagger. His is a workaday Théroigne, not one embellished by a murderous mythology. Baudot compares her in some detail to Claire Lacombe, so as to emphasize that the republican woman citizen 'tended not to draw such large crowds as Mlle Théroigne, because she had none of the bizarre characteristics of her rival. Beauty counted for little in such circumstances.'[17] He therefore noticed her madness, and her peculiarity, but Baudot, who was a doctor, also noticed something which had escaped the attention of everyone else: according to him, Théroigne was not clean. Baudot saw this negligence as politically motivated. The woman from the Ardennes did not wish, he said, to resemble a coquette. This detail is an interesting one and, if it is to be believed, it should either be related to the realities of the time — Théroigne had kept her peasant habits — or interpreted in the light of the rites of pollution and purification which she engaged in at La Salpêtrière. Here is Baudot's portrait:

> I saw much of Mlle Théroigne de Méricourt during the gatherings in the Tuileries. She tended to speak confidentially rather than with the rhetoric of an orator. She was almost always dressed in a riding-habit; her cloth attire

was perfectly commonplace, and dark green in colour. She had a hat with a black feather. Those who have described her as wearing a bizarre or elegant costume have been reading too many novels. She was fairly small, with a good figure, a mean countenance, with no especially good features but with no faults either. Her complexion had the tint of a russet pear, very probably because of her continual excursions in the open air; all in all, not too bad, but without any real attractions. She was far from claiming the particular merit of professional coquettes, namely cleanliness; this was very probably a political calculation, but she tended to take it a little too far.[18]

Edgar Quinet, whose protestant ethic may perhaps have made him something of a puritan, was very probably embarrassed by this question of cleanliness, and therefore did not mention it. On the other hand, his concern for accuracy was such that he sought to rehabilitate Théroigne, refusing to treat her as a bacchante. He accepted Baudot's view that a bizarre woman would be more likely to fascinate a crowd than a beautiful one. The woman from the Ardennes therefore owed her power to some 'extraordinary' or even religious quality. In addition, Quinet emphasized the notion of 'speaking in confidence', as suggested by Baudot, and therefore depicted Théroigne as a woman who preferred to act in secret rather than in the public domain. He particularly stressed her low voice and her 'insinuations'. This is an interesting notion, not least because we now know, through the Austrian archives, which were still unknown in 1865, how much Théroigne feared being immersed in crowds. Moreover, the references to the art of whispering and to her timid voice call to mind her failed career as a singer, and her inability to write her memoirs, whose contents, had they ever been published, might well have revealed what should have remained masked: humiliation, the pox, a dark melancholy, and still other things perhaps. Being unable to 'project her voice', finding it difficult to speak and to write correct French, as much because of her Walloon accent as because of her lack of education, she would therefore have been condemned to resort to confidences. This was already an alienation, and was to be followed by a confinement, and later by a form of 'automatic' speech. However, Quinet saw this propensity to whisper as one of the characteristics of a bizarre *grisette* with a pleasant enough little face, who seemed to anticipate the *midinette* of the Belle Époque. There had thus been a curious reversal in the myth. Where Michelet and Lamartine had seen either a sublime or a bloodthirsty amazon, we are now concerned with an ordinary woman who is just a touch deranged. Quinet's account reads as follows:

> Who was their leader? They had none, unless we grant this title to Mlle
> Théroigne de Méricourt, whom rumour, irrespective of the actual truth of
> the matter, depicted as the sole heroine of the October Days. Some said that
> she had been glimpsed, in the morning, hauled along in triumph on a
> cannon; others claimed that she emerged, no one knows how, on the place de
> Versailles. Be this as it may, Théroigne de Méricourt was not the bacchante
> that she is usually represented as being. It was not so much her face as the
> black feather on her hat that made her stand out from a distance. She was
> small, and cut a good figure in her amazon garb, but her features were mean,
> though pleasing enough, her complexion the tint of a russet pear, and she did
> not seem suited to represent the anger of the people. For she always spoke in
> a low voice, as if in confidence, and was capable of none of the bold flights of
> the orator discoursing in the public square. She tended rather to insinuate a
> word or two into the ear of each person, and seemed to be entrusting every-
> one with a great secret. Was this perhaps the source of her power? It is not
> beauty which influences a crowd, but the unusual.[19]

There are many anecdotal treatments of the history of the Revolution, but
here I want to consider only the Goncourt brothers' description of
Théroigne, which was published in 1856, in their *Portraits intimes du XVIIIe
siècle*. If we are to grasp its meaning, however, we need also to take account
of the biography of Marie-Antoinette and the *Histoire de la société française
pendant la Révolution*.[20] Since they hated bourgeois society as much as Balzac
himself had done, the brothers execrated the Revolution which had given
birth to it. It was their misfortune, however, that they lacked the genius of
the author of the *Comédie humaine* and, unlike him, did not know how to
decipher the specific characteristics of the pain suffered by women on every
rung of the social hierarchy. To the vilenesses of the century in which they
lived, the Goncourts opposed a fetishized account of the absolute greatness
of the preceding century. Being inveterate collectors, obsessed both by *objets
d'art* and by pictures, these two misogynists, who frequented only whores,
their servant-girl, Madame Daudet and the Princess Mathilde, spent their
days browsing in secondhand shops and bookshops in search of vestiges of
their favourite period. They were thus historians, *avant la lettre*, of manners,
fashion and private life. Élisabeth Badinter has demonstrated quite convincingly how their method seems to anticipate the 'new history', just when

positivist historiography, narrative and political, was being forged.[21] Like Michelet, they took woman as their object, but their symbolic model was the woman of the eighteenth century. Indeed, they were so adept at delving into her intimacy, her boudoirs or her rouge that Michelet himself upon one occasion advised them in all seriousness to write a 'history of housemaids'.[22]

In the hierarchy of values to which Jules and Edmond Goncourt subscribed, the noblewoman of the Ancien Régime embodied the finest qualities of civilization. By contrast, the bourgeois woman, with her eye fixed on her progeny, seemed a stuffed animal, caught between the crudeness of her class and the virtues of her household, which distanced her from the corruptions of the world and rendered her, if not stupid, at any rate devoid of all charm. On the very lowest rung, the woman of the people resembled a coarsened Hottentot, while the sole ambition of the kept woman, living in the shadow of La Salpêtrière, was to become a young lady of fashion.

As for the revolutionary woman, the Goncourts saw her as afflicted with all the taints of an epoch which, fortunately, had passed. Such women were much to be pitied. By launching themselves into politics, they had ceased to be women at all, and in adopting the disguise of a Roman citizen or in defending lofty ideas about emancipation, they were making themselves appear simply ridiculous. But the two brothers did not stop short at such clichés. Their commitment to research and their cult of the archive were such that, irrespective of their actual theories, they made a genuinely original contribution to the history of manners. Their portrait of Théroigne rested upon a cheerful mixture of Michelet, Peltier, Lamartine and the royalist tradition, and they therefore represented her as a humiliated, blood-thirsty cutthroat, wallowing in the midst of the riff-raff. However, they were also the first to quote from, and to publish, a number of new sources, in particular, the Salpêtrière death certificate, the speech delivered at the *Société fraternelle des Minimes*, the Appeal to the Forty-Eight Sections and the letter to Saint-Just. Here are a number of extracts from the Goncourts' account:

> Théroigne, in an inebriated state, ran furiously, brandishing death in the face of the theories of the faubourgs. Riots were her element, and she had the instinct and appetite of a wild animal, a 'panther' as Camille Desmoulins called her. She was avid to overcome and to kill. She was armed at the Invalides; she had played her part at the Bastille; October sounds; to horse! and with her red plume, her overcoat of red silk, this radiant Penthesilea, this

Rubenesque amazon, riding-whip in hand, pistols in her belt, galloping in triumph at the head of her hordes and smiling at the upraised arms — this was how the woman from Liège appeared, as she led the pikes to Versailles. Those with pikes called for heads, while the females demanded the queen's 'guts'.... Théroigne had been so shocked by the turn of events and by the words that were used that her mind had caught fire; and from her head, where every kind of conflicting reading clashed, from her mouth, where the French language faltered, there poured out a singularly bold and unbridled eloquence, which gave way before the image and, helter-skelter, rolled, in the torrent of its grandiloquence, the lofty utterances of Pindar and the solemn tones of the Bible. Her voice gave the commands, together with the threats of an angry people, when, running through the Palais-Royal, shop-keepers were rebuked for displaying royalist caricatures. She thundered in the Deseine bookshop. She spoke at the Jacobins; she spoke at the *Société fraternelle.* She mounted the rostrum at the Cordeliers, and her bearing was like that of Herodias....

Théroigne was the bearer of a particular idea. In the Revolution, she represented the party of woman. As Liberty was unleashed, she called woman to emancipation, and to usurpation. She demanded that civism allocated duties to her, and that her heroism should win her rights. Her desire for such changes was fervent, and she was the first to argue that her sex should leave the household and enter the fatherland. This is an aspect of this bloodthirsty figure, and indeed her historical soul, which history has not even reclaimed. Two sheets of paper, which are of the utmost rarity and which may even be unique, will reveal to us Théroigne's views, aspirations and paradoxes, which have since come to seem ridiculous, but at the time seemed generous....

On 10 August, Théroigne cut Suleau's throat.

When, in September, the Mountain broke with the Gironde, Théroigne followed Brissot. A few days before, on 31 May, Théroigne had been at the Tuileries. Some women of the people yelled: 'Down with the Brissotins!' Brissot passed by. The *sans-jupons* screamed at him. Théroigne came forward to defend him. 'So you too are a Brissotin', cried the women, 'you will pay the price for all of them'. Théroigne was then whipped. After that, she dis-appeared from public view. The whipping had driven her mad. A hospital had shut its gates behind her. Her reason had gone. Her ideas still lived, but in a confused, scrambled state ...'[23]

We have already seen how Michelet, in his description of Théroigne, relied upon a portrait engraved by Charles Dewritz in 1845, after an anonymous drawing.[24] He was wrong to suppose that this was a genuine 'trace' of the now mad heroine, and he failed to mention Gabriel's sketch. Dewritz's Théroigne, which was probably not drawn from life, is a woman of the people with a sensuous, vulgar mouth. She displays all the anger of the Revolution, all of its dreams, and all its despair. Her face is turned to the right, her forehead is bound in a Madras from which a few coal-black curls escape. Her left breast is bare and emerges from a bodice whose border merges with a hard, round nipple. In short, this Théroigne is a woman in a state of crisis, a marginal woman, on the very edge of madness, who seems to have come straight out of Michelet's feminary.

Although Michelet sometimes refers to portraits, there is no precise iconography informing his narrative of the Revolution. His language is sufficiently pictorial, and his style sufficiently visual, to dispense with any actual illustrations. Michelet did not create an 'image' so much as an imaginary, commenting upon the iconography when the need arose. If proof of this were necessary, consider his lengthy analysis of David's paintings, where he chooses to discuss the artist's drawings rather than his representations of Antiquity.

Conversely, Lamartine, in his *Histoire des Girondins*, prefers the shock of the image to the power of a purely verbal imaginary. His style, the shaping of his sentences and the construction of his narrative are related less to Michelet's visualization through language than to a kind of montage of scenes, which reminds the present-day reader of the great Hollywood productions. As we read Lamartine, we are reminded of the colours of a director like Vincent Minelli or of the frescoes of someone like King Vidor, whereas our reading of Michelet tends rather to conjure up the sort of staging of the revolutionary idea attempted by Jean Renoir in *La Marseillaise*.

Since Lamartine was forever referring to images, it made sense to provide an iconography to accompany the text, which would serve, as was customary with the *feuilletons* of the period, to popularize the heroes featured in the book. The painter Auguste Raffet was commissioned to draw the characters, which were then engraved by Bosselman. Raffet was born in 1804, and had known none of the principal actors of the Revolution, but he was able, using the existing iconography or eye-witness accounts, to reinvent them. He saw Théroigne as the legendary figure of collective memory, dressed as an amazon, with her left fist on her thigh and with her right fist clenched around the handle of a drawn sabre which was pointed towards the ground. Her hair escaped from a plumed hat of the Henri IV style. Her face was touched with a thoroughly oriental kind of beauty, in accord with the lyricism of Lamartine, but totally at odds with the arrogant popular figure featured in Michelet's account.[25]

The Goncourt brothers make no reference to any portrait of Théroigne, but they have no hesitation in evoking Rubens so as to match the 'blood-coloured fabric' dreamed up by Lamartine with a 'plume' of the same colour. For them, Théroigne has literally become 'unrepresentable'. How in fact could one combine within the same frame the fleshy nakedness of the great Flemish painter, a silk overcoat in the eighteenth-century style, the spectacle of the queen's 'guts', Herodias, Pindar, the Bible, Penthesilea — the whole thing coated in a mass of haemoglobin? At this stage in the legend, the wretched woman from the Ardennes would seem to be floundering under the weight of an excess of signifiers which only the surrealist genius could have reinvented, had one charged Max Ernst or Salvador Dali with the task of deconstructing, to the point of absurdity, the rambling prose of two bachelor brothers. One thing, however, is clear. This prose serves as a perfect illustration of the Goncourts' historical method, which was based upon the art of narrating *la grande histoire* through the piling up of its apparently insignificant details. Their 'unrepresentable' Théroigne may perhaps be a premonition that the mythological hotchpotch with which history had burdened the woman from the Ardennes was now dissolving, and another, more accurate and more banal representation was replacing it, as the work of Edgar Quinet and Louis Blanc to some extent suggests.

Charles Baudelaire took possession of the myth at a time when it was being swamped by the excesses of the Goncourt brothers. In a sonnet entitled 'Sisina', which was first published in April 1859, and then included in the second edition of *Les Fleurs du mal*, the poet summons up the figure of Elisa Neri, friend of Madame Sabatier. When he sent the manuscript to his editor, he referred to this female adventurer, who was something of a spy, as the 'Lady who drinks the health of Orsini in Van Swieten water'. The liquor in question had anti-syphilitic and prophylactic properties, while Orsini had been executed in March 1858, after having made an attempt upon the life of Napoleon III. Associating the name of the miracle-working liquid with that of a 'foreigner' who had become a *Sisina*, and who had herself paid homage to the murderer of a tyrant, Baudelaire fashioned his poem around two legendary women, Diana the huntress, 'elated with the chase', and Théroigne de Méricourt, 'by blood and fire enraged'.

SISINA

Picture Diana, gallantly arrayed,
Ranging the woods, elated with the chase,
With flying hair and naked breasts displayed,
Defying fleetest horsemen with her pace.

See Théroigne, by blood and fire enraged,
Hounding a shoeless rabble to the fray,
Who plays herself on a flaming stage,
As she climbs, sword in hand, the royal stairway.

Such is Sisina. Terrible her arms.
But charity restrains her killing charms.
Though rolling drums and scent of power madden

Her courage, — laying by its pikes and spears,
For those who merit, her scorched heart will sadden,
And span in its depth, a well of tears.[26]

Baudelaire was undoubtedly inspired by Raffet's drawing rather than by a specific text. However, instead of overloading the image and amplifying the legend, he deconstructed them. Théroigne is no longer reduced to the clichés of blood and debauchery. She is neither the humiliated woman dear to Michelet, nor the impure Joan of Arc delineated by Lamartine. Instead, Baudelaire apprehends her in all the excess of a femininity condemned to masquerade, forever divided between a ritual of appearances and an aesthetics of unveiling. In this alternating rhyme scheme, the poet imagines that Théroigne 'plays herself' (*joue son personnage*). Now, through this act of clairvoyance, he advances a new representation of the heroine, and one which is truer to nature. Indeed, before him, no historian had ever noticed the degree to which Théroigne had become identified in her own lifetime with the mythical figure which she had become through her entrance into the Revolution. Baudelaire is therefore the first to cast a ray of modernity upon her, which only our contemporary gaze is capable of reinventing with the aid of archives, an analysis of the collective imaginary and a Freudian interpretation of identifications.[27]

With the publication, from 1875 onwards, of Hippolyte Taine's *Origines de la France contemporaine*,[28] an interpretation of the Revolution in terms of mental pathology was launched. Disillusioned by various personal setbacks, Taine had already displayed great hostility towards the Revolution of 1848, and although he did not approve of the coup d'état of 2 December, he submitted to the imperial dictatorship. In later years, he was to benefit greatly from the Second Empire. An admirer of English literature, and aware of German philosophy, he was passionately interested in the observation of societies and wished to place his method on a 'scientific' footing. He drew his inspiration from clinical discourse and followed the teaching at La Salpêtrière of François Baillarger, an alienist who had himself been a pupil of Esquirol.

Baillarger believed that a psycho-pathological fact was essentially differ-ent in nature from so-called 'normal' functioning. As a consequence, madness was interpreted solely in terms of organic deviance. We can thus see how, around 1850, what was already operative in the Esquirolean revision of Pinel's doctrine, namely, an organicist emphasis, became increas-ingly dominant. The distinction between the normal and the pathological informed Taine's entire theory of the analysis of societies, as it did his conception of a Revolution as the source of deviance and anomaly.

France's defeat at the Battle of Sedan transformed Taine's intellectual trajectory. He had been a Germanist, and an admirer of Kant and Hegel, but now he became an ardent patriot, convinced of the greatness, indeed, of the superiority, of French civilization. But the turning-point of the Paris Commune also served to reinforce his instinctive hatred of crowds, which he theorized by linking France's misfortunes to its revolutionary 'origins'. The people of 1793 was described by him as an 'animal wallowing on a carpet of crimson', and the Revolution was likened to the 'onset of an alcoholic delirium'. As for its main protagonists, they were beasts, syphilitics or outlaws.

Taine therefore could not help but regard Marat as the most spectacular symbol of popular fury. In his attempts to situate his madness in particular, and that of the Revolution in general, Taine drew upon the arguments of his friend Ulysse Trélat, another pupil of Esquirol, and the inventor of the notion of 'lucid madness'. Trélat believed that those madmen who were 'invisible' and who were endowed with reason would prove more dangerous than those who were ordinarily insane, because they were more adept at deceiving those around them. In association with the concept of mono-mania, this theory was much favoured by criminologists, because it made it easier to 'track down' the pathology of the murderer. This did not make it any the less pernicious, however, for the limitless extension of the criteria serving to identify deviance was an abuse of medical science. After all, if madness was an invisible condition, each and every individual could become a suspect. What was to prevent one from sending anyone before the court of mental medicine who was judged to be somewhat out of the ordinary? Flaubert, Baudelaire, Verlaine and Rimbaud might all be afflicted with this illness. Similarly, if the revolutionaries resembled such deviants, it was because they were sometimes liars or charlatans, and sometimes dangerous criminals whose essential harmfulness required unmasking. From Taine's perspective, Marat therefore fitted Trélat's category and was a 'lucid madman'. Danton, however, was a 'covetous barbarian', Robespierre a 'freak of the first order', La Fayette a 'milksop', etc.

This denigratory vocabulary allowed Taine to employ the discourse of royalist historiography, while at the same time investing it with a spurious scientificity. He thus established a continuity between the old counter-revolutionary representations, still in the grip of the art of journalistic reportage, and a 'false' theory of history based upon crowd psychology and upon typologies of deviance.

As someone who had frequented La Salpêtrière in the 1850s, Taine could not have been unaware of the 'case' of Théroigne, as described by Esquirol. The latter had become famous in the annals of mental medicine. It is there-fore legitimate to inquire just why, twenty-five years later, the author of the *Origines* made no mention of the story of this madness, while he was at the same time exploiting the discourse of the direct heirs of Esquirolean alienism to examine the Revolution in the light of an organicist doctrine of deviance.

In order to answer this question, one must first of all show how Taine's observation of the case of Marat evolved in the course of his writings. To begin with, the 'Friend of the People' was described in terms of the Esquirolean terminology which Lamothe-Langon had already employed, and he was therefore seen as 'homicidal monomaniac'. Thus, as Taine's judgement of Marat grew increasingly negative, he drew upon Ulysse Trélat's arguments. The fact that Marat's madness remained invisible made him seem all the more dangerous. He was afflicted, it was claimed, with 'delusions of ambition', 'recurring nightmares' and a 'persecution mania'. In addition, his skin complaint was seen as a corollary of his mental derange-ment. One of the key signs of madness was therefore an organic substratum, which was itself the symptom of a 'logic' of lucid madness. By way of conclusion, Taine added that, if the Revolution had been suppressed, Marat would have ended his life in an asylum.[29]

Every one of these arguments is absurd. Taine's approach here is that of a censor. Just as he selected from among the archives those which lent credence to his own theses,[30] so too he drew from the clinical discourse of his own period those elements which would serve to bolster his own theory of revolutionary pathology. This is why he chose to pit Trélat's terminology against that of Esquirol. The notion of 'lucid madness' in fact made it possible to 'forget' a crucial fact: not only was Marat's madness not invisible to his contemporaries, but everyone had noticed it. As a consequence, Trélat's terminology, which presupposed invisibility, was wholly unsuited to account for the 'case' of Marat as it appeared in the history of the Revolution, save under the pen of Taine, where it became operative, not in order to interpret a reality, but rather to impose an interpretation of the Revolution.

The problem of Marat's madness should anyway on no account be seen in the light of a theory of deviance. It cannot be true that, without the Revolution, Marat, an authentic madman, and recognized as such by his own contemporaries, would have ended his life in an asylum. For, had it not been for the Revolution, the Esquirolean asylum would not have assumed its familiar form. Anyway, if Marat was mad, and often delusional, his language and his opinions were no more 'mad' than those of the other protagonists on the revolutionary stage. It is almost certain that, as the case of Théroigne shows, the so-called periods of 'troubles' favour not so much the onset of madness as the exhaustion of symptoms. Ordinary suicides are less frequent when war authorizes a heroism of death, and mental disorders proliferate, and are more apparent, when the society in which they feature gives every sign of being stable. Charcot gave hysteria a theatrical form fifteen years after the Commune, at a time when republican calm seemed to have triumphed over revolutionary 'convulsions'. By the same token, Freud identified the sexual causes of neurosis within a society that was apparently plunged in the torpor of its bourgeois tranquillity. As for the traumas associated with war, torture, confinement and revolutionary violence, fairly thorough study of such phenomena has shown that they are to a great extent particular to a given situation and symptomatic of the circumstances of specific individuals. One cannot go mad just because one wishes to do so, nor can one choose when one is to go insane. Each individual will react differently to a collective event.

This being so, neither the traumatic causality conjured up by Esquirol with respect to the Revolution, nor Trélat's theory will account for the relations between madness and the 'Revolution-as-event'. Esquirol's lype-maniac Théroigne is no truer than Trélat's lucid Marat. However, these arguments are an exact expression of the manner in which alienists represented the Revolution for the whole of the period which runs from the revision of the Pinelian heritage to the establishment of the organicist legitimacy. In this respect, the Esquirolean lineage added a new element to the vision which the master had had of the 'Revolution-as-bad-object'. The harmful qualities of the Revolution, in Esquirol's view, stemmed from the fact that it was no longer 'curable', since each social conflict which referred back to it seemed to supply the proof of its persistence. Faced with the lost sheep of the barricades, alienists after Esquirol had therefore to choose either an ideal of pardon (Descuret), which favoured integration within the asylum, or a repressive attitude, which used 'tracking down' and organic aetiologies to exclude deviance. As we shall see, this latter tendency became the rule during the second half of the nineteenth century. And, as it justified a representation of the revolutionary disorder in terms of incurable taints, it enabled Taine to 'prove' that the Revolution and its actors were criminal by their very nature.

One can now hazard a hypothesis as to why Taine did not use Théroigne's madness for his demonstrations. Even Taine was unable to shift from an Esquirolean terminology to that of Trélat, for there was no way in which Théroigne could be classified in terms of the category of 'lucid madness', since her madness had in reality led her to the asylum, and her case had been the object of an actual clinical observation, duly entered in the annals of mental medicine. No one could claim that such a madness was invisible or dangerous, for it had been punished by confinement. Indeed, because the case did not support Taine's hypotheses regarding the invisible harmfulness of the revolutionary pathology, it was quite simply repressed.

On the other hand, the myth of Théroigne as a debauchee and rabble-rouser illustrated to perfection Taine's crowd theories. This is why, in *Les Origines de la France contemporaine*, Théroigne was stripped of all vestiges of her history and her legend. There was therefore no trace of her riding-habit, of her purple cloak or of her sabre, and both her flagellation and the murder of Suleau went unmentioned. For Taine, she was a mere grain of sand, immersed in the instinctual depths of the mob. The relevant passages read as follows:

In addition there were the women of the street, led by Théroigne de

Méricourt, a virago and a courtesan, who distributed places and gave the signal for boos or for claps (National Assembly, August 1789).... Three or four are known by name, one because she brandished a sword, another who was the famous Théroigne (the October Days).... One should add to this list the filthy tail-end of every agitation, insurrection or popular dictatorship, the beasts of prey such as Jourdan d'Avignon and Fournier the American, the women — such as Théroigne, Rose Lacombe and the *tricoteuses* of the Convention — who had disavowed their own sex, the amnestied outlaws, and all those gaol-birds who roamed free in such unpoliced times, layabouts, a host of vagabonds who refused all subordination and work, and who, in the midst of civilization, preserved the instincts of savage life, and pleaded the sovereignty of the people in order to assuage their native habits of idleness, licence and ferocity (the Jacobins).... The rest was a mob similar to that of 14 July, 5 October and 20 June. 'The château', said Napoleon Bonaparte, 'was attacked by the vilest riff-raff.' By professional rioters, by Maillard's gang, by Fournier's gang, by Lazowski's gang, by Théroigne's gang, by all of the assassins of the previous day ... (*journée* of 10 August). He [Danton] had set up in his own quarter a small, independent republic, aggressive and domineering, a centre for faction, an asylum for lost children, a meeting-place for every energumen, a pandemonium for all the crackpots and for all the available knaves, visionaries and bravos, hacks and tubthumpers, drawing-room or public murderers, Camille Desmoulins, Fréron, Hébert, Chaumette, Cloots, Théroigne, Marat ...[31]

Michelet argued that Théroigne's fate should be analysed in the light of the history of Liège. His wish was answered in Belgium after the publication of the *Femmes de la Révolution*. In this country, which was unified in 1830, reference to the founding act of the Revolution did not play the same role as in France. The case of Théroigne was therefore not subject to the same projections as had been evident in French historiography. What the large number of articles published on the woman from the Ardennes, from 1852 onwards, supply us with is information, anecdotal in nature but nevertheless very valuable, regarding her family, her jewels, her material resources and her relations with the Baron de Sélys-Fanson. In short, they throw light on Théroigne's peasant origins and upon her finances, without therefore revealing how it was that the milieu in which she lived could have prepared the subsequent onset of her madness. Although the humiliations, moral unhappiness, illusions and disappointments which she suffered were severe, and although they are the major signifiers of this heroine's unhappy childhood, they do not themselves provide an adequate explanation for her melancholic fate. There were other Walloon women in the eighteenth century, and other women involved in the Revolution, who had difficult lives, but who did not go mad. We shall no doubt have to wait until new research is undertaken, and new documents uncovered, before we are in a position to identify the primordial determinants, affective and sexual, of such a psychosis. We have already identified several such determinants above. However, if all subsequent researches were one day to prove that no psychoticizing genealogy, susceptible to recurrences, no crucial deficiency, no pathogenic terrain lay behind Théroigne's madness, one would have to conclude, as we have known since Freud and his heirs, that madness is closely dependent upon 'normality', even in its details. Consequently, as both Esquirol's autopsy and the hypotheses that we have advanced show, it is feasible to claim that the aetiology of this madness should be related to a multiplicity of different determinations, among which organic causation counts for nothing and the signifying detail for everything. This will give no pleasure to the present-day advocates of the genetic or biological aetiology of the psychoses.

I want briefly to consider two articles from the Belgian historiography of Théroigne: that by Thomas Fuss, entitled 'Théroigne de Méricourt, dite "la belle Liégoise"' (1854), and Joseph Demarteau's 'Théroigne de Méricour [*sic*] lettres inédites, prison, bijoux'.[32] Both authors were hostile to the Revolution and depicted Théroigne as a ruined, greedy and debauched courtesan. However, they present valuable information regarding the manner in which the heroine's legend was transmitted in the Ardennes. Fuss went to Marcourt in 1849, and burrowed in the archives. He found the Terwagnes' marriage certificate, together with Anne-Josèphe's baptismal certificate. The villagers showed him the family house, which stood opposite the church, and told him the rumours, which Mengin-Salabert had earlier communicated to François de Blanc regarding Marie-Antoinette's famous necklace, the English seducer and the October Days. In 1850, these men were therefore unable to perceive the real fate of the country child. They retained from her story only those elements which accorded with their own peasant phantasies, namely, wealth, ruin, poverty, social climbing, kings, queens and courtesans.

In 1882, Demarteau was to prove more prolix than Fuss. His account is imbued with a visceral hatred of the Revolution, and his testimony is marred by a series of massive errors, and yet he contributed a number of fresh items to the documentation of Théroigne's life. In particular, he published numerous letters written by Théroigne and the Baron de Sélys-Fanson, which he had uncovered in the archives of the latter's grandson. I have made use of these documents in my own account. In addition, Demarteau suggests, on the basis of a remark by the baron, that Théroigne had had incestuous relations with her elder brother, Pierre-Joseph, and that it was this episode which had 'maddened' her. There is no proof of this, however. Even if this detail were accurate, one would still need to know what kind of incest it was. It may well have been an excessive and exclusive love, but who is to say that it was or was not a carnal relation? In any case, this detail tells us nothing that we did not already know about Théroigne's 'cold' sexuality.

On the other hand, these documents prove conclusively that the baron spied upon Théroigne on behalf of the agents of the Emigration. The amiable Belgian chronicler concludes that the poor man paid dearly for his contribution to the cause, since he ended up a victim of the heroine's rapacity. Demarteau thus depicts Théroigne as miserly and incestuous, and as someone who fully deserved the horrible punishment which she was to suffer for twenty-three long years.

FEMINISM OR HEREDITARY DEGENERATIONISM?

In 1853, when Alphonse Aulard was four years old, his path crossed that of one of the last surviving representatives of the Convention. 'Remember, little one', his father said to him, 'what you have just seen: a *Conventionnel*. Store it up in your memory.' Never having heard the word before, the child asked his nanny what a *Conventionnel* was. 'He must be a red', she answered, 'like Monsieur Rivière.' The good woman had often pointed out this republican lawyer with the pleasant face. 'I came to the conclusion', said Aulard, 'that this red had a fine face, and that if a *Conventionnel* was a red, he was nevertheless a good man.'[33]

Thirty years later, Aulard set out, together with a number of others, to found a positive history, which rested upon the return to sources, the criticism of erroneous interpretations and the accurate establishment of facts. For Aulard's generation, history could be reduced to a collection of events, and the historian's task was to pronounce upon the truth or falsity of facts. In 1929, Marc Bloch and Lucien Febvre, the founders of the Annales school, sought to destroy this positivist 'tyranny', which had by that time become a dogma.

However, at the end of the nineteenth century, the issue was primarily one of introducing a 'true' history of the Revolution into the universities. Given Taine's incantations, and the disastrous impact of his widely read writings, a 'positivist tyranny' seemed attractive, necessary even. In order, therefore, to prepare a suitable celebration of the centenary, Aulard founded a review with the title *La Révolution française*. With the support of Alexandre Millerand, a socialist, his campaign for the creation of a course at the

Sorbonne devoted to the founding act of the Republic was also crowned with success. In 1891, the course became a professorial chair.

Ten years later, Aulard published his *Histoire politique de la Révolution française*. In the very same year, Jean Jaurès brought out his own account, which was entitled *Histoire socialiste de la Révolution française*. Claiming kinship both with Marx, for his materialism, with Condorcet, for his intellectual engagement, and with Mirabeau, for his verbal genius, Jaurès also demonstrated the major role of German culture in publicizing the Revolution to the rest of the world. Kant and Fichte had founded 'moral' socialism, and Hegel had been the forerunner of 'dialectical' socialism. Thus, in their inheritance from the Revolution of 1789, German socialism and French socialism had converged. While he was writing his book, Jaurès became aware of the inadequacy of the documents that had been published to date in the domains of social and economic history. This is why, in 1903, he put a bill before Parliament calling upon the government to make the funds available for the creation of an institution responsible for researching into and publishing the archives concerned with economic life under the Revolution. The bill became law. Alphonse Aulard later succeeded Jaurès at the head of this commission, which featured a galaxy of historians.[34]

If Jaurès was the first historian of the Revolution to conceive of it in terms of the economy, socialism and philosophy, Aulard was the first to attribute to the women of this period a pioneering role in the history of feminism. While Michelet had 'sexualized' revolutionary history, Aulard 'politicized' it, so as to accentuate, behind the role of women, that of an original feminism. He formulated his position in an article published in 1898, which was entitled 'Le feminisme pendant la Révolution française', and which ascribed a crucial role to Condorcet.

Inspired by Aulard, in 1900 Léopold Lacour published his monumental work, *Les Origines du feminisme français*, which was devoted both to the origins of French feminism and to its three main heroines, Olympe de Gouges, Théroigne de Méricourt and Claire Lacombe. Not only did he establish the facts, on the basis of archival research, but he also corrected all the errors of the historiography by marshalling all the information then available.

Lacour was the first to unearth the file dealing with the period of Théroigne's confinement. He also quoted extensively from the royalist press and from *Le Moniteur*, commented on the documents from the Bibliothèque nationale, presented valuable information regarding the authenticity or otherwise of the various portraits, made use of the Belgian sources and reproduced a part of the material from the Viennese archives. In short, he brought to light the 'hidden face' of the woman from the Ardennes, and the real part played by her in the origins of feminism.

However, the positivist scouring in which he indulged, no matter how necessary it may have been, was itself informed by yet another mythological construction. By ridding Théroigne of the last vestiges of her legend, Lacour was relying upon a vision of femininity and feminism which accorded with that of his own period.

When we read Lacour, the iconography which springs to mind is no longer that of Raffet or Dewritz, or even Chrétien or Lagrenée, but rather that of Antoine Vestier and Joseph Ducreux.[35] These two painters, each in their own fashion, had invented a Théroigne who was well-suited to serve as an illustration to Lacour's text. Vestier paints a frontal portrait of her, with her powdered hair held by a ribbon. Her dark eyes do not so much suggest a passion in the soul as a languorous state, midway between spleen and vapours. Ducreux, on the other hand, depicts her as a bourgeois woman from the provinces, who takes pride in her appearance. She wears a blue dress, scalloped at the throat and edged with a flounce, which matches both the white belt tied at her stomach and her gauze Charlotte, which is placed on her abundant hair.

If one compares these two portraits with Lacour's account of Théroigne, one will readily appreciate just how far removed such representations are from the 'woman-as-the-people' depicted by Michelet and Dewritz, or from the oriental amazon delineated by Lamartine and Raffet. There is no longer anything 'unrepresentable' about her, as there had been in the prose of the Goncourt brothers; she is not the 'hallucinated' creature of Baudelaire's sonnet, nor is she the 'whisperer' identified by Quinet. Still less does she wallow in the mire, as in Taine's version.

Lacour's punctilious research in the archives seems to recover a Théroigne who is a 'true' woman of the Revolution, dressed according to the fashion of the day. However, though the portraits by Vestier and Ducreux may reflect this truth, on to it another truth came to be grafted, namely, that of the feminism of the first decade of the twentieth century. Lacour thus seems to paint Théroigne in the image of this feminism, as a suffragette of the Belle Époque, part mournful *grisette*, part miniature Madame Roland for the boulevard theatres.

Given this perspective, Lacour has some difficulty in accounting for

Théroigne's madness. He can neither regard it as mere eccentricity, nor interpret it in terms of *déclassement*, nor attribute it to the persecutions of the royalist press. He sees quite clearly that neither before nor during the Revolution had Théroigne presented any explicit symptoms of madness. He also noted that it had been the flagellation which had precipitated her madness. Finally, being ever concerned with accuracy, he never envisaged, quite rightly, attributing this madness to the 'Revolution-as-event'. Théroigne being neither a courtesan nor a criminal, he could not see why her involvement in the Revolution should have led her to the asylum. Even the murderous acting out of 10 August did not convince him.

There remained the organicist hypothesis. Lacour observed that Théroigne was afflicted with a 'strange illness' during her stay in Genoa. But as his knowledge of the Viennese archives was very incomplete, he was unaware, even though he may have had intimations of it, that she had caught the pox. In order to have a clear conscience, Lacour, being a good rationalist, decided to place his trust in the medical science of the day. He therefore asked a brilliant specialist in mental illness for his professional opinion. He showed this man, a Doctor Garnier, the autopsy contained in Esquirol's report. Garnier, who was head doctor at the Infirmerie spéciale du Dépôt, replied as follows:

> The cerebral lesions found in Théroigne's case are in a sense a commonplace feature among insane persons who have lived long years in the most absolute dementia. All that I would venture to say is that Théroigne belonged to the army of unbalanced people who enter the lists in periods of unrest.... She was exalted, as is well known, and she had her red page in history, owing to the effect upon her of morbid cerebral dispositions — possibly hereditary in nature — which were in their initial stage of development during the revolutionary period, which were later exacerbated, and which eventually brought about the complete ruin of her intelligence, which was not lacking in a certain brilliance but which had never had any equilibrium. Théroigne's miscalculations respecting her own popularity could also have served to hasten her irremediable ruin.

This letter seemed to confirm Lacour's hypothesis that Théroigne had been branded with madness by a 'taint' transmitted by her forebears or through an 'illness' contracted at Genoa. However, he refused to let himself be fooled by the idiocies of such a discourse:

Doctor Garnier ended his letter by stating that 'she was a degenerate, but not exactly inferior.' Scientific terminology is a terrible thing. It should also be said that Monsieur Garnier has taken his view of Théroigne's role from the historical preamble to Esquirol's 'observation'. If we had forewarned the doctor, and represented to him the charm and brilliance of the heroine's intellectual faculties, he would still have described her as degenerate, albeit of the superior sort. So men of genius were degenerates ... of a very superior sort. Was there genius in this head, where reason had capsized? That this question can be asked is already a fact of some significance. Unfortunately, however, the legend of the Penthesilea of October being wholly false, the name of the ardent democrat was in reality not connected to any major political fact, aside from the likewise negligible role that she played in the assault upon the Tuileries. Moreover, given the strange nature of her proposals, she only merits a place of the second rank in the history of the origins of feminism.[36]

We can see from Doctor Garnier's hypotheses just how far the French alienism which stemmed from Esquirol had developed. In a single generation, medical discourse on madness had shifted from a situation in which the organicist thesis had some currency, to one in which the theory of heredity and degeneration was dominant. This new configuration had arisen out of an encounter between Antoine Bayle's doctrine on general paralysis and that of Benedict Augustin Morel regarding degeneration. The Frenchman Valentin Magnan effected a synthesis of these two currents, while the Italian Cesare Lombroso applied the approach as a whole to criminology.

In 1822, Bayle identified general paralysis, which he regarded as but one among a range of mental illnesses, and as the culmination of the syphilitic process. This thesis was, however, unanimously rejected at the time, and it was only twenty-two years later that the discovery was recognized for its true worth. Ten years after that, this same discovery occasioned a complete upheaval in the science of mental illness, which had itself been invaded by organicism.

Morel's work may be seen as the a posteriori consequence of Bayle's original discovery. If sexually transmitted illnesses were a major scourge of modern society, a prophylactic which was not merely defensive would be needed to overcome them. It would no longer be sufficient simply to isolate mad persons or dangerous individuals. One would seek, rather, to create a preservative prophylactic by attempting to alter the physical, moral and intellectual conditions of those who might ultimately contaminate others.

Thus, in his *Traité des dégénérescences*, which was published in 1857, Morel placed his theory under the sign of Genesis, for it was the Fall which had set man adrift. Degeneration was thus connected with sin, and it presented itself as an unhealthy deviation from a primitive and normal type of humanity. Every deviation was thus a degradation inflicted upon man by external circumstances. The essence of the primitive type lay in the domination of the physical by the moral or, in other terms, in the subject's acceptance of the moral law or of the conviction of duty in order to arrive at his social destination in a free and reasoned manner, the body being merely the instrument of the intelligence. In mental illness, there occurs an inversion of this hierarchy, which has the consequence of reducing man to the level of an animal and of alienating his mind from the sick organism. But degeneration may be hereditary and therefore threaten one's lineage. The 'germ' was thought to be progressive and would therefore spread, very much in the image of syphilitic illness. When a pathology is transmitted, its effects are exacerbated and the heirs are threatened with a still graver physical ruin. In order to safeguard the normality of the race, Morel recommended the prevention of marriages between degenerates.

One can see here how, after 1860, under the influence of Darwinism, a shift had occurred from an organicist theory of madness to one based upon hereditary transmission. As a consequence, the 'taint' of madness could well exist in 'normal' subjects, as a kind of stigma liable to manifest itself in specific circumstances. Esquirol's clinical theories — or that aspect which had survived in the work of his heirs — were thus entirely subverted by this new configuration, around which Magnan was to organize his doctrine. Magnan's theory turned upon four main principles: the predisposition, or initial state of the degeneration, the disequilibrium, or loss of synergy, the stigmas, or signs of regression, and the episodic syndromes. The idea then arose of individualizing the concept of partial genius, then of showing that genius was a neurosis which shared a common source with madness. There were thus 'superior degenerates' and 'inferior degenerates'. In criminology, Lombroso formulated the notion of the 'born criminal', which enabled one to differentiate between the 'accidental criminal', who was untouched by mental illness and who was therefore responsible, and the 'degenerate criminal', who was judged not responsible for his actions.[37]

Armed with this new terminology, Garnier had ranked Théroigne in the class of degenerates, without having to justify his classification by looking for some organic proof in the autopsy. The crucial reference to heredity enabled him to dispense with any such substratum. But, once he had revived the legend of the 'bloodthirsty courtesan', the doctor became eager to show that the Revolution was itself formed in the image of a degeneration, since it had mobilized a whole army of 'unbalanced persons'. It is easy to guess what this eminent specialist's judgement would have been if he had known of Théroigne's venereal disease. He would have believed that he had found the 'proof' which he lacked, not so much of a general paralysis — for there was none — but of a degeneration, on to which had been grafted all the phantasies characteristic of advanced syphilis.

MELODRAMA AND NEUROSIS

Between 1900 and 1914, owing to Aulard's pioneering works on feminism, and the development of the feminist movement itself, numerous books and articles on the place of women in the French Revolution were published. These studies may not have actually 'rehabilitated' the women of the Revolution, but they did at least promote the serious study of their history, and of the part they had played in the clubs. There thus developed a feminist vision of woman which led to a projection of contemporary preoccupations on to the revolutionary period. Lacour's book created something of a stir, and helped to popularize this conception. The article on Théroigne in the *Grande Larousse* of 1905 reflects this shift of opinion: although it contains a number of errors, Théroigne is no longer seen as a legend; instead, a conscientious attempt is made to present a truthful picture of her life, based upon accurate research in the archives:

THÉROIGNE DE MÉRICOURT (real name, Anne-Josèphe Terwagne); heroine of the French Revolution, born at Marcourt (Belgian Luxembourg) in 1762, died in Paris in 1817. From a family of rich peasants, she left the family home at the age of seventeen, either because of a hostile stepmother, or because she had been seduced by a young nobleman. She went from England to France and held a salon at the rue de Tournon, which Sieyès, Romme, Danton, Mirabeau and Camille Desmoulins attended. She was full of enthusiasm for revolutionary ideas and was present at the storming of the Bastille. From that time on, she became known as 'the Amazon of liberty', and won the admiration of the crowd, though she also attracted the raillery of the journalist Suleau. Her supporters called her *la belle Liégoise*; her red riding-habit and her large plumed felt hat were to be glimpsed at every uprising. From the Cordeliers, she requested the right to a consultative vote at the sessions of the Constituent Assembly, and she offered her jewels, in order to help finance the building of a palace at the Constituent Assembly. Having to leave Paris, she went to Liège, and then to Austria, where she was imprisoned; the emperor spoke with her, and then ordered her release. Upon her return to Paris, she knew a few moments of enthusiastic popularity. On 10 August, she denounced Suleau to the crowd, which tore him to pieces. But she began to preach moderation, at a time when the Mountain was beginning to triumph; she lost whatever influence she had previously had. On 31 May 1793, she was surrounded and whipped by some *poissardes*, on the Feuillants terrace. It has been claimed that she went mad there and then, but this is doubtful. She was confined at La Salpêtrière, where she died. Bibliography: Léopold Lacour, *Trois Femmes de la Révolution* (1900). Paul Hervieu, *Théroigne de Méricourt, drame en cinq actes* (1902).[38]

Thus, regardless of the sort of diagnosis which Garnier had advanced, the public image of Théroigne in this period was not that of a degenerate. This was both because the theory of hereditary degeneration was on the wane when Lacour's book was published, and because the women of the revolutionary period were a particularly attractive topic to a public which was greedy for melodrama, and which lived the Revolution retrospectively as the founding act of the modern republic.

The danger which threatened bourgeois society during the Belle Époque, and which has been so well described by Proust, was not posed by kings, who no longer existed, nor by the Constituents of 1789, nor even by the Girondins and Montagnards, but by socialists, Marxists, proletarians, Jews, foreigners and, finally, the German, who was the hereditary enemy and therefore a focus for hatred and patriotic intolerance. Thus, although the theory of hereditary degeneration was on the wane in the discourse of mental illness, owing to the arguments of Charcot, Janet and Freud, it was as virulent as ever in the social domain. It effectively provided a so-called 'scientific' basis to fundamentally inegalitarian theories of race, and it is well known what use the anti-Dreyfusards made of such arguments in their pursuit of the 'stigma' of Jewishness.

Since the monarchy no longer existed, and since the revolutionary threat was perceived as issuing from another quarter, the kings and regicides of yesteryear could now become the heroes of a great founding drama. The century of Versailles had had its Racine, the English monarchy had had its Shakespeare, why then should the Revolution not have its own dramatist, who would if possible be an Academician?

For a modern sensibility, Théroigne now appeared to be the quint-essential heroine. She had won glory for herself, she had raised herself above her own condition and she had been in the company of the 'great' of this world, whether crowned heads or revolutionaries. In short, she was seen both as an enigma, whose meaning remained masked, and a 'self-made woman' whose merit was now acknowledged. As she also bore a masquerade name, she could be the expression, in the theatre, of the attitudes of the new bourgeois class, which, in aping the manners of the old nobility, through borrowing titles and etiquette, reduced them to nothing more than the deceptive appearances of a social success.

In 1901, shortly after the publication of Lacour's book, Sarah Bernhardt, the famous actress, who was already fifty-seven years old, and had her own theatre, asked an Academician, Paul Hervieu, to write a drama featuring the heroine of the Revolution, in which she herself would play the leading role. The writer accepted and wrote a play in six acts entitled *Théroigne de Méricourt.*[39] It was a very grand production, a triumphant success with sumptuous costumes, the 'Marseillaise' as a fanfare and a huge number of extras.

Hervieu followed Lacour's narrative faithfully, but he added a phantas-magoria which deprived this Aulardian historian's careful work of all credibility. The play was undoubtedly heightened on the stage by the sublime playing of Sarah Bernhardt, who, in her interpretation of Théroigne's madness, had been inspired by Charcot's iconography of hysteria. The text, such as we have it today, is utterly absurd. Nevertheless, it helped to form an image of the heroine — a figure with something of a carnival air, yet still a soul in torment — which was to last for over fifty years.[40]

The first act depicts the meeting between Théroigne and Leopold at the end of 1791. In the corridors of the imperial palace, the good Suleau encounters the wicked La Valette. He refuses to denounce the activities of the supposed spy for, even if he detests her, he is too proud and too noble to stoop to such a deed. Sarah Bernhardt, who is dressed in eighteenth-century fashions but in the taste of the Belle Époque, addresses a sovereign who is straight out of an operetta, and whose eyes, darkened by an excessive use of make-up, were supposed to express the oppressive qualities of the Teutonic mind. Théroigne is represented as a beautiful lady, the incarnation of the nation, and she tries to convince the emperor not to invade French territory, for, if he does, he will have to fight a glorious people, committed to the defence of its liberty. Although persuaded for a brief moment, the sovereign wavers, but then reminds his subject of the 'faults' which she has committed, namely, she has been an unmarried mother and has given birth in a state of sin. Upon hearing these words, Théroigne breaks down and sobs, and complains bitterly about her former predicament as an abandoned courtesan.

In the second act, the scene shifts to the Tuileries on the night of 9 and 10 August 1792. Théroigne does not make an appearance but Marie-Antoinette, dressed in a flounced skirt, serves as a simplified version of the Germanic spirit. Seen as less Teutonic than her brother, she resembles a Princess palatine on a visit to Madame Verdurin. Louis XVI is an ass of a husband, who refuses to wear the protective breastplate made by his wife.

In the third act, it is still the night of 9 and 10 August, but this time we are in Théroigne's salon, in rue de Tournon. This act counterbalances the previous one, with the bourgeois simplicity of the decor contrasting with the outmoded luxury of the tyrants' palace, and symbolizing the rise to power of the new political class. The puppet queen is contrasted with a woman who was queen for just a day. Having become the covert adviser of the leaders of the Mountain, Théroigne attempts, in the presence of Romme and Fabre d'Églantine, to reconcile Danton and Robespierre. The former is depicted as a pleasant buffoon, and the latter as a kind of fugitive, who advocates transferring the Revolution to the South of France in order to regenerate it through contact with 'Latin blood'. He resembles a sort of fervently Christian but leftist Maurras. At this point, Théroigne's idol, Sieyès, comes on stage, represented as an infamous Richelieu, both sinister and cowardly. The heroine suggests that he ascend the throne, and embody beside her the 'radiant' future of the Revolution. He slips away, refusing to sign the 'founding pact of the Republic', by which the assembled Montagnard leaders decide, for good or ill, to call upon the people to rise up. Meanwhile, Pétion, in a state of abject terror, plies back and forth between the deposed king and queen and Théroigne. Théroigne hides the precious pact in her corset at the very moment that Suleau calls in at her house to wrest it from her. At the sight of her enemy, she becomes a Zolaesque heroine and feels 'a beast's ferocious instinct' welling up in her. She checks herself, however, and recovers her human form.

The fourth act is set on the Feuillants terrace on the morning of 10 August. Théroigne urges the crowd not to storm the palace. However, when she learns that the soldiers have opened fire on the people, she hurls herself into the assault upon the monarchy, carrying the enraged populace with her. At first, she tries to stop Suleau being murdered. Then she remembers that it was he who had stolen the famous pact. Reverting to Zolaesque bestiality, she points him out; after the murder, however, she repents bitterly over his corpse.

In the fifth act, which takes place on 15 May 1793, Théroigne, who is by now stricken with remorse, tries to halt the inexorable march of the Revolution towards the Terror. She calls upon Sieyès in order to persuade him to effect a reconciliation between the good Girondins, the 'heirs of the Enlightenment', and the terrible Montagnards, the signatories of the famous pact. The wicked Sieyès slips away again; she describes him as the 'mole of the Revolution' and compares him to Robespierre. Stirred up by the 'former Marquis de Sade', who makes a brief appearance here, some Jacobin shrews then rise up, as if from some infernal Sodom, and assault Théroigne. Marat comes to her aid, pleading indulgence for 'the weakness of an inoffensive sex'. Théroigne falls to her knees and cries out: 'Kill me, but do not degrade me!' The queen for a day is thus dethroned in her turn.

The sixth act is set in La Salpêtrière in 1808. Taking his cue from one of Lacour's hypotheses, Paul Hervieu imagines Sieyès paying a visit to Théroigne in her padded cell. Dressed in a long white straitjacket, she is under the very harsh supervision of one of the women who had whipped her, citizeness Blanchu, now versed in a particular theory of madness which involves a mixture of Esquirolean terminology and the degenerationism of Émile Zola. 'People are mad from birth', she says, 'and it is merely a question of waiting for a pretext for the thing to declare itself.' Sieyès, who is now laden with honours, repudiates the Revolution and parodies the historian Beaulieu's famous sentence: 'There she [Théroigne] now is, the very image of the Revolution. When she first set out, she was dashing and beautiful, then she became a horrible shrew, who has toppled over into absurdity.... Now she is in a cage!' In her delusions, the madwoman conjures up the founders of the Republic, who are disguised as ghosts. Then, confronted with this Aeschylean chorus, she chases the infamous politician from the pantheon of the gods: 'Drive him from the great Convention, where only the dead deserve a place.' The curtain falls.

At the dawn of the twentieth century, Théroigne had therefore become, beneath the dome of the Academy, a modern neurotic who had 'toppled over into absurdity' because of her reprehensible drives. She is also formed in this period in the image of a Republic which, after having 'toppled over' into the bourgeois drama, felt itself threatened on all sides. It felt at risk on its borders from German nationalism (Leopold), in its institutions, because of shady politicians (Sieyès), and in the streets, through the supporters of Maurras (Robespierre). In this respect, it is only too easy to imagine how Hervieu could have come to depict Sieyès as a sordid Richelieu, and Leopold as a carbuncular Bismarck. In his depiction of the former, he took his cue from Dumas, whereas his treatment of the latter was inspired by the prevalent anti-German feeling. On the other hand, it is hard to see what legerdemain could have prompted him to attribute a Maurrasian ideology to Robespierre. One explanation springs to mind. The Academician had no choice but to place the Dreyfus Affair at the heart of the drama, since Sarah Bernhardt had asked him to write it. This was partly because the 'affair' had become the major event of the whole period, and partly because the great tragic actress had stood shoulder to shoulder with Zola in the struggle to rehabilitate Captain Dreyfus. Since he could not put on the stage a character from the Revolution who embodied 'the anti-semitism of the forces', Hervieu had decided to come down heavily upon the Montagnard leader whom he detested the most. This is why he showed no hesitation in making the citizen from Arras a fervent defender of Maurrasian Latinity. But to concoct an imbroglio of this order, the author of the melodrama could not help but 'topple over' into absurdity himself.

As the second movement of dynamic psychiatry was establishing itself on the ruins of hereditary degenerationism, on the basis of works by Emil Kraepelin, Martin Charcot, Sigmund Freud and Pierre Janet, a new terminology, centred on the concepts of neurosis, paranoia and hysteria, began to emerge. Mesmer's intellectual inheritance was reappraised, but the notion of degeneration was maintained, either in order to invoke, as was the case in Zola's writings, a 'heredity', or to signify the hereditary character of the pathology. In contrast to Janet, however, Freud's discovery of the unconscious dealt a fatal blow to the notion of hereditary degenerationism, which collapsed in France around the 1930s.

Although the advance of Freudianism was a factor of the greatest importance in these changes, the works of Eugen Bleuler were also highly influential. Thus, in 1911, the latter coined the term 'schizophrenia' in order to replace the category of dementia praecox. Through these developments, the classical structure of psychiatric and psychoanalytic clinical medicine was established, with the domain of the psychoses on one side (schizophrenia, paranoia, manic-depression), and the domain of the neuroses on the other. Psychosis referred to madness in general, whereas neurosis designated those illnesses which had previously been termed nervous (hysteria, obsession, etc.). Within this new configuration, melancholia enjoyed a paradoxical status. Freud saw the 'sad madness' as linked to the process of mourning, of which it was the pathological form. Whereas, in the process of mourning, the subject succeeds in detaching itself step by step from the lost object, in melancholia it regards itself as guilty for the death that has occurred, denies it and believes itself to be possessed by the defunct person or affected by the illness which led to their death. In short, the ego identifies with the lost object.[41]

The Freudian perspective has the advantage of restoring a formidable vigour to the 'black humour' so vividly described by the Ancients, inasmuch as it views the sad madness as a historical destiny rather than as a sickness associated with a climate, a period or an organic substratum. This perspective has made it possible, in the present work, not so much to explain Théroigne's madness as to understand how her entrance into psychosis occurred, through the loss of the ideal object, the Revolution, with which she had identified, and which, when it had toppled over into the Terror, she had failed to mourn.

We have seen how Hervieu, in drawing his inspiration from Lacour, turned Théroigne into a modern neurotic. However, the writer borrowed the style of the melodrama and the vocabulary of Zola just as the discourse of mental medicine was turning towards the terminology of Charcot, Janet and Kraepelin. When, therefore, Doctors Cabanès, Nass and Guillois began to study revolutionary pathology, much as Descuret, Trélat and Taine had done before them, they too relied upon 'scientific discourse' to reflect upon the Revolution in terms of the category of madness. This time, however, their writings were dominated by terms such as neurosis, hysteria and paranoia.

In reviving the hypothesis that every revolution is a source of madness, these psychiatrists no longer knew how to distinguish the genuinely mad from ordinary neurotics, nor how to theorize the clinical form of each individual madness. Indeed, if the Revolution were in itself a madness, all the protagonists on the revolutionary stage would be authentic madmen. Distinctions were no longer drawn between Marat and Dom Gerle, Théroigne de Méricourt and Charlotte Corday, Robespierre and Catherine

Théot, for each and every one of them were now seen as authentic madmen and madwomen caught up in the torment of the Revolution.

This mode of thinking was a revival of the old Rousseauist argument that women possessed a much greater degree of madness than men. Being judged by their nature more hysterical than men, they therefore appeared by nature to be much more mad than their male equivalents, since the Revolution was likened through its nature to a fit of collective hysteria. One can appreciate what a distortion of the classical doctrine this is, for neither Charcot nor Freud ever uttered such nonsense. Indeed, they were the first to theorize the existence of a male hysteria, in order to wrench this neurosis more effectively from its supposed uterine substratum.

This did not stop Doctor Guillois, in his psychiatry thesis (published in 1904), from describing the unfortunate Olympe de Gouges as 'paranoiac with reforming ideas', and then as a 'hysteric', before proceeding to extend these notions to all the women of the Revolution.[42] A year later, Doctors Cabanès and Nass revived the same old story in *La Névrose révolutionnaire*:

> However, rising above this seething sea, we can identify a few dominant individuals. Out of all these eccentrics, some stood out as still more eccentric. These were the Illuminists, the only persons capable of precipitating revolutionary periods. Need one add that we find them among the women, who are always less balanced than the men, and who have an inborn tendency to exaltation, and to the exaggeration of the affective and imaginative faculties.[43]

After Cabanès and Nass have put Suzette Labrousse and Catherine Théot in the Illuminists' basket, they show no hesitation in including Théroigne de Méricourt, Olympe de Gouges and Claire Lacombe, who are themselves likened to Charlotte Corday. There should be no need to point out that each of these women was wholly different from the others, and that only one of them had actually sunk into madness. Moreover, whereas Suzette Labrousse and Catherine Théot were genuine Illuminists, neither Olympe de Gouges nor Claire Lacombe were. Charlotte Corday was so far from being mad that she refused to allow this label to be pinned to her by the Revolutionary Tribunal, so that she might assume full responsibility for her deed and therefore die on the scaffold 'like everyone else'. Her murderous deed had stemmed from political fanaticism but in no sense could it be attributed to a psychosis, a delusion or a specific 'mental derangement'. Where Olympe de

Gouges was concerned, the two doctors used the term 'zoophilia' to describe her love of animals, as if such a love was irrefutable proof of a genuine perversion.

Nass and Cabanès were therefore interested in Théroigne de Méricourt. But as she had already been duly filed as an 'Esquirolean lypemaniac', they no longer knew quite how to diagnose her. This is why, after having expressed delight at the fact that she had 'toppled over into dementia', they applied the label 'erostratism' to her, a catch-all term, named after a figure from Greek Antiquity. In 356 BC, Erostratus had sought to win fame by burning down the temple of Artemis. He was burned in his turn, and anyone who mentioned his name would themselves be put to death:

> We shall merely recall that Théroigne was a victim of events; if it is not accurate to claim that the shame of being publicly whipped was the precipitating cause of her madness, we can at least argue that the amazon's reason foundered totally because of the tragic events in which she had been involved. She was the fly on the wheel of the Revolution, getting tipsy from her own buzzing. She toppled over into dementia; much like those young girls who, in their games, turn round faster and faster until they come crashing down, their heads all in a spin, from whirling their skirts round in the 'cheese-making' game. This wretched madwoman, who was also afflicted with *erostratism*, and who believed herself to be the glorious instigator of the risings of October and of 10 August, did at least have her story told by a writer who caused her lustreless personality to gleam in the footlights. Paul Hervieu has shown us an enthusiastic Théroigne, genuinely embodying patriotism and republicanism, whose unbalanced nature was not apparent in the popular tumult which, on the evening of 9 August, led to the sack of the Tuileries, nor on that memorable day when the *tricoteuses* whipped the over-zealous Girondin. This is a character put on the stage by the dramatist, who recalls a few of the heroine's features, but who is still very far removed from reality.[44]

So it was that in 1905 Théroigne was, on the one hand, an anti-Marie-Antoinette, bathed in the glory of her French nationalism, and, on the other, a hysterical female, part Marat, part whirling dervish.

After the First World War, the women of the Revolution disappeared altogether from the discourse of mental medicine. In France, through the initiative of the *Évolution Psychiatrique* group, a great boost was given to the

Freudian discovery and to the organization of madness in terms of the ideals of dynamic psychology. Pinel's gesture was once again a matter of contemporary relevance, and was regarded as an authentically revolutionary act; the legend of abolition as a utopia was at long last to be realized. It was no longer necessary for the Revolution to be catalogued in terms of madness, since the study of the recent war traumas made it possible to elaborate a genuine theory of trauma. In a word, Marat's madness, or the affairs of original feminism, were no longer of abiding interest to psychiatrists. And when a form of psychobiography of Freudian inspiration developed, it was very little concerned with revolutionary France.

After Jaurès's contributions had brought about a change in the scholarly study of the French Revolution, there was a tendency to concentrate upon economic and social problems, notably in the works of Albert Mathiez and Georges Lefèbvre. Although there were exceptions,[45] historians in general had ceased to regard the women of the Revolution as an object of specific interest, even though their role was recognized. The problem had not been annulled, but there had been a change of perspective; the topic no longer seemed to be part of the preserve of historians of the Revolution, and was now treated by specialists in women's questions, who integrated the revolutionary period within a general history of feminism, conceived in a long-term perspective.[46] In short, in the period after 1914, the advances made by Aulard were to prove more fruitful for the opening up of a special field devoted to the history of women than for a renewal of the study of the women involved in the revolutionary saga.

It is worth noting, in passing, Jaurès's complete silence on this question. In his *Histoire socialiste de la Révolution française*, he neither mentions the names of the main heroines of original feminism nor the positions adopted by Condorcet, although he studied the history of the *enragés* at great length, and although his attitude towards the feminist movement of his own time was identical with that of the philosopher at the beginning of the Revolution. In 1912, in an article in *L'Humanité*, he called for a debate on the subject of women's rights in the Chamber. Two years later, he insisted that it was

> humanity as a whole that should act, think and live, and it is quite mistaken
> to fear that the granting of women's suffrage would give more power to the
> forces of reaction, for it is their passivity and their servitude which has
> weighed upon human progress.[47]

It may be that, at the time he was writing his history of the Revolution, he had not yet pondered the women's question in sufficient depth, and that he preferred to abstain altogether rather than to handle the subject in too frivolous a manner. It should also be noted that, after the great suffragette meeting of 1910, it became a matter of some urgency for him to take a position within the socialist camp, in which many were still markedly hostile to the idea of giving the vote to women.

Although, in the interwar period, the women of the Revolution ceased to be a topic of interest to mental medicine, and although original feminism was less and less part of revolutionary historiography, one can readily understand why Théroigne de Méricourt's fate should still have provided raw material for phantasies. Aside from scholarly history and romantic biography, two works were published between 1930 and 1939, one in Belgium and the other in Austria. The former, entitled *La Vie trépidante de Théroigne de Méricourt*, was written by the Ardennais author Georges Laport, who compiled an inventory of all the Belgian documents and presented the heroine as akin to La Traviata, thus reviving the melodramatic vision of her presented by Hervieu. The latter, written by Otto Ernst, uncovered for the first time a pile of valuable documents drawn from the Austrian State Archives and made known, save for a few details, almost the whole of the file concerned with her trial at Kufstein. However, being more than a little in love with his heroine, Ernst could not resist making her play a role which she never had. He therefore depicted her as a sublime vamp, whose beauty set alight the hearts of the 'great men' of history. The Aulic councillor threw himself at her feet, stricken with love for her, the emperor Leopold threw himself into her arms and old Kaunitz cast lustful glances at her. Otto Ernst declared his own, posthumous passion for her:

> Every author is a little in love with his heroine. I must confess to this also but, for excuse, my pretext is — inelegant though it may seem — that my heroine would today be one hundred and seventy years old, whereas at the time she was but twenty-seven.[48]

The emphatic character of this declaration explains why the author is careful not to mention Théroigne's venereal disease.

In the aftermath of the Second World War, the heroines of the original feminism crossed a kind of desert. For twenty or so years, they aroused virtually no interest, either as legends or as objects of study for historical scholarship. Evidence of this is supplied by the negative judgement of them passed by Gérard Walter in his critical edition of Michelet. This excellent historian ridicules the three women whom Lacour had studied, and ascribes his interest in them to Michelet's own eccentric concerns. He admits that he is not really competent to judge these matters, but he describes Olympe de Gouges as a 'hysterical quadragenarian, whose widowhood seemed to have weighed somewhat heavily upon her'. Likewise, Claire Lacombe is seen by him as 'impulsively fantastical', and a woman who 'sank finally into absurdity' after she had importuned Robespierre.[49] Walter, who was plainly very frightened by sexual matters, saw hysteria not as an ordinary neurosis but as a uterine affair. These remarks would seem to reflect, at least implicitly, the hostility which this sympathetic historian felt towards psychoanalysis during the 1950s, at a time when the Freudian discovery was scoring direct hits on the ideals of the French far left. His attitude towards Théroigne seems to have been neutral, and he made no allusion at all to her madness.[50]

It was not until the 1960s that the heroines of early feminism once more aroused the interest of scholars. This time, it was almost exclusively women who took up the pen to pay homage to those who now seemed to them to have been the mothers of radical feminism.[51] Two perspectives were in evidence within this new configuration. The first took its inspiration from Mathiez's works on Robespierre, and from Albert Soboul's studies of the Paris *sans-culotte* movement, and sought to place the emphasis, in terms of class struggle, upon the study of revolutionary women citizens. The latter then seemed to be the most advanced representatives of revolutionary femininity.[52] Conversely, the second focused on all of the women of the period, in order to conceive of the Revolution in terms of a struggle between the sexes. Imbued with radical feminism, this second tendency overturned the classical argument about inegalitarianism, by opposing a supposed feminine nature, which had always been devalued, to a hypothetical masculine nature, which was always inflated by a phallocratic narcissism.[53]

In either case, accurate archival research had served to 'rehabilitate' the women of the Revolution. Although this was clearly a major step forward, it had entailed an exclusively feminine representation of the condition of such women during the Revolution. Théroigne de Méricourt was sometimes depicted as a pioneer, because of her involvement in the activity of the clubs, and sometimes as a victim, because she had suffered throughout her life.[54]

Today, she has therefore lost almost all the radiance of her legend, and is only mentioned as a 'bird of passage' in almost all of the works devoted to the famous figures of the Revolution, but she is tending to disappear altogether from the encyclopaedias and the general dictionaries.[55] In the context of a psychohistory, she is depicted as having served as a support for formidable sexual projections, much like Marie-Antoinette, or as having projected herself upon the ideals of 1789.[56] Posterity readily forgives her for her deed of 10 August, on account of her tragic fate, and sees her as the quintessential symbol of a Revolution which devours its own children. If mention at all is made of her 'presence' during the October Days, it is almost always left an open question as to whether she was in fact there at all.[57] Aulard's sand-blasting exercise has therefore borne fruit, to a greater extent than one could ever have hoped for.

Nowadays, it is rare indeed for a writer to place Théroigne at Versailles, at the head of a squadron of 'proletarian amazons', or to describe her, in hackneyed terms, as a 'priestess of Eros, who, for want of a lover, became the mistress of liberty'.[58]

Epilogue

Epilogue

Beneath the snow, the village seems to have preserved intact the signs of its memory. There are no advertisement hoardings, no businesses and no neon lights. The history of the countryside seems frozen in a motionless time, rather like the madness of the asylum, in which one could endlessly inscribe the unfolding of past events. Marcourt is an abandoned relic.

For household goods and everyday purchases, the inhabitants of Marcourt visit La Roche-en-Ardenne, an interesting medieval town which was rebuilt in 1944. The 'Nature and Health' park, designed for walking, is a made-to-measure green space, with Hungarian boars and convalescent deer. A placard refers to La Boverie. There is no sign of the White Cross Inn. In summer, this ill-defined area becomes a camping-site. A handful of white caravans, sunk deep in the snow, remind one of holiday rituals, of hunting, fishing, swimming and visits to the caves.

As I look at the guide-book, I reflect that the abduction of January 1791 did not happen here, but in the Parc de la Boverie, which is now part of the town of Liège, to the south of an island watered by the river Meuse. Xhoris is some dozens of kilometres away, and Stavelot is further still. Apollinaire spent the summer there in 1899, at the Hôtel du Mal Aimé. What was he doing in Théroigne's country? Did he even know of her existence? Had he read 'Sisina'?

Olivier came with me to Marcourt, bringing his daughter, little Hélène. The *Journal des Enfants* had asked her to write an account of her journey. Why Belgium? What relation was there with the Bicentenary? Did the Revolution happen at Marcourt? Who was this 'Trémoigne'? What were women's rights? Are dotty people sent to asylums? The answers to these questions proved to be interlocking. I thought of my mother's death, of the *Union des femmes françaises*, in which she was involved for a period, after the war. I thought of my aunt too, who had been a suffragette in the very early days. I thought of my other aunt, who had emigrated from Romania, and who spoke several different languages. I thought of Françoise Dolto, who was not afraid to die. I had never needed to be 'feminist', since all the women who had featured in my childhood had already been so. Fortunately. The women's struggle has ended. The Revolution is over. I sent a postcard to my god-daughter Alice. I sent another card to my friend Élisabeth Badinter, who had insisted that I make the journey to Marcourt.

Had Théroigne been schizophrenic or manic-depressive? The terminology matters little. Mourning and melancholia have no need of science. I feel that I have invented everything, and that I have pondered over the celebration of a *trompe l'oeil* bicentenary and of a nostalgic centenary. Which had I been concerned with, Revolution or psychoanalysis? Had I been searching for Freud behind Pinel, and for Ferenczi after Mesmer? It would be claimed nowadays that this whole story had simply been a question of 'neurones' and of the power of the media.

The dominant memory at Marcourt was of the horrors of war. In September 1944, the patriots of the Belgian Resistance had pitched camp above Marcourt, with a view to linking up with the American army, which was stationed at Hotton. At the crossroads, on the La Roche road, they attacked two enemy machine-gun carriers. The first was destroyed, but the second managed to escape. For some time afterwards, the head of a decapitated soldier was to be seen in a sunken road, a grim symbol of this final struggle against barbarism. The German retaliation was terrible. Troops marched into the village and set fire to thirty-odd houses. Prisoners were burnt alive in an old barn. Each year, on 9 September, friends and relatives gather in a votive chapel, to remember the massacre.

Théroigne, the patriot of yesteryear, has never been associated with this celebration.

In Hodister, which is in the mountains, Noëlle Mormont lives surrounded by her memories. She is a lovely old lady, a former teacher who is familiar with Théroigne's story. In order to remind the inhabitants of Marcourt of their ancestors, she has written a chronicle, in which she describes the circumstances and deeds of the two local celebrities. Before Théroigne, there had been Evrard Mercurian, general of the Jesuit order. His surname encompassed Marcourt, which was derived from the Latin Mercurium and Mercury, god of journeys and of communication. It is a curious repetition: two children of this 'mercurial' village — the Jesuit Mercurian and the Amazon of Méricourt — had won glory by escaping and conquering the world in search of a new faith.

We took Noëlle to visit Marcourt cemetery. I inspected every grave, hoping to find some inscription, date or portrait which might conjure up the presence of the Terwagnes. There was nothing, no shadow or shade, not even the slightest trace of this huge family. Even the dead have disappeared.

The presbytery was inhabited by a private person, who rented it from the parish. Every Sunday, the only *curé* in the area did his rounds, celebrating several masses on the same day. Those with a religious vocation are rare, and the faithful are elderly. Nevertheless, the church is in very good repair, with a baroque choir, pious images and ultra-modern heating. The main door overlooks some waste-ground, flanked by some huts serving as a tourist information bureau. With René Moureau as our guide, we visited the tawdry corrugated-iron structure in which this sympathetic man struggled to harvest a few fragments of local culture. He proudly showed us Anne-Josèphe's original baptismal certificate, which was kept under glass. Suddenly, Hélène asked where 'Trémoigne' had lived, where her house and that of her parents had been. It had been on that very spot, opposite the church, where the tourist information bureau now was.

The house had changed hands several times in the course of the nineteenth century until finally, in 1873, at the request of Houba, the *curé*, it had been demolished. He felt that it was attracting too many visitors. By effacing the last living trace of the amazon, the priest had sought to banish all record of the Revolution from human memory. He believed that archives were silent, forgot that a church document could restore Théroigne's legal existence, in the very place where it had been destroyed. Did he perhaps dream at night of Michelet's imprecations? Did he fear the spread of a new contagion, coming from France, from Liège or from the Brabant? Did he perhaps see the great Sabbath of the Bastille danced beneath his windows? History does not tell us. But, at Marcourt, aside from a baptismal certificate, Théroigne is nowhere to be found.

Notes

Notes

In my reconstruction of Théroigne de Méricourt's life, I have used the following sources: (1) Manuscript sources held by the Bibliothèque nationale and by the Archives nationales in Paris. (2) Alexandre Tuetey, *Répertoire des sources manuscrites de la Révolution Française*, 1890–1914, I, IV, IX. (3) Unpublished documents from the State Archives in Vienna, complemented by those already published in Otto Ernst, *Théroigne de Méricourt*, Paris, 1935, and in Ferdinand Strobol von Ravelsberg, *Les Confessions de Théroigne de Méricourt, la fameuse amazone révolutionnaire*, Paris 1898. (4) Printed sources from Belgian historiography: Warlomont, 'Notice sur Théroigne de Méricourt', *Annales de la Société pour la conservation des monuments historiques dans la province du Luxembourg*, 1852–53; Thomas Fuss, 'Théroigne de Méricourt, dite "la belle Liégoise"', an extract from the *Bulletin de la Société scientifique et littéraire du Limbourg*, Liège 1854; Joseph Demarteau, 'Théroigne de Méricour' [*sic*], unpublished letters, prison, jewellery', *Revue générale*, new series 2, Brussels 1882; Felix Magnette, 'Théroigne de Méricourt, la belle Liégoise, légendes littéraires et réalitiés historiques', *Wallonia*, XXIᵉ Année, March 1913; Théodore Gobert, 'Documents inédits', *Bulletin de l'Institut archéologique liégeois*, vol. 44, 1914, p. 131; J. Falise, 'Théroigne de Méricourt', *Bulletin de la Société royale du vieux Liège*, 57, April 1939, pp. 420–24; Marcel Florkin, 'Episodes de la médecine liégeoise. Caractère, démence et phrénologie de Théroigne de Méricourt', *Revue médicale de Liège*, vol. XIII, 1958, pp. 854–6; Usmard Legros, *Le Double Destin de Théroigne de Marcourt dite de Méricourt*, Hovine, Marquain, 1969. (5) Printed sources from French historiography: Marcellin Pellet, *Étude historique et biographique sur Théroigne de Méricourt*, Paris 1886; A. Grégoire, *Mémoires de l'exécuteur des hautes oeuvres, pour servir à l'histoire de Paris pendant le règne de la Terreur*, Paris and Brussels 1830 (republished, n.d., Paris); Marc-Antoine Baudot, *Notes historiques*, Paris 1893; Restif de la Bretonne, *Année des dames nationales*, BN Y²62097 62099; Léopold Lacour, *Les Origines du feminisme français. Trois femmes de la Révolution, Olympe de Gouges, Théroigne de Méricourt, Claire Lacombe*, Paris 1900; Maurice Dreyfous, *Les Femmes de la Révolution*, Paris 1903. Finally, I consulted F. Hamel, *A Woman of the Revolution*, n.d., BN 8° LN 2782540, and I plundered the royalist press. I have not had access to a number of English sources, but these will be used by Helga Grübitzsch in a book due to appear soon in Germany. This work should shed light on Théroigne's life in England on the eve of the Revolution. Other works will be referred to in the course of the narrative. Philippe Raxhon's work on Belgian historiography is also due to be published shortly: *La Révolution liégeoise de 1789 et les Historiens belges de*

1805 à nos jours, 2 vols, and *Théroigne de Méricourt 'la belle Liégeoise', les traces du souvenir, les supports d'une légende, la naissance d'un mythe dans l'histoire belge.*

I THE CONQUEST OF LIBERTY

1. Henri Pirenne, *Histoire de la Belgique*, Brussels 1900–32, 7 vols. See also Jean Jaurès, *Histoire socialiste de la Révolution française*, Paris 1970, 6 vols and an index, with presentation and commentary by Albert Soboul.

2. Jules Michelet, *Les Femmes de la Révolution*, in *Oeuvres Complètes*, Paris 1980, vol. XVI, with an introduction by Mireille Simon. See also, by the same author, *Histoire de la Révolution française*, Paris 1952, 2 vols, with presentation and commentary by Gérard Walter.

3. Now rue Hérold. Prior to this date, Théroigne lived in rue Bourbon-Villeneuve, which is now rue d'Aboukir.

4. Ernst, p. 89. The work is based upon some unpublished documents drawn from the secret archives of the house of Austria.

5. Jean-Paul Bertaud, *Camille et Lucile Desmoulins*, Paris 1985, p. 40.

6. Ernst, p. 75.

7. The description of her face is taken from Baudot, and that of her hands and feet from the executioner, see ibid.

8. Quoted by Lacour, p. 140. The full text of the contract between the Marquis and Théroigne is reproduced in Gobert.

9. Von Ravelsberg, p. 178.

10. For further information on Tenducci, see Pierre Villiers, *Souvenirs d'un déporté*, Paris 1803. For the contract, see Vienna State Archives, second list in Théroigne's portfolio, Konvolut III, unpublished.

11. Vienna State Archives, three doctors' letters, 6 January 1788, 14 May 1788, 23 March 1789, Konvolut I, unpublished.

12. Pellet, p. 14, together with a document from the Consulate in Genoa, dated 2 March 1789, BN : n.a.f. 1308.

13. Lacour, p. 150.

14. See Pierre Roussel, *Système physique et moral de la femme*, 1775; Y. Knibiehler and C. Fouquet, *La Femme et les Médicins*, Paris 1983; Paul Hoffmann, *Le Femme dans la pensée des Lumières*, Strasbourg 1976; Pierre Darmon, *Mythologie de la femme dans l'ancienne France*, Paris 1983.

15. Poullain de la Barre, *De l'égalité des deux sexes*, 1673.

16. See Élisabeth de Fontenay, 'Pour Émile et par Émile, Sophie ou l'invention du ménage', *Les Temps modernes*, 358, May 1976; Élisabeth Badinter, *Émile, ou l'ambition féminine au XVIIIe siècle*, Paris 1983. See also M. Albistur and D. Armogathe, *Histoire du feminisme français*, Paris 1977.

17. See Élisabeth and Robert Badinter, *Condorcet, un intellectuel en politique*, Paris 1988.

18. J.-P. Bertaud, *En France au temps de la Révolution*, Paris 1985, p. 207.

19. Alphonse Aulard, 'Le feminisme pendant la Révolution Française', *La Revue bleue*, 12, March 1898, pp. 361–6.

20. See Jacques Godechot, *Les Institutions de la France sous la Révolution et l'Empire*, Paris, 1968.

21. Madame Roland, letter to Bancal, quoted by Paul-Marie Duhet, *Les Femmes et la*

Révolution 1789–1794, Paris 1977, p. 78.

22. See Edmond et Jules de Goncourt, *La Femme au XVIIIᵉ siècle*, with a preface by Élisabeth Badinter, Paris 1982.

23. On the subject of melancholy, see Jean Starobinski, 'La mélancholie au jardin des racines grecques', *Le Magazine littéraire*, 244, July–August 1987; *Histoire du traitement de la mélancholie dès origines à 1900*, Geigy SA, Switzerland, November 1960; Marie-Claude Lambotte, *Esthétique de la mélancholie*, Paris 1984; Aristotle, *L'Homme de génie*, with preface and introduction by J. Pigeaud, Paris 1988; Julia Kristeva, *Le Soleil noir de la Mélancholie*, Paris 1987; 'Tradition de la mélancolie', *Le Débat*, 29, March 1984.

24. Quoted by Benedetta Craveri, *Madame du Deffand et son monde*, Paris 1987, p. 99.

25. On Mesmer, see H. Ellenberger, *A la découverte de l'inconscient*, Villeurbanne 1974; Jacques Postel, *Genèse de la psychiatrie*, Paris 1981; Robert Darnton, *Mesmerism and the End of the Enlightenment*, Cambridge, Mass. 1968. In order to move his fluid, Mesmer used a tub, around which twenty or so people would sit. A rope served to establish communication between the tub and one of these persons, and then with each of the others in turn.

26. Condorcet, *Oeuvres complètes*, published by A. Condorcet, O'Connor and M.F. Arago, Paris 1847–49, vol. IX, pp. 1–93 and vol. VIII, pp. 115–659.

27. Condorcet, *Oeuvres complètes*, vol. VIII, p. 141.

28. *Cahiers de doléances des femmes*, Paris 1789 (republished Paris 1981), p. 28. Hostility towards prostitutes may in part be explained by the fact that during this period men were encroaching upon trades which had up until then been regarded as exclusively feminine. This gave rise to unemployment and prostitution among women.

29. Ibid., p. 47.

30. Michelet, *Histoire de la Révolution française*, vol. 1, p. 266.

31. Emmanuel Sieyès, *Qu'est-ce que le Tiers État?*, presented by Roberto Zapperi, Geneva 1970. See also J.-D. Bredin, *Sieyès, la clé de la Révolution française*, Paris 1988.

32. Albert Soboul, *An I de la liberté*, Paris 1973, p. 24.

33. Ernst, p. 89.

34. Michelet, *Histoire de la Révolution française*, vol. 1, pp. 248, 280.

35. Ernst, p. 90. The *Dictionnaire des rues de Paris*, Paris 1964, vol. 2, suggests that Théroigne would have been living at No. 5, at the Hôtel du Bouloir. However, in her *Confessions*, she mentions the Hôtel de Grenoble, rue du Bouloir, which is now rue de Bouloi.

36. *Histoire de la révolution par deux amis de la liberté*, Paris 1791–1803, vol. VIII, pp. 77–8.

37. Ernst, pp. 91–2.

38. J.-P. Bertaud, *Les Amis du roi*, Paris 1984, 29. For information on the whole of the movement, see Jacques Godechot, *La Contre-Révolution*, Paris 1984.

39. Bertaud, *Les Amis du Roi*, p. 24.

40. Ibid., p. 25.

41. Ibid.

42. *Les Actes des Apôtres*, November 1789. It was published in Paris between 1789 and 1791 [BN, 8⁰ LC² 273]. The term 'Arcades' is an allusion to the Palais-Royal, which was known as a haunt for prostitutes.

43. *Théroigne et Populus*, A.A, 24 and 38.

44. Quoted by Pellet.

45. Quoted by Ernst, p. 256. The Bishop of Autun was Talleyrand.

46. Quoted by Alessandro Galante Garrone, *Gilbert Romme, histoire d'un révolutionnaire, 1750–1795*, Paris 1971, pp. 203–4.

47. Ibid. Romme was to commit suicide with a dagger, on 17 June 1794, together with the last of the Montagnards.

48. Ibid; A. Soboul, in *Romme et son temps*, Proceedings of the Conference held at Riom and Clermont in June 1965, Paris 1966.

49. Quoted by Pellet, p. 39.

50. The monastery of the Feuillants, located on rue Saint-Honoré, on the axis of place Vendôme, was decreed national property on 2 November 1789.

51. Garrone, p. 208.

52. Ibid., p. 211.

53. Ibid.

54. Minutes of the session of 13 January 1790. Ibid., p. 449.

55. See Godechot, *Les institutions de la France*, and Tulard, Fayard, Fierro, *Histoire et Diction-naire de la Révolution Française*, Paris 1987.

56. Condorcet, 'Adresse à l'Assemblée du 20 Avril 1790', published in the *Journal de la Société de 1789*; Robespierre, 'Discours du 5 juin 1790', in *Discours et Rapports*, Paris 1908, p. 87.

57. Minutes, quoted by Garrone, pp. 455–7.

58. Godechot, p. 54; See also D. Feuerwerker, *L'Émancipation des Juifs de France de l'Ancien Régime à la fin du second Empire*, Paris 1976.

59. Minutes of 29 January 1790, quoted by Garrone, p. 258.

60. See Godechot, pp. 59–65.

61. Minutes of 29 January 1790, quoted by Garrone, pp. 451–2.

62. Unpublished letters of Augier and Chalier, in the Vienna State Archives, Konvolut III, and an undated note of Marat, mentioned in the 2nd list of Théroigne's portfolio, unpublished.

63. Minutes of the session of 31 January 1790, quoted by Garrone.

64. Vienna State Archives, 2nd list of Théroigne's portfolio Konvolut III, unpublished.

65. Ernst, p. 94.

66. Ibid., pp. 92–3.

67. Camille Desmoulins, *Les Révolutions de France et de Brabant*, 14, 27 February 1790.

68. Ibid., quoted by Lacour and Pellet. In 585, several bishops at the Council of Mâcon had questioned whether woman in fact belonged to the human species. They thought her inferior to man and doubted whether Jesus had died for her. After some discussion, they decreed that women did not form part of the animal kingdom.

69. Lacour, p. 202.

70. The le Châtelet proceedings are included in the Viennese archives. See also Tuetey, *Repértoire des sources manuscrites*, I, 1009 and 1039. There is a fairly complete commentary in Pellet, and in Lacour.

71. Ernst, p. 95.

72. See Louis Devance, 'Le feminisme pendant la Révolution française', *Annales de l'histoire de la Révolution française*, vol. 49, 299, 1977, pp. 351–76.

73. Condorcet, 'Sur l'admission des femmes au droit de cité', *Journal de la Société de 1789*, 5, 3 July 1970, pp. 1–13, BN: 8⁰ LC²402. See also A. Dessens, *les Revendications des droits de la femme au point de vue politique, civil, économique, pendant la Révolution*, law thesis, Toulouse 1905.

74. Baron Marc de Villiers, *Histoire des clubs de femmes et des legions d'amazones, 1793–1848–1871*, Paris 1910.

75. Ibid., pp. 43–44.

II EXILE AND RETURN

1. The term 'Belgian' referred at this period to the northern part of the Imperial Low Countries.

2. See letters published by Demarteau; Dreyfous, p. 132; Laport, p. 50; von Ravelsberg, p. 127.

3. List of objects taken from Théroigne, together with documents, Konvolut III, Vienna State Archives, unpublished.

4. Letter of 21 January 1791, quoted by Ernst, pp. 19–20.

5. Letter of 21 February 1791, quoted by Ernst, p. 42.

6. *Le Journal général*, 28 February 1791, quoted by Pellet, p. 68. This newspaper was founded by Fontenai and appeared between 1 February 1791 and 10 August 1792. BN : 3 vol. 4 Lc² 538.

7. *Actes des Apôtres*, 257.

8. *Catechisme libertin*, republished in 1799, BN: Reserve 51.

9. *Le Moniteur*, 10 April 1791.

10. Letter quoted by Demarteau, pp. 861–2; manuscript letter of Pierre Terwagne, April 1791, BN : n.a.f. 1308.

11. Letter of Kaunitz to F. de Blanc, 9 May 1791, quoted by Ernst, pp. 59–61.

12. Letter of de Blanc to Kaunitz, 30 May 1791, Ernst, pp. 197–8.

13. See von Ravelsberg.

14. 2nd list of letters, Konvolut III, Vienna State Archives, unpublished.

15. Letter of de Blanc to Kaunitz, 3 June 1791, Ernst, p. 200.

16. Letter of de Blanc to Kaunitz, 3 June 1791, Ernst, p. 201.

17. Letter of de Blanc to Kaunitz, 3 June 1791, Ernst, p. 202. The *Statements and Admissions* are reproduced in their entirety in Ernst.

18. Minutes of 2 July 1791, Ernst, p. 146.

19. Ernst, p. 128.

20. Minutes for 27 June 1791, Ernst, p. 127.

21. Minutes for 6 July 1791, Ernst, p. 159.

22. Ibid.

23. Ibid., p. 164.

24. The text is reproduced in its entirety in ibid., pp. 166–73.

25. Ibid., p. 168 (emphases added).

26. Ibid., p. 169.

27. Ibid., p. 173.

28. Ibid., pp. 189–90.

29. 2nd list of Théroigne's portfolio, Konvolut III, Vienna State Archives, unpublished.

30. De Blanc's report to Kaunitz, Ernst, p. 208.

31. Letter of Kaunitz to de Blanc, 4 August 1791 and of de Blanc to Kaunitz, 6 August 1791 October 1791, Ernst, pp. 213, 215.

32. Letters of Théroigne to Kaunitz and to de Blanc, 4 October 1791 and 6 October 1791, Konvolut V, Vienna State Archive, unpublished.

33. De Blanc's proposals to Kaunitz regarding Théroigne's possible release, 7 October 1791, Ernst, p. 235.

34. Ernst, p. 236.

35. Letter of Kaunitz to Metternich, 23 November 1791, ibid., p. 243.

36. *Schlitter Briefe des Erzherzögin Marie Christine auf Leopold II*, Vienna 1896, p. 211, quoted by Pirenne, p. 277.

37. See Demarteau.

38. Letter of Théroigne to Perregaux, BN: n.a.f. 1308.

39. Pellet, p. 75; Legros, pp. 75; Legros, pp. 75, 100–1.

40. Quoted by Pellet, pp. 76–7.

41. Jaurès, *Histoire socialiste*, vol. 2, p. 75.

42. *Actes du colloque Girondins et Montagnards*, Sorbonne 14 December 1975, edited by Albert Soboul, *Société des études robespierristes*, Paris 1980, p. 19.

43. J. Chaumie, ibid., p. 51; E. and R. Badinter, pp. 372–3.

44. Tulard, Fayard, Fierro, p. 81.

45. A. Aulard, *L'Éloquence parlementaire pendant la Révolution française*, Paris 1982, p. 249, and E. and R. Badinter, pp. 372–3.

46. Robespierre, 'Discours du 5 juin 1790', p. 125.

47. Villiers, *Histoire des clubs.*

48. Michelet, *Les Femmes de la Révolution*, p. 247; Villiers, *Histoire des clubs*, p. 49; and A. Aulard, *Histoire politique de la Révolution française*, Paris 1909, pp. 88–90. At this date, Condorcet also thought in terms of a Republic, see E. and R. Badinter.

49. *Les Révolutions de Paris*, 5 February 1791. See also Aulard, 'Le feminisme pendant la Révolution Française'.

50. Villiers, *Histoire des clubs*, p. 39.

51. *Cahiers de doléances*, p. 205.

52. On Olympe de Gouges, see Lacour. She had never read Condorcet.

53. *Cahiers de doléances*, pp. 211–12.

54. *Journal des débats et de la correspondence de la Société des amis de la Constitution*, 4 February 1792. See Lacour, p. 254.

55. *Journal des débats et de la correspondance de la Société des amis de la Constitution*, 4 February 1792, and Lacour, p. 253.

56. Michelet, *Histoire de la Révolution française*, vol. 1, pp. 877–8.

57. *Le Journal général*, 6 March 1792. The Marquis de Vilette was commonly assumed to be a hermaphrodite.

58. Quoted by Pellet.

59. On the liaison between Basire and Etta Palm, see Lacour, and Marie Cerati, *Le Club des citoyennes républicaines révolutionnaires*, Paris 1966.

60. BN : L³³e3xt1, quoted by Lacour. Upon the women's *sans-culotte* movement, the best source is Dominique Godineau, 'Les femmes des milieux populaires parisiens pendant la Révolution française (1793–Messidor Year III)', history doctorate supervised by Michel Vovelle, University of Paris I, 1986, This thesis has been published under the title *Citoyennes tricoteuses*, Aix-en-Provence 1989.

61. Published originally by the Goncourt brothers, *Portraits intimes du XVIIIᵉ siècle*, Paris 1856.

62. See Baron de Villiers, *Reine Audu*, Paris 1917.

63. *Les Sabbats jacobites*, 65, April 1792, a newspaper belonging to Marchant. See André Martin and G. Walter *Catalogue de l'histoire de la Révolution française*, Paris 1943. *La Chronique de Paris* featured Condorcet as its chief correspondent. See Lacour, pp. 368–70.

64. A. Aulard, *La Société des Jacobins*, Paris 1889–95, vol. III; Legros, p. 115; Lacour, pp. 266–7.

65. The abbé Bouyon's newspaper was originally called *A deux liards, à deux liards*, then *A deux liards, à deux liards, mon journal*. The title page each month featured 'One month's madnesses at two *liards* a day'. The abbé Bouyon was murdered at the same time as Suleau. See below.

66. *Actes des Apôtres*, 119.

67. Lacour, p. 275; Pellet, pp. 90–2; Michelet, *Histoire de la Révolution française*, vol. 1, pp. 443–57. The eighth verse of the 'Marseillaise' is devoted to this event. Bouillé was also responsible for the Flight to Varennes.

68. Michelet, *Histoire de la Révolution française*, vol. 1, p. 875; Jaurès, *Histoire socialiste*, vol. 1, p. 840 and vol. 2, p. 251.

69. Jaurès, *Histoire socialiste*, vol. 2, p. 271; E. and R. Badinter, pp. 400–5.

70. *Journal des débats et de la correspondence de la Société des amis de la Constitution*, April 1792. E. and R. Badinter, pp. 405–7.

71. Michelet, *Histoire de la Révolution française*, vol. 1, p. 865.

72. Pellet, pp. 93–4; Ernst, p. 262; Legros, p. 118.

73. *Journal de la Cour et de la Ville* or *Petit Gautier*, 16 May 1792. This paper was published between 16 September 1789 and 10 August 1792. See also Lacour, p. 280.

74. Charles François Dumouriez, *Mémoires du general Dumouriez écrits par lui-même*, Paris 1794, vol. 2, p. 78.

75. *Journal de Suleau*, 13 April 1792. This paper ran for only thirteen issues, between April 1791 and April 1792. BN : 8LC² 588–589 A and B and Reserve: 8LC² 589, in octavo.

76. Quoted by Tulard, Fayard and Fierro, p. 93.

77. Jaurès, *Histoire socialiste*, vol. 2, p. 551.

78. Jean Renoir's film, *La Marseillaise* (1938) narrates this episode from the Revolution, which lasted from 22 June to 10 August, through the story of the Marseillais *fédérés*.

79. Police report A.N.F.⁷ 4387, and Tuetey, *Repertoire des sources manuscrites*, IV, 752 (20 June).

80. Quoted by Bertaud, *Les Amis du roi*, p. 235.

81. The manifesto was not in fact composed by Brunswick himself. Louis XVI had commissioned the Genevan journalist Mallet du Pan to draft it at the time of his departure from Paris in April 1792. But the final draft was the work of a French emigré. The Duke would seem to have been unaware of the phrase which threatened Paris and, upon his learning of it, he tore up the document, without however repudiating it. See Jaurès, *Histoire socialiste*, vol. 2, p. 683.

82. BN : L³³et 3x; quoted for the first time by Lacour, p. 324.

83. See Bertaud, *Les Amis du roi*, p. 249. And L. Meister, *Un champion de la royauté au début de la Révolution française: Suleau*, Beauvais 1909, p. 280. On the *journée* of 10 August, see M. Reinhard, *La Chute de la royauté*, Paris 1969.

84. In *Le Tocsin de la nécessité*; Bertaud, *Les Amis du Roi*, p. 196.

85. J.-G. Peltier, *Le Dernier Tableau de Paris ou récit historique de la Révolution du 10 août*, London 1793, pp. 102–3. On Peltier himself, see Hélène Maspero-Clerc, *Un journaliste contre-révolutionnaire: J.G. Peltier (1760–1825)*, with a preface by Jacques Godechot, *Société des études robespierristes*, Paris 1973.

86. Baron General Thiébault, *Mémoires*, vol. 1, Paris 1893–95. Thiébault describes what Théroigne was wearing on the day of 10 August, and all subsequent accounts would rely on his description, together with that of Peltier. The identities of the five other victims are unknown. See also Dreyfous, p. 146. Citizen Paul Bonjour, attached to the fourth division of the Ministry of the Navy, was denounced in Frimaire Year II by the Poissonière popular society, not so much for being employed as first footman of the former Monsieur, as for having kept the demeanour and manners of 'a heart corrupted by aristocracy'. See A. Soboul, *Les Sans-culottes parisiens en l'an II*, Paris 1962, p. 409.

87. *Le Moniteur*, 28 August 1792.

88. Beaulieu, *Essais historiques sur les causes et les effets de la Révolution*, Paris 1801–02, vol. 2,

p. 54.

    89. Quoted by Legros, *Le double destin*, p. 157.

    90. Maton de la Varenne, *Histoire particulière des événements qui ont eu lieu pendant les mois de juillet, août et septembre 1792*, Paris 1806.

III HISTORY OF MADNESS

    1. Alphonse Aulard, *Le Christianisme et la Révolution*, Paris 1925.

    2. *La Chronique de Paris*, 31 August 1791; quoted by Badinter, p. 475.

    3. Tulard, Fayard and Fierro, p. 103.

    4. Théroigne's name does not feature in the list of participants in the massacre compiled by Granier de Cassagnac in 1860, *Histoire des Girondins et des massacres de septembre*, vol. 2, pp. 502–16.

    5. On this topic, consult Pierre Caron, *Les Massacres de septembre*, Paris 1935.

    6. *La Chronique de Paris*, 4 September 1792, quoted by Badinter, p. 475.

    7. Jaurès, *Histoire socialiste*, vol. 3, pp. 100–2.

    8. Ibid., p. 259.

    9. Ibid., p. 265.

    10. Ibid., p. 258.

    11. Michelet, *Histoire de la Révolution française*, vol. 1, p. 1132.

    12. Quoted by Lacour, pp. 289–90. See also Pirenne, and *Occupants et Occupés 1792–1815*, a conference held at Brussels, 29 and 30 January 1968, Brussels 1969.

    13. A letter reproduced in facsimile by Pellet.

    14. A letter reproduced by Demarteau, p. 874. It was signed 'La citoïenne Théroigne, rue Saint-Honoré, no 273, près des Jacobins'.

    15. Quoted in its entirety by Lacour from a document in the Archives nationales.

    16. Edgar Quinet, *La Révolution*, Paris 1987, pp. 350–1. On Quinet's discussion of Théroigne, see part IV.

    17. An anecdote recounted by Dreyfous and by Lacour.

    18. For the whole of this period, see Godineau.

    19. See *La Mort de Marat*, Paris 1986, a collective work, and J. Guilhaumou's essay in particular.

    20. Villiers, *Histoire des clubs*, p. 224.

    21. See G. Rudé, *The Crowd in the French Revolution*, London 1967, pp. 114–16.

    22. The term *tricoteuses* referred to those women who used to assemble beside the guillotine and knit, or to follow the tumbril; the *flagellantes* were women who used to whip their political adversaries in public.

    23. See Godineau, 'Les femmes des milieux populaires' and Jaurès, *Histoire socialiste*, vol. 5, p. 281. The term *enragé* had referred from 1789 to extremists, and from 1790 to the Jacobins. However, in February 1793, it designated popular leaders who called for measures against the rising cost of living.

    24. See Aulard, *Histoire politique de la Révolution française*, p. 288, and E. and R. Badinter, p. 534, 537.

    25. BN : Lb⁴¹ /2981 in 8⁰. See also Devance.

    26. BN : 8⁰ R 5648. And Godineau 'Les femmes des milieux populaires', vol. II, pp. 799, 802.

27. A. Aulard, *Histoire politique de la Révolution française*, p. 289.

28. Villiers, *Histoire des clubs*, and Godineau, 'Les femmes des milieux populaires'.

29. BN : L^b40, 2411 and Villiers, *Histoire des clubs*, p. 239.

30. For the chronology of the club, see Godineau, 'Les femmes des milieux populaires', vol. II, pp. 440–2.

31. BN : L^b41–4940. This is the first complete publication of this document.

32. Michel Vovelle, *La Mentalité révolutionnaire*, Paris 1985, p. 185.

33. Michelet, *Histoire de la Révolution française*, vol. 2, p. 543.

34. Lenôtre, *Paris révolutionnaire*, Paris 1928, pp. 91–101.

35. *Histoire de la Révolution par deux amis de la liberté*, vol. VIII, p. 200.

36. Although the details differ somewhat, the same narrative is given by Lacour, Pellet, Dreyfous and Legros.

37. Quoted by E. and R. Badinter, p. 560.

38. AN : F^IV 1470 and AF^II 45, no. 351. See Also Tuetey, *Répertoire des sources manuscrites*, IX, 597, 13, and 598, I. See also Ch. A. Dauban, *La Démagogie en 1793 à Paris*, Paris 1868, pp. 189–90.

39. Quoted in its entirety by Lacour and Legros. This version is also given in Maurice Barras, *Mémoires*, introduced by G. Duruy, Paris 1895–96, p. 121.

40. Restif de la Bretonne, p. 3807.

41. A detail from Louis Léopold Boilly's painting, 'Triomphe de Marat', see list of illustrations.

42. *La Mort de Marat*, and Godineau, 'Les femmes de milieux populaires'.

43. Document published by Demarteau, p. 853, and used again by Lacour, p. 298.

44. See D. Godineau, 'Vision de la participation collective des femmes à la Révolution française (93–Year II)', conference at the University of Paris VII, CNRS, Paris 1985.

45. Godineau, 'Les femmes des milieux populaires', vol. II, p. 538.

46. Legros, p. 139.

47. Godineau, 'Les femmes des milieux populaires', vol. II, p. 549.

48. The Amar report is printed in another thesis by D. Godineau, 'Subsistance et Politique, les femmes du Fg. Saint-Marcel et Saint-Marceau (sept 93–messidor an II)', supervised by A. Soboul, Paris 1979–80.

49. Duhet, p. 206.

50. *Les Révolutions de Paris*, 216, 29 Brumaire Year II, and Lacour, pp. 3 and 4.

51. Godineau, 'Les femmes des milieux populaires', vol. II, p. 677. On the many different causes for this ban, see also J. Godechot, review of the book by P.-M. Duhet, *Annales historiques de la Révolution française*, 1971, pp. 635–6.

52. The entire file dealing with Théroigne's arrest and confinement may be found at AN : F^7 4775^27. It consists of fifteen documents in manuscript, and was mentioned for the first time by Lacour. A certificate dated 14 Vendémiaire Year III shows that Nicholas-Joseph Terwagne was seeking to protect himself: 'This is to certify that citizen Joseph Terwagne owner of the laundry "toile du clos payen" is an upstanding citizen who enjoys the trust of his fellow citizens, and that we have heard of no complaint regarding him, etc.'

53. Mentioned for the first time by Pellet and published in its entirety by Lacour, on the basis of the Benjamin Fillon exhibition. I have not managed to trace the original.

54. Saint-Just, *Oeuvres complètes*, Paris 1984, pp. 698–707.

55. Quoted by Lacour, p. 305.

56. Villiers, *Souvenirs*, p. 225.

57. Entry, exit and death certificates, Documentation et Archives de l'Assistance publique, Cote I Q2 132, 10 I 114,3 Q2 34.

58. Jean Colombier and François Doublet, *Instructions sur la manière de gouverner les insensés*, 1785. See Marthe Henry, 'La Salpêtrière sous l'Ancien Régime', thesis in medicine, Le François 1902.

59. See Louis Boucher, 'La Salpêtrière de 1656 à 1790', thesis in medicine, Paris 1883, and René Semelaigne, *Les Pionniers de la psychiatrie française avant et après Pinel*, Paris 1932, vol. 1, p. 127.

60. Étienne Esquirol, *Des maladies mentales*, Paris 1938, 2 vols, vol. 1, p. 447. Lacour suggests that the visitor may have been Sieyès.

61. Quoted by Pellet, p. 117.

62. Ibid., p. 119; letter of 28 April 1808, delivered 18 May.

63. See Georges Gusdorf, *La conscience révolutionnaire des Idéologues*, Paris 1978.

64. See Monique Dumas, 'E. Esquirol, sa famille, ses origines et ses années de formation', thesis, Toulouse 1971, and C. Regnier, 'Sort de l'insensé et évolution de la médicine aliéniste pendant la Révolution française', thesis in medicine, Paris VI 1983; *La Loi de 1838 sur les alienés*, Paris 1988, 2 vols; Gladys Swain, *Le Sujet de la folie, naissance de la psychiatrie*, Toulouse 1978; J. Postel and C. Quetel, eds, *Nouvelle histoire de la psychiatrie*, Toulouse 1983.

65. See the quotation from Barère in the exergue, dated 23 messidor Year II. This statement was made at a time when hospital property was being sold. The Girondins had tended to be suspicious of the organization of a national system of medicine because they feared that it would involve imposing a state framework upon the poor. The Montagnards, on the other hand, were in favour.

66. P. Pinel, *Variété (Révolution)*; *Journal de Paris*, 18 January 1790, quoted by Postel, pp. 196–7.

67. P. Pinel, *Traité médico-philosophique sur l'aliénation mentale ou la manie*, reprint of the first edition of 1800, Geneva and Paris 1980.

68. See Paul Bercherie, *Les Fondements de la clinique*, Paris 1987.

69. In particular, Louis Daquin, *La Philosophie de la folie*, Paris 1987.

70. Quoted by R. Semelaigne, 'Philippe Pinel et son oeuvre au point de vue de la médecine mentale', thesis in medicine, Paris 1888, p. 166.

71. P. Pinel, *Traité de l'aliénation*, pp. 235–7.

72. Esquirol, *Des maladies mentales*.

73. Georges Gabriel, *Portraits de criminels et d'aliénés*, BN : Na 58 4[0], works AA[1] and Jf 29. See also the plates to Esquirol, *Des maladies mentales*, vol. II, and C. Quetel and P. Morel, 'Art et Folie, Littérature, médecine, société', University of Nantes, 6, 1984.

74. Portrait of Théroigne by Gabriel, see list of illustrations.

75. Esquirol, *Des maladies mentales*, vol. 1, p. 43.

76. Ibid., pp. 1 and 2. For the whole of this period, see G. de Berthier de Sauvigny, *Au soir de la monarchie*, Paris 1955.

77. Quoted by Swain, p. 155.

78. Esquirol, *Des maladies mentales*, vol. 2, p. 446.

79. Postel, p. 51; For the renewal of the myth as a founding act, see Michel Foucault, *Histoire de la folie à l'âge classique*, 2nd edn, Paris 1972.

80. Two profiles by Louis Chrétien, after a drawing by Fouquet dated 1792. The carved wooden medallion is in the Curtius museum in Liège. The physionotrace, invented by Chrétien, enabled one to reproduce a model by tracing and then to reproduce it mechanically on the pantograph. For the profiles, see the list of illustrations.

81. Professor Pierre Morel advanced the hypothesis that it was a schizophrenia of the 'circular' type. This deduction was based upon the extreme length of Théroigne's confinement. Marcel Florkin, in 1958, preferred to think in terms of manic-depressive psychosis.

82. Esquirol, *Des maladies mentales*, vol. 1, pp. 445–51.

83. Marcel Florkin ('Episodes de la médecine liégoise') was the first to mention this cast, and to publish the plate (see list of illustrations). On Dumoutier, one should consult E.H. Ackerknecht, 'Dumoutier et sa collection phrénologique du musée de l'Homme', *Bull. soc. d'anthropologie*, vol. VII, pp. 289–308. And *Collections anthropologiques du Museum*, vol. III, *Aliénés, idiots*, musée de l'Homme, Paris, pp. 363–5.

84. Published by Varicléry, Paris 1936, BN: Y²71332–71323.

85. See also Robert Castel, *L'Ordre psychiatrique*, Paris 1978; *Moi, Pierre Rivière*, Paris 1973; and Yannick Ripa, *La Ronde des Folles*, Paris 1986.

86. Lamothe-Langon, *La jolie Liégoise*, vol. II, pp. 56–7.

87. Ibid., p. 58.

88. J.B. Descuret, *La Médicine des passions*, 2nd edn, Paris-Lyons, 1844, pp. 758–65.

IV THE HISTORIOGRAPHY OF THÉROIGNE

1. Adolphe Thiers and Pierre Mignet brought out the first volumes of their histories in 1823, whereas those of Carlyle, Tocqueville and Quinet appeared in 1837, 1856 and 1865 respectively. Michelet's work was published between 1847 and 1853. Lamartine's *Histoire des Girondins*, first published in 1847, appeared in an English translation by H.T. Ryde, in three volumes, in 1847. Louis Blanc's *Histoire de la Révolution française*, was published in twelve volumes, Paris 1847–62. On this subject, see Jacques Godechot, *Un jury pour la Révolution*, Paris 1974.

2. A. Aulard, in the various works mentioned above.

3. Among the works not yet mentioned: Dulaure, *Esquisses historiques des principaux événements de la Révolution française*, Paris 1823–24; Lairtullier, *Les Femmes célèbres de 1789 à 1795*, Paris 1840; Adolphe Mathieu, *Théroigne de Méricourt, poème et prose*, Paris and Mons, 1847–48; Auguste Barthélemy, *Douze Journées de la Révolution*, 1832; Emmanuel des Essarts, 'L'amazone du 20 Juin', *Poèmes de la Révolution française*, Paris 1879; Baron de Stassart, *Bulletin du bibliophile belge*, vol. 7, 1848, p. 461; A. Dumas, *La Comtesse de Charny*, Paris 1860.

4. All the biographies have been mentioned. For the theatre and for mental medicine, see below. V. Blasco Ibanez wrote a novel about Théroigne entitled *La Belle Liégoise*, Paris 1903.

5. Michelet, *Les Femmes de la Révolution*, pp. 353–563.

6. J. Michelet, *Journal*, Paris 1976, vol. II, p. xi.

7. R. Barthes, *Michelet*, trans. R. Howard, Oxford 1987.

8. Michelet, *Les Femmes de la Révolution*, pp. 402–5. In his *Histoire de la Révolution française*, Michelet attributes Théroigne's humiliation to the Montagnards, but here he merely uses the pronoun *on*. For a comparison between the two texts, see the table drawn up by M. Simon on pp. 491–555. For a commentary on the portrait, see below.

9. Godechot, *Un jury pour la Révolution*.

10. See J.-P. Jacques' preface to Lamartine, *Histoire des Girondins*.

11. Lamartine, *History of the Girondists*, vol. I.

12. Ibid., vol. I.

13. Ibid., vol. I, pp. 490–2; vol. II, pp. 68–70.

14. Blanc, *Histoire de la Révolution française*, vol. 3, pp. 218–19 (1852); vol. 6, p. 24 (1854); vol. 7, pp. 70–1 (1855); vol. 8, p. 357 (1856). The English historian mentioned here is Carlyle.

15. Michelet, *Histoire de la Révolution française*, vol. 2, p. 1224.

16. Portrait of Théroigne by Louis Lagrenée, see list of illustrations.

17. Lacour, p. 108.

18. Ibid., p. 104.

19. Quinet, pp. 118–19.

20. Works by the Goncourt brothers published between 1858 and 1862.

21. Badinter, Preface.

22. Ibid., p. 40.

23. Edmond and Jules Goncourt, *Portraits intimes*, Paris 1856, pp. 166–92.

24. Anonymous portrait, see list of illustrations.

25. Raffet's drawing, see list of illustrations.

26. *Poems of Baudelaire, a translation of 'Les Fleurs du mal'*, trans. Roy Campbell (with modifications), London 1952.

27. Legros noticed this detail in Baudelaire.

28. H. Taine, *Les Origines de la France contemporaine*, Paris 1986.

29. Ibid., vol. 1, pp. 707, 719, 822; vol. 2, pp. 97, 100, 102, 105, 116.

30. See, in this respect, Godechot, *Un jury pour la Révolution*.

31. Taine, *Les Origines de la France contemporaine*, vol. 1, pp. 379, 383, 385, 586, 696; vol. 2, p. 109.

32. See Fuss, and J. Demarteau.

33. Told by Godechot, *Un jury pour la Révolution*, p. 233.

34. Aulard, *Histoire politique de la Révolution française*, Jaurès, *Histoire socialiste*.

35. Portrait of Théroigne by Antoine Vestier, see list of illustrations. Another portrait by Pierre-Nicolas Selles depicts her as a woman of the period, but somewhat more harshly, and with an air of madness reminiscent of certain works by Goya. See list of illustrations.

36. Lacour, pp. 309–12.

37. On these questions, see E. Roudinesco, *Histoire de la psychanalyse en France, la bataille de cent ans*, Paris 1986, vol. I.

38. Quoted by Legros, pp. 157–8. In spite of all the inaccuracies of this article, there is no cause to doubt the truth of the story.

39. Paul Hervieu, *Théroigne de Méricourt*, Paris 1902. Photographs of this production were published in *Le Théatre*, 98, special issue devoted to the play, January 1903. For Sarah Bernhardt in the part of Théroigne, see list of illustrations.

40. For the polemics occasioned by the play, see Vicomte de Reiset, *Le Carnet*, 1903, followed by an exchange of letters with L. Lacour in February and April. See also Armand Bourgeois, *Théroigne de Méricourt et le Marquis de Saint-Huruge*, Paris 1903.

41. S. Freud, 'Mourning and Melancholia', in *Standard Edition*, vol. XIV, London 1957, pp. 243–58.

42. Guillois, *Étude médico-psychologique sur Olympe de Gouges, considérations générales sur la mentalité des femmes pendant la Révolution française*, Paris 1904.

43. Nass and Cabanès, *La Névrose révolutionnaire*, Paris 1905, pp. 343–4.

44. Ibid., pp. 366–9.

45. Jeanne Bouvier, *Les Femmes pendant la Révolution*, Paris 1931, and Yvonne Bruhat, *Les Femmes de la Révolution française*, Paris 1939.

46. See Léon Abensour, *Histoire générale du feminisme, des origines à nos jours*, Paris 1921.

47. Albistur and Armogathe, p. 380.

48. Ernst, p. 7.

49. Michelet, *Histoire de la Révolution française*, vol. 2, pp. 1427 and 1467.

50. Ibid., vol. 2, p. 1574.

51. Only one text during this period reopened the question of Théroigne's madness,

namely, Florkin.

52. The first work to discuss this issue was M. Cerati, *Le Club des citoyennes républicaines révolutionnaires*, Paris 1966, which was originally a dissertation for a diploma, supervised by Mathiez (prior to 1932), then revised and corrected thirty years later, under the supervision of Albert Soboul. For the same perspective, twenty years on, see Godineau, 'Vision de la participation collective'.

53. This perspective is typified by Duhet and Ripa.

54. Legros carried out a survey, in 1969, of the works which had appeared up until that date.

55. She features neither in the *Petit Robert* nor in the *Encyclopaedia Universalis*. The heroines of original feminism are not mentioned in the *Dictionnaire de la Révolution française*, Paris 1988, but they are all mentioned in the forthcoming *Dictionnaire historique de la Révolution française*.

56. See Vovelle, and J.-C. Bonnet, ed., *La Carmagnole des muses*, Paris 1988, which contains some interesting allusions to Théroigne's relations with the Assembly.

57. In Tulard in particular.

58. Guy Chaussinand-Nogaret, *Mirabeau*, Paris 1981, p. 181.

Chronology

Chronology

1731	Birth of Pierre Terwagne.
1732	Birth of Anne-Élisabeth Lahaye.
1743	Birth of Etta Lubina Johanna Aelders, subsequently Etta Palm.
1745	Birth of Philippe Pinel.
1748	Birth of Sieyès and of Marie Gouze, subsequently Olympe de Gouges.
1750	Birth of Gilbert Romme.
1754	Birth of Marie-Jeanne Phlipon, subsequently Manon Roland.
1758	Birth of Louise Robert-Kéralio.
1761	Marriage of Pierre Terwagne and Élisabeth Lahaye.
1762	Publication of *Émile*, by Jean-Jacques Rousseau. Birth, on 13 August, of Anne-Josèphe Terwagne, later known as Théroigne de Méricourt.
1764	Birth of Pierre-Joseph Terwagne.
1765	Birth of Claire Lacombe.
1767	Birth of Nicolas-Joseph Terwagne. Death of Élisabeth Lahaye.
1768	Birth of Pauline Léon.
1767-73	Théroigne lives with her aunt, and in a convent.
1772	Birth of Étienne Esquirol.
1773	Marriage of Pierre Terwagne and Thérèse Ponsard.
1778	Arrival in Paris of Franz Anton Mesmer. Théroigne meets Madame Colbert.
1782-9	Théroigne's liaison with her English lover, relations with the Marquis de Persan. London–Paris.
1784	Pinel and Mesmer meet.
1786	Death of Pierre Terwagne.
1787	Publication of Condorcet's *Lettres d'un bourgeois de New Haven sur l'inutilité de partager les pouvoirs législatifs entre plusieurs corps*.
1788	Death of Théroigne's daughter. Publication of Condorcet's *L'Essai sur la constitution et la fonction des assemblées provinciales*.
1789	Théroigne's journey to Italy.

1789

1 JANUARY	The women of the Third Estate petition the king.
5 MAY	Opening session of the Estates-General.

11 May	Return of Théroigne to Paris.
9 July	The National Assembly adopts the name of Constituent Assembly.
14 July	The storming of the Bastille.
17 July	Royal visit to Versailles. Théroigne is present, dressed as an amazon.
20 July	The 'Great Fear' begins.
4 August	Abolition of privileges.
18 August	Insurrection in Liège.
20 August	Théroigne moves to Versailles, in the rue de Noailles.
26 August	Proclamation of the Declaration of Rights of Man and the Citizen.
7 September	Artists' wives come to offer their jewels to the Constituent Assembly.
12 September	Marat launches his newspaper.
5 October	The women's march on Versailles.
6 October	The king brought back to Paris.
19 October	The Assembly is established in Paris, in the salle du Manège. Théroigne now lives in rue du Bouloi.
22 October	The Assembly rules that the vote will be granted only to 'active citizens'.
24 October	Insurrection in Brabant. The Belgian insurgents proclaim their country independent, and declare that the emperor Joseph II's sovereignty is null and void. Brissot takes part in the insurrection.
2 November	First issue of the *Actes des Apôtres*.
9 November	First session of the Assembly to be held at the Manège.
10 November	First of the attacks which the Apostles directed at Théroigne.
11 December	The court of Le Châtelet commences proceedings against those who had made an attempt on the queen's life during the October Days.

1790

11 January	Proclamation at Brussels of the 'United States of Belgium'.
10–15 January	Théroigne and Gilbert Romme found the *Société des amis de la loi*. Théroigne is still hounded by the Apostles.
18 January	Article by Pinel on the Revolution.
20 January	Sieyès's report on the liberty of the press.

25 JANUARY	Robespierre's motion at the Assembly regarding the rights of the active citizen.
28 JANUARY	The Jews are granted civil rights.
4 FEBRUARY	The deputies swear the civic oath before the king. Théroigne is present.
13 FEBRUARY	Suppression of monastic vows.
20 FEBRUARY	Death of the Emperor Joseph II. Théroigne's reception at the Cordeliers Club. She calls for the building of a temple of the nation on the ruins of the Bastille. Her speech is transcribed by Camille Desmoulins.
15 MARCH	*Droits d'ainesse et masculinité* abolished.
16 MARCH	*Lettres de cachet* abolished.
18 MARCH	At Brussels, the 'Vonckists' are defeated by the conservative supporters of Van der Noot.
20–30 MARCH	The *Société des amis de la loi* closes.
27 MARCH	Article 9 of the law: 'Those persons who are detained on the grounds of dementia will be interrogated by the judges, examined by doctors and, if they are found to be mad, will be treated in hospitals.'
30 MAY	Decree on the elimination of begging and on the creation of *ateliers de charité*.
3 JULY	Condorcet: *Sur l'admission des femmes au droit de cité*. Discussion on this topic begins in the Assembly.
14 JULY	Festival of the Federation.
27 JULY	The revolution in Brabant is crushed.
AUGUST	Warrant for Théroigne's arrest issued by the court of Le Châtelet.
OCTOBER	Claude Dansard founds the *Société fraternelle des amis de la Constitution*. Théroigne returns to Marcourt, Xhoris and Liège. Baron de Sélys-Fanson spies on Théroigne, and passes on what he discovers to emigré agents.
22 NOVEMBER	Austrian troops occupy Belgium.
20–26 NOVEMBER	Etta Palm delivers a series of speeches at the *Cercle social*, which was founded by the abbé Fauchet.
21 DECEMBER	The Assembly, 'mindful of all that it owes to the memory of J.-J. Rousseau', decrees that: 'A statue to the author of *Émile* and of the *Social Contract* will be raised, and it will bear the following inscription: "The free French nation to J.-J. Rousseau …" Marie-Thérèse Levasseur, widow of J.-J. Rousseau, will be kept at the state's expense …'.

1791

12 JANUARY	Austrian troops occupy Liège and reinstate the prince-bishop.
15 JANUARY	Théroigne is abducted by French aristocrats.
5 FEBRUARY	Beginning of the anti-feminist campaign waged by the *Révolutions de Paris*.
MARCH	Etta Palm founds the *Société des amies de la vérité*, the first exclusively feminine club.
9 MARCH	Théroigne leaves for Kufstein.
2 APRIL	Death of Mirabeau.
15 MAY	Decree granting Blacks resident in the colonies equal rights to whites. Slavery, however, is maintained.
28 MAY	Arrival of Aulic councillor François de Blanc at Kufstein.
30 MAY	Robespierre proposes the abolition of the death penalty at the Assembly.
20 JUNE	The Flight to Varennes.
22 JUNE	The king is arrested.
25 JUNE	The king returns to Paris.
26 JUNE	The Marquis de Bouillé is declared responsible for the flight of the king.
6 JULY	Leopold II invites the sovereigns of Europe to join with him in declaring war upon France, and to make Louis XIV's cause their own.
8 JULY	At the Jacobin Club, Condorcet declares himself to be in favour of the Republic.
15 JULY	The National Assembly declares the king inviolable. The people take a petition calling for his overthrow to the Champ-de-Mars.
17 JULY	Popular demonstration on the Champ-de-Mars. La Fayette opens fire on the demonstrators.
21 JULY	'Those who are guilty of letting the insane or the demented or dangerous or ferocious animals wander at large' will be liable to prison sentences.
15–30 AUGUST	Théroigne is transferred to Vienna.
27 AUGUST	The Pillnitz Declaration.
4 SEPTEMBER	The Constitution of 1791.
15 SEPTEMBER	Law of amnesty.
SEPTEMBER	Olympe de Gouges: *Les Droits de la femme et de la citoyenne*.
EARLY OCTOBER	Théroigne meets Prince Kaunitz.
2 OCTOBER	The new legislative body declares itself to be the National Legislative Assembly.

5 OCTOBER	The National Legislative Assembly suppresses the words 'Sire' and 'Majesty' and confirms that the title of king of France is to be replaced with that of king of the French.
END OF OCTOBER	Théroigne meets Leopold II.
14 NOVEMBER	Pétion is elected mayor of Paris.
25 NOVEMBER	The Legislative Assembly sets up a watch committee (*comité de surveillance*).
12 DECEMBER	Robespierre's first speech against the war.
28 DECEMBER	Decree on the organization and formation of battalions of volunteers.

1792

EARLY JANUARY	Théroigne returns to Paris, lives in rue de Tournon.
17 JANUARY	Brissot urges the Assembly to declare war upon the German emperor.
JANUARY–FEBRUARY	The royalist press subjects Théroigne to violent attacks.
1 FEBRUARY	Théroigne recounts the story of her persecutions at the Jacobin Club.
1 MARCH	Death of Leopold II. His son, Francis II, succeeds him.
6 MARCH	The women of Paris, Pauline Léon among them, mount a petition calling for the levying of women's battalions.
7 MARCH	The Duke of Brunswick is appointed Major-General of the Austrian troops.
15 MARCH	Dumouriez is appointed Minister of Foreign Affairs.
23 MARCH	Louis XVI summons the Girondin ministers.
25 MARCH	Théroigne's speech at the *Société fraternelle des Minimes* on the need for battalions of amazons.
1 APRIL	Etta Palm advocates equality for women at the Assembly.
14 APRIL	The National Assembly decrees: 'The French nation renounces its intention of embarking upon any war of conquest and will never employ its forces against the liberty of any people.'
15 APRIL	Festival of Liberty in honour of the Swiss of Chateauvieux, organized by David, on Théroigne's initiative.
20 APRIL	France declares war upon the 'King of Bohemia and Hungary' (Francis II).
21 APRIL	The Assembly orders the printing of Condorcet's draft plan for education. The *Révolutions de Paris*'s anti-feminist campaign continues.

23 APRIL	Collot d'Herbois attacks Théroigne.
25 APRIL	At Strasbourg, Rouget de Lisle composes and sings his 'War song for the Army of the Rhine', which in July was to become the 'Marseillaise'.
23 MAY	Brissot denounces the 'Austrian committee' at the Assembly.
8 JUNE	Muster of 20,000 *fédérés*, who camp outside the walls of Paris.
12 JUNE	The king sacks the three Girondon ministers. Dumouriez becomes Minister of War.
17 JUNE	A deputation from the Croix-Rouge section appears before the Assembly and accuses Louis XVI of treason.
20 JUNE	The people of Paris invade the Tuileries and force Louis XVI to don the red cap. During the night, Théroigne helps to prepare the insurrection.
30 JUNE	La Fayette leaves Paris. He is burnt in effigy at the Palais-Royal.
11 JULY	The fatherland is declared to be in danger.
17 JULY	The *fédérés* present a petition to the Assembly calling for the suspension of the king.
25 JULY	Claire Lacombe makes a declaration at the bar of the Assembly, advocating the arming of women.
28 JULY	Paris learns of the existence of the *Brunswick Manifesto*.
29 JULY	At the Jacobin Club, Robespierre calls for the overthrow of the monarchy.
30 JULY	The Marseillais battalion arrives in Paris.
10 AUGUST	The fall of the monarchy. The French people storm the Tuileries. Théroigne initiates the killing of Suleau, and plays a part in the capture of the Tuileries. A decree passed by the Assembly invites the French people to form a National Convention, and declares the king provisionally relieved of his functions.
11 AUGUST	Calling of the primary assemblies. Suppression of the distinction between active and passive citizen. Danton becomes Minister of Justice.
16 AUGUST	The *armée du Nord* beats a retreat. The enemy invades France.
19 AUGUST	La Fayette goes over to the Prussians.
21 AUGUST	The guillotine is set in motion.
22 AUGUST	Insurrection breaks out in the Vendée.
27 AUGUST	The primary elections begin. Universal male suffrage in two stages.
30 AUGUST	Divorce is made legal.
1 SEPTEMBER	Verdun capitulates.

2 SEPTEMBER	Beginning of the September Massacres in Paris. Théroigne plays no part in them.
9 SEPTEMBER	Marat is elected to the Convention as deputy for Paris.
20 SEPTEMBER	Bombardment of Valmy. Women are granted the right to testify in civil cases.
21 SEPTEMBER	Abolition of the monarchy. Opening session of the National Convention.
22 SEPTEMBER	Year I of the French Republic.
25 SEPTEMBER	The Girondins accuse Robespierre of aspiring to be dictator.
24 OCTOBER	The French army invades Belgium.
6 NOVEMBER	Battle of Jemappes. The Austrians withdraw from Belgium.
13 NOVEMBER	First debates on the trial of Louis XVI. Saint-Just's maiden speech.
14 NOVEMBER	The French army enters Brussels.
28 NOVEMBER	Dumouriez enters Liège.
4 DECEMBER	A number of Belgian deputies plead the cause of their country's independence at the bar of the Convention.
12 DECEMBER	The Convention accepts Tronchet, de Sèze and Malesherbes as council for the king's defence. Olympe de Gouges offers to assist Malesherbes.
15 DECEMBER	Decree concerning the treatment of Belgium, which was to be followed by several decrees of annexation.

1793

JANUARY	Etta Palm leaves Paris. Théroigne lives in room 1449 at 273 rue Saint-Honoré.
21 JANUARY	At 10.22, Louis XVI mounts the scaffold. Pinel is present at the execution.
26 JANUARY	The Belgian deputies complain to the Convention about its decree of 15 December 1792.
24 FEBRUARY	The laundrywomen of Paris have soap distributed at pre-Revolution prices.
25 FEBRUARY	The grocers' shops are invaded by the people, who regulate the prices of the goods on sale.
2 MARCH	The *Comté* of Hainaut is annexed to France, under the name of the department of Jemappes. The Convention also decrees the annexation of the *pays* of Stavelot, Franchimont and Logne, the principality of Salm and the town of Gand.
5 MARCH	Liège is recaptured by the Austrians.

10 March	The Convention creates the emergency criminal Tribunal, later known as the Revolutionary Tribunal.
11 March	Outbreak of Vendée rebellion. Republicans are massacred at Machecoul.
12 March	Dumouriez's letter to the Convention.
18 March	Dumouriez's army is defeated by the troops of Saxe-Cobourg. The French withdraw from Belgium.
21 March	Creation of the Revolutionary Watch Committees.
3 April	Claire Lacombe calls for the arrest of all aristocrats and their families. The Convention outlaws Dumouriez.
4 April	Dumouriez defects to the Austrians, after having attempted a march on Paris. The Commission of Six discuss the rights of women.
6 April	The Committee of Defence becomes the Committee of Public Safety.
13 April	Decree accusing Marat.
15 April	At the Convention, the Paris sections request the proscription of twenty-two Girondon deputies.
24 April	Marat is acquitted by the Revolutionary Tribunal. Women's worship of Marat.
10 May	Pauline Léon and Claire Lacombe found the *Club des citoyennes républicaines révolutionnaires*, the second exclusively feminine club. The Convention abandons the Manège and sits at the Tuileries in the machine room. It rules that executions will no longer be held in place du Carrousel but in place Louis XV, which has been renamed place de la Révolution (now place de la Concorde).
May	Théroigne's poster advocating a magistracy for peace, to be held by women.
15 May	Théroigne publicly whipped by Jacobin women at the door to the Convention. Marat protects her.
18 May	The Girondins denounce the women's action and call for their removal from the galleries of the Convention.
26 May	At the Jacobin Club, Marat calls for an insurrection against the Girondins.
31 May	Insurrection in Paris.
2 June	Arrest of twenty-seven Girondin representatives.
6 June	Upon hearing the news of the arrest of the Girondins, their friends in the provinces set the federalist movement in motion.
20 June	The *enragés* protest against the lacunae in the draft

constitution regarding economic and social questions.

24 JUNE The Constitution of 1793 voted, although it was never to be implemented. Men accorded the right to vote at the age of twenty-one, but servants still excluded.

5 JULY Théroigne resolves her dispute with the Baron de Sélys.

8 JULY A warrant issued for the arrest of Condorcet.

10 JULY The Committee of Public Safety now has nine members; in September, it will have twelve.

13 JULY Marat assassinated by Charlotte Corday. *Sans-culotte* women worship Marat's body in the days following his death.

17 JULY Condemnation and execution of Charlotte Corday.

27 JULY Robespierre joins the Committee of Public Safety.

28 JULY 'Translation' of Marat's heart by the *sans-culotte* women.

1 AUGUST The Convention resolves to destroy the Vendée. It adopts the metric system.

10 AUGUST First anniversary of the fall of the monarchy: destruction of all 'signs of the feudal order'.

23 AUGUST The Convention decrees a *levée en masse* of all Frenchmen.

30 AUGUST Terror 'the order of the day'.

5 SEPTEMBER *Sans-culotte* invasion of the Convention.

11 SEPTEMBER The Convention appoints Pinel head doctor at Bicêtre.

12 SEPTEMBER The Committee of General Security overhauled.

17 SEPTEMBER The Convention votes the law on suspects.

21 SEPTEMBER The Convention decrees that women are obliged to wear the tricolour cockade.

22 SEPTEMBER Year II of the Republic.

29 SEPTEMBER The Convention decrees the *Maximum général* on commodities and wages.

2 OCTOBER The Convention decrees the transfer of Descartes's body to the Panthéon. Dechristianization begins.

3 OCTOBER Marie-Antoinette appears before the Revolutionary Tribunal.

4 OCTOBER Chaumette's crusade against women of the streets. Accusations are levelled against republican women citizens who 'dress as men'.

5 OCTOBER Adoption of the revolutionary calendar as drawn up by Gilbert Romme.

16 OCTOBER Execution of Marie-Antoinette; Jourdan and Carnot defeat Austrians at Wattignies.

24 OCTOBER A new system of naming the months adopted, on the basis of a report by Fabre d'Églantine.

30 OCTOBER	Amar report presented to the Convention. Ban on women's clubs.
31 OCTOBER	Twenty-one Girondin representatives executed, Vergniaud and Brissot among them.
6 NOVEMBER	Olympe de Gouges executed.
7 NOVEMBER	Manon Roland executed.
10 NOVEMBER	Festival of Liberty and Reason at Notre-Dame in Paris. The apogée of dechristianization.
19 NOVEMBER	Anti-feminist article in the *Moniteur*.
20 NOVEMBER	Danton launches his campaign for indulgence, in order to halt the Terror.
24 NOVEMBER	From this day, the revolutionary names for the months of the year become compulsory for public announcements.
19 DECEMBER (*29 Frimaire*)	Toulon recaptured by Bonaparte.
23 DECEMBER (*3 Nivôse*)	Vendéens defeated at Savenay.

1794

4 FEBRUARY (*16 Pluviôse*)	Slavery abolished in the French colonies.
6 FEBRUARY (*18 Pluviôse*)	Bonaparte appointed general at the age of twenty-five.
26 FEBRUARY (*8 Ventôse*)	Saint-Just's report on the confiscation of the property of 'enemies of the Revolution'.
28 MARCH (*8 Germinal*)	Death of Condorcet.
29 MARCH (*9 Germinal*)	Arrest of the Indulgents, Danton among them.
1 APRIL (*12 Germinal*)	Beginning of the Great Terror.
2 APRIL (*13 Germinal*)	Claire Lacombe arrested.
5 APRIL (*16 Germinal*)	Danton's supporters executed.
13 APRIL (*23 Germinal*)	Chaumette's execution, between that of Lucile Desmoulins and of Hébert's widow.
7 MAY (*18 Floréal*)	The Convention recognizes the Supreme Being.

10 JUNE *(22 Prairial)*	Law of Prairial. The Great Terror intensifies.
26 JUNE *(8 Messidor)*	Victory of Fleurus.
27 JUNE *(9 Messidor)*	Théroigne arrested.
11 JULY *(23 Messidor)*	Hospital property is put on sale as *biens nationaux*. Barère's speech on the end of the asylum.
24 JULY *(6 Thermidor)*	Pichegru and Jourdan's armies enter Anvers and Liège.
26 JULY *(8 Thermidor)*	Robespierre's last speech to the Convention. Théroigne's letter to Saint-Just.
27 JULY *(9 Thermidor)*	Fall of Robespierre.
28 JULY	Robespierre, and twenty-one Robespierrists, are guillotined.
29 JULY *(11 Thermidor)*	Seventy-one Robespierrists executed.
21 AUGUST *(4 Fructidor)*	Pauline Léon disappears without trace.
29 AUGUST *(12 Fructidor)*	First demonstration of the *muscadins*.
18 SEPTEMBER *(second complementary day)*	Church and state separated for the first time.
20 SEPTEMBER *(fourth complementary day)*	Théroigne's madness officially acknowledged.
22 SEPTEMBER	Year III of the Republic.
5 OCTOBER *(14 Vendémiaire)*	Babeuf expounds his 'communist' ideas in *Le Tribun du peuple*.
12 NOVEMBER *(22 Brumaire)*	Closure of the Jacobin Club.
20 NOVEMBER *(30 Brumaire)*	Arrest in Austria of Jacobin suspects.

1795

7 FEBRUARY *(19 Pluviôse)*	Babeuf arrested.

8 FEBRUARY *(20 Pluviôse)*	Beginning of the White Terror.
15 FEBRUARY *(27 Pluviôse)*	Pacification of the Vendée.
24 FEBRUARY *(6 Ventôse)*	Creation of the *Écoles centrales.*
1 APRIL *(12 Germinal)*	First insurrection of the Parisian *sans-culottes.*
10 APRIL *(21 Germinal)*	Intensification of the White Terror.
13 MAY *(24 Floréal)*	Pinel appointed head doctor at La Salpêtrière.
20 MAY *(1 Prairial)*	Second insurrection of the Parisian *sans-culottes.*
24 MAY *(4 Prairial)*	Ban upon women's participation in political assemblies. Arrest of the last Montagnards, Gilbert Romme among them.
8 JUNE *(20 Prairial)*	Death of the dauphin, Louis XVII. The comte de Provence is declared king, under the name of Louis XVIII.
17 JUNE *(29 Prairial)*	Suicide of the last Montagnards, Gilbert Romme among them.
26 JULY *(8 Thermidor)*	Courtois's speech to the Convention regarding Saint-Just's papers. He announces that Théroigne is at the Maison des folles in faubourg Saint-Marceau.
15 AUGUST *(28 Thermidor)*	The franc becomes the legal currency of France.
22 AUGUST *(5 Fructidor)*	The Convention adopts the Constitution of Year III. It is preceded by a Declaration of Rights and Duties. Voting rights are granted to all men paying direct taxes. The Constitution will survive four years.
30 AUGUST *(13 Fructidor)*	All trace is lost of Claire Lacombe.
22 SEPTEMBER	Year IV of the Republic.
1 OCTOBER *(9 Vendémiaire)*	The Convention votes the annexation of Belgium to France.
26 OCTOBER *(4 Brumaire)*	The Convention dissolved.
3 NOVEMBER *(12 Brumaire)*	The Directory established.

1796

8 MARCH *(12 Ventôse)*	Bonaparte appointed general in chief of the Army of Italy.
30 MARCH *(10 Germinal)*	Conspiracy of the Equals, known as Babeuf's Conspiracy.
11 APRIL *(22 Germinal)*	Beginning of the Italian Campaign.
15 MAY *(26 Floréal)*	Entry of Bonaparte's army into Milan.
22 SEPTEMBER	Year V of the Republic.
15–17 NOVEMBER *(25–27 Brumaire)*	Battle of Arcole.

1797–1840

1797	Théroigne confined in the Hôtel-Dieu.
SEPTEMBER	Second Directory.
22 SEPTEMBER	Year VI of the Republic.
17 OCTOBER *(26 Vendemiaire)*	Signing of the Treaty of Campoformio between France and Austria.
26 OCTOBER *(5 Brumaire)*	Triumphal return of Bonaparte to Paris.

1798	Egyptian Campaign.
21 JULY *(3 Thermidor)*	Battle of the Pyramids.
1 AUGUST *(14 Thermidor)*	Defeat of Aboukir.
5 SEPTEMBER *(19 Fructidor)*	Compulsory military service introduced.
22 SEPTEMBER	Year VII of the Republic.

1799	Esquirol, Pinel's pupil, at La Salpêtrière.
12 MARCH *(22 Ventôse)*	France declares war on Austria.
16 MAY *(27 Floreal)*	Sieyès elected to the Directory.
26 MAY *(7 Prairial)*	The Directory recalls Bonaparte to France.

12 June	Coup d'état of 30 Prairial. Third Directory.
6 July *(18 Messidor)*	Reopening in Paris of the Jacobin Club, in the Manège.
13 August *(28 Thermidor)*	Closure of the Jacobin Club by Sieyès.
23 August *(6 Fructidor)*	Return of Bonaparte from Egypt.
22 September	Year VIII of the Republic.
9 November	Coup d'état of 18 Brumaire. The end of the Revolution.
9 December *(19 Frimaire)*	First transfer of Théroigne to La Salpêtrière.

1800 — Publication of Pinel's *Traité médico-philosophique de l'aliénation mentale.*

1805 — Esquirol defends his thesis. Pinel is appointed consultant doctor to the emperor.

1807 — Esquirol's tour of France.
7 December — Second transfer of Théroigne to La Salpêtrière.

1808 — Régnault de Saint-Jean-d'Angély's letter requesting information regarding Théroigne's fate. A former party leader pays a visit to La Salpêtrière.

1810 — Article 64 of the Penal Code. Théroigne in a state of chronic dementia.

1811 — Esquirol replaces Pussin as supervisory doctor of the mad section of La Salpêtrière.

1812–17 — Esquirol's observation of Théroigne.

1816 — Gabriel's drawing of Théroigne, the only portrait of her taken from the life.

1817
8 June — Death of Théroigne.
10 June — Autopsy of Théroigne's body performed by Esquirol's pupils. Dumontier takes a cast of her skull.

1820		Esquirol writes up the case of Théroigne.
1826		Death of Pinel.
1836		Death of Sieyès.
1838		Esquirol's *Des maladies mentales* published.
	30 JUNE	Law regarding the insane.
1840		Death of Esquirol.

INDEX